Political Blackness
in Multiracial Britain

THE ETHNOGRAPHY OF POLITICAL VIOLENCE

Tobias Kelly, Series Editor

A complete list of books in the series
is available from the publisher.

Political
Blackness
in Multiracial
Britain

Mohan Ambikaipaker

PENN

UNIVERSITY OF PENNSYLVANIA PRESS

PHILADELPHIA

Published by
University of Pennsylvania Press
Philadelphia, Pennsylvania 19104-4112
www.upenn.edu/pennpress

Printed in the United States of America on acid-free paper
1 3 5 7 9 10 8 6 4 2

Library of Congress Cataloging-in-Publication Data
ISBN 978-0-8122-5030-5

For Ashwin and Mallika,
and in memory of my father,
Ambikaipaker Arunasalam

CONTENTS

====

The Parable of "Paki Ali"

Amina did not tell me her family's story of arrival in Britain until our very last meeting. In some ways, this was to be expected. Why would people whom you meet as part of fieldwork want to confide their family secrets to you? And yet the strange thing about doing my fieldwork among people who had suffered racial and state violence was that it seemed to lead to moments when folks would narrate their personal accounts of British history. These were histories that arose from intergenerational memories of confronting race and racism.

Amina was of British Indian descent, in her thirties, and lived with her eleven-year-old son in a small public housing apartment block. She had been suffering abuse and harassment from a set of white neighbors for more than a year.

In desperation, she had turned to the Newham Monitoring Project (NMP), a community-based antiracist organization, located in the east London borough of Newham. I was her caseworker and our work together consisted in engaging the police, the local council, and the courts to remedy her situation.

It all began when neighbors were caught making fraudulent claims for welfare benefits. They were convinced that it was Amina who had "grassed" on them. Her comings and goings were met with daily verbal abuse, and her front door had recently been scrawled over with racist graffiti. One of her neighbors, who claimed to be HIV positive, had also smeared his blood on the door and threatened to infect her son.

Luckily, Amina had videotaped this particular attack through her peep-hole and the evidence led to charges that were before Snaresbrook Crown Court. But the abuse did not end and we were still trying to find a way to ensure her safety. I was attempting to convince various authorities to place a restraining order against her neighbors.

The story of her father's journey to Britain was not directly connected to her present predicament, and perhaps this is why she had not told me before. But in a few weeks I would return to the United States and another caseworker would take over. It seemed important for her to unburden this tale.

Her father, Mr. Azlan, had been in his early twenties when he first came to London in the late 1960s. Mr. Azlan was from a rural village that was located between the once-thriving medieval Islamic trading ports of Surat and Ahmedabad in the state of Gujarat in India. This region had become severely impoverished during successive western imperial conquests and colonial rule.

Amina remembered her dad recounting that his childhood village was a place where "people didn't know what they were going to eat until the day." Some of Mr. Azlan's village friends had already migrated to London. They called him to come over, saying that there was loads of work that English people did not want to do. He could sweep airport floors and work in factories, they said.

When he first arrived, it was difficult for Amina's dad to find a room to rent. English people did not want blacks in their houses, he told her. They had notices on their doors that read "No Wogs," he explained. "Wog" was a racist slur that white Britons used against any non-white person.

Eventually Amina's father secured steady factory work. He married and had five daughters, including Amina. The family was assigned their first public housing flat in a project in North Woolwich.

As one of the first South Asians in the area, he was nicknamed "Paki Ali" by his neighbors. "That was normal," Amina explained. "They weren't trying to be funny. Whenever people talked about him they would say 'Paki Ali.' Women liked him. He was a handsome man.

"Old ladies loved my dad!" Amina said and then became pensive. "It is—really easy. To call someone 'Paki.' Even if that person is Sikh, Hindu," and then looking up at me, she added, "Malaysian, Sri Lankan, or whatever. How sad," she added, becoming thoughtful again.

"I used to get told—what was it—'oh, you're all right, we don't mean you, you're one of us.' But I'm not. Definitely. I'm not one of them," she said. "At the end of the day I have brown skin and I am very proud of who I am, of my background.

"Black people were called 'gollywogs'; it was awful," she continued. "But—people used to come around, though! To have my mom's cooking. She was such a fantastic cook," Amina said, breaking into a smile again. "And Dad used to do odd jobs for people around there. He was such a good gardener," she added.

Amina grew up in east London in the 1970s and 1980s, when hers was one of only three South Asian families in her school. There was also one African Caribbean family. "I remember a song that comes to mind. It was 'Ding dong the bells are ringing, we're a going a-Paki-bashing!' The people upstairs, they were singing it. And you know we were probably the cleanest family there. I mean they talk about Asians being smelly and all, but we were the cleanest family there. Simply ridiculous.

"My dad did not see himself as a black man, other people—they just see a wog," Amina continued. "I mean when push came to shove, they make everyone a Paki or a black bastard. To them you're not white, so you're all these other things because you're not white. Because they are superior."

Despite the racism he experienced, Amina's father did not want to isolate himself or his family. He took a "liberal" approach, Amina explained. He allowed his daughters to dress as they pleased and to mix widely. Amina described her social circle growing up as comprising people from many different racial backgrounds, which included many white friends from school.

Amina married her son's father, a white man, who had also converted to her family's Islamic faith. The marriage had not worked out and she had recently divorced her husband.

In contrast to the stereotypes of British Asians and Muslims as self-segregating communities, Amina pointed to her own cosmopolitan family: one of her sisters was married to a black Grenadian man; another was married to a Pakistani man; and another had married a man from South Africa and emigrated there.

She described the openness of her upbringing and how her parents had taught her not to look down on anybody. She remembered her father telling her, "You've got to take people as they come."

According to Amina, her father initially didn't care about the racism he faced. "He would go down to the local pub and have drinks with these people, play darts and even bowl," Amina said. Victoria Park, near where Amina lived as a child, had a lawn bowling club. But it did not allow African

Caribbean or South Asian people to play. And yet she remembered how her father would simply enter uninvited and join in the games.

One day, however, Mr. Azlan's nonchalance reached its breaking point. "Well, the people who lived above us, in the flat above, they used to call my dad names. Racial comments and stuff like that," Amina said. "My dad would always stick up for himself and his family, you know, protect his family and whatnot," she added. "We came home from school one day, well, I came home from nursery and my elder sisters came home from school. Our mum was walking with us, and we could see smoke coming out. They had put all our things, well, my dad's things in the middle of the room, poured something on there and set them on fire," she said. "And wrote 'Paki' on the wall and things like that. Other people were making off with our things," she remembered. The year was 1978. Amina was four years old.

"They basically wanted us out, wanted us out of the area," she said. "Before this I didn't take anything on board really. My sisters were tough cookies because they had become immune to being called names and things. My eldest sister went to Cumberland School in Canning Town and experienced such bad, bad racism. It was unbelievable—putting things in her hair, setting her bag on fire, calling her names all the time," she added.

"Things were really turning around for my dad before then. Although men were threatened by him because, you know, in their eyes, he was a black man or whatever," Amina said. After the fire, Mr. Azlan's life and outlook changed. Amina did not want to get into the details, and I did not have the heart to press on. She said that eventually he ended up in prison. And there, when Amina was nine years old, he hanged himself with his belt and socks.

In his last letter from prison, he told his family that he was killing himself to spare them any further pain. "Was he right in doing this?" Amina asked. "Little did he know what would happen to us. I don't know. Maybe it would have been worse if he had been around," Amina added, sinking deeper into her own thoughts.

But then, remembering my presence, she looked up.

"I have been through a lot, haven't I?" she asked.

Noticing my fallen look, she broke out into a smile and told me, "Don't take all of this on board."

This ethnography starts with the reality that, under present racial and political conditions in Britain, Mr. Azlan, Amina, and many others whose stories

I will tell lack the power to right the wrongs they endured. Ethnography has been critiqued as a colonial form of knowledge production, rooted in the performance of dispassionate objectivity and objectification of the people we work with (Harrison 1997; Smith 2012).[1] Heeding these critiques, I situated my research ethics and methodology within an activist anthropology approach, where I would carry out "observant participation" on the front lines of the struggle for racial justice in Britain (Hale 2006; Vargas 2008). In contrast to positivistic arguments that view advocacy and activism as impediments to research about race, I agreed with Satya P. Mohanty's (1997:127) formulation that the very task of trying to objectively explain racism is "necessarily continuous with oppositional political struggle." I had hoped that by departing from a "fly-on-the-wall" objectivistic approach in fieldwork research I would be able to contribute to more positive racial justice outcomes for the people I worked with. However, the more I experienced my work as an antiracist activist working within the liberal channels of justice in Britain, the more elusive the outcomes of racial justice seemed to be. I discovered that these official antiracist processes that purport to preside over and adjudicate racism are themselves race-making sites, embedded in domination. They rarely provided effective remedies for ethnic, racial, and religious minorities who experienced white racial violence or state violence.

This ethnography cross-culturally examines the lived experiences of racial violence and racialized state violence as well as the lived experience of engaging in antiracist activism against these forms of violence in Britain.[2] People don't simply experience racism passively or uncritically, but rather they are actively involved in constructing meaning and narratives about their experiences of oppression and their collective efforts to resist and recover their violated humanity.

In 2005 and 2006 I worked as a caseworker and carried out self-reflective fieldwork as I observed and participated daily in NMP's antiracist activism. I was an unpaid caseworker along with three other full-time caseworkers. I initially apprenticed myself to a senior activist, Zareena Mustapha, and later teamed up with another caseworker, Titilayo Folashade Aloba, while working with the east Londoners whom I describe in this book. There was also a white British director, Estelle du Boulay, who did casework and was responsible for grant writing and development. Community outreach workshops and high-profile campaigning leadership drew upon a close-knit circle of senior NMP activists, most of who chose to live

in Newham. These senior activists contributed their labor to the organization through their mentoring and supervision work on the management
council.

NMP's staff included a cadre of activists focused on two forms of antiracist mobilizations. They constructed casework for victims of racial violence and police abuse who sought immediate remedies from the
institutions of the British state. They also campaigned for justice in high-
profile cases of police abuse and racial attacks. Campaigning work pursued
changes to collective patterns of institutional racism and discrimination
found in state policies and practices.

From 2003 to 2016 I built a relationship with NMP, its circle of activists,
and residents of the Newham community. NMP often engaged antiracist
politics at a national level, but its day-to-day work was grounded in the
local realities of racial, religious, and ethnic minorities in Newham, both
recent immigrants and second- or third-generation British. The stories in
this book come from my interactions with people who have complex identities: they are British Indian and Muslim; African Caribbean / St. Lucian
and British; Tanzanian and Gujarati / Pakistani and Palestinian; Bangladeshi and Muslim; Sri Lankan Tamil and Malaysian; Nigerian and German,
white British and Jewish; and many others. These identities, however, are
not the subject of this ethnography, which focuses instead on the lived
experiences of white British racism and British state violence.[3]

Introduction

The people's stories and struggles for justice described in this book take place in the London borough of Newham. Newham is situated five miles east of central London and is one of the thirty-two boroughs that, along with the iconic city center, make up the metropolitan area of greater London. Newham is bounded by the River Thames on the south, by the River Lea on the west, the River Roding on the east, and Wanstead Flats on the north. At the edges of Newham's recently redeveloped western boundary is the site of the 2012 Olympic Park. The Westfield Stratford City Mall—the largest retail mall in Europe—is adjacent to the park and also the Stratford train, bus, and subway stations, which form a major transportation hub in the city.

These highly capitalized mega-projects, situated behind Stratford Station, were built at the former site of low-income public housing estates. The inhabitants of these dwellings had been "Travellers" who were categorized in the 2011 Census as "White Gypsy" and "Irish Traveller." "Travellers" is a term that refers to the nonsedentary lifeways of this particular ethnic group and to other low-income residents strongly identified with the Clays Lane community, a place that no longer exists. This long-standing community was broken up and displaced through compulsory purchase, known as eminent domain in the United States, of land, homes, and small businesses. Former residents experienced considerable distress and loss in the relocation process (Bernstock 2014). As Penny Bernstock (2014:63) argued, "Residents found themselves in the way of a prestigious national project [and] the need to expedite the project meant that [residents] had to respond to a very tight and highly pressurized timetable" of two years.

Today tourists and Londoners from other parts of the city flock to the Westfield Mall, oblivious of this violent history that displaced a group of poor east Londoners. Furthermore, the vast majority of the other inhabitants of Newham have not benefited in any way from the Olympic redevelopment. On follow-up visits to my field site in 2013 and 2016, I was struck

Figure 1. Post–2012 Olympics gentrification in Newham, 2013.
Photo by the author.

by how unchanged the rest of the borough appeared once I left the areas containing the Olympic Park and Westfield Mall.

Initially east Londoners I talked with saw promise in the winning Olympic bid, because they believed that they would themselves benefit from the massive capital investments in the borough. By 2013, it was clear that the over ten billion pounds spent on the Olympics, four billion of that from public funds, had not profited the majority of Newham's residents or improved the borough's long-standing systemic inequalities. Newham in 2015 continued to have the lowest median income, highest income inequality, highest overcrowding, and highest homelessness rate in London (Aldridge, Bon, Tinson, and MacInness 2015). It also has exceptionally high rates of ill health, child poverty, and premature death. However, since 2016 a new narrative about the borough's climb out of poverty began to emerge as the borough became more gentrified. Newham Council stated that "Newham is no longer in the 20 most deprived local authorities" (Newham Council 2015a; New Policy Institute 2015). In past decades, Newham ranked in the top three of the most deprived boroughs in England, and its ranking is said to have improved to the rank of the twenty-fifth most deprived municipality in 2015. Along with the processes of gentrification,

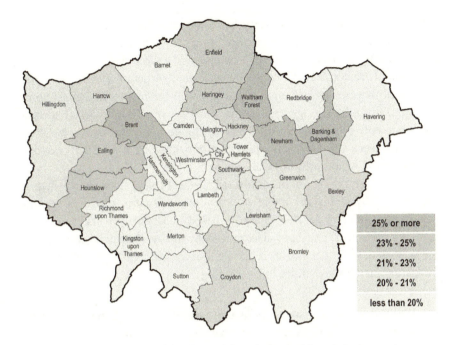

Figure 2. Proportion of London residents in low-paid work, by borough,
2015. The borough of Newham is in the upper-right section of the map.
Map courtesy of New Policy Institute.

which obscured the indices of poverty, the character of poverty in east London also changed to include a majority of full-time but underpaid working families, as well as high rates of unemployed residents and workless households[1] (New Policy Institute 2015b).

Moving deeper into Newham's inner wards, you leave behind the relatively gentrified character of Stratford and the Olympic Park. Newham's population today mainly comprises various South Asian, African, and African Caribbean communities made up of British-born and recent immigrants, asylum seekers, and refugees. This complex diversity creates a rich and unique environment for antiracist politics.

The antipathy to new immigrants, for example, which is often heard in everyday conversation, reflects some of the powerful, internalized racial discourses that have depicted Newham as a crime-ridden "ghetto," perennially inhabited by unruly and nonnormative British communities. Since the late nineteenth century, when the pioneering sociologist and ethnographer

Charles Booth researched poverty here, the area has been constructed in the academic and media imagination as a dangerous and deviant urban space. Booth, in fact, described Newham as "lowest class; vicious, semi-criminal" (Presser 2016). When I began extended fieldwork in 2006 I was surprised that many residents of Newham saw themselves and their home borough from these long-running elite perspectives. They shared in a common perception that areas with white-dominated, middle- and upper-class residents were superior, and their own working-class, multiethnic, and multicultural neighborhoods were inferior.

In contrast, the Newham Monitoring Project (NMP) viewed the diverse context of Newham as one of its attractive strengths and a promising ground on which to develop solidarity-based social movements against racism. NMP, in fact, conceptualized and defined the struggle against "white racist society" (NMP 1985:44) in the light of the complex racial, ethnic, and religious minority dynamics in Newham:

> We understand racism to be a political concept that involves the defence of assumptions of "superiority" by the majority in this country over the minority on the basis of the colour of people's skin. Prejudice, religious and cultural intolerance and communalism are not the same as racism (although they can be used to perpetrate racism). To characterize black-on-black violence, although a vitally important issue, as "racial harassment" ignores the central role that racism against black communities plays in British society. . . . And it is precisely because racism is about race (rather than just nationality or religion) that we have always talked about "black communities" rather than ethnic minorities.[2]

Many of NMP's activists had also chosen to move into the borough in order to participate in its culturally vibrant everyday life as well as its strong tradition of grassroots antiracist resistance. In the 1980s, the borough was made famous by high-profile mass mobilizations, especially around the Newham 8 and Newham 7 cases, two landmark antiracist campaigns that helped assert the legal right of racial and ethnic minority communities to engage in self-defense when racially attacked. Both cases involved South Asian youths who had tried to defend themselves from violent racist attacks. The police had acted in alignment with the white perpetrators by

arresting and charging the South Asian victims who had organized themselves to fight back.

In 1984 a sixteen-year-old African Caribbean teenager, Eustace Pryce,
was killed by a member of a local white racist gang from Canning Town, a
predominantly white British area in the south of the borough. NMP was
similarly involved in organizing the Justice for the Pryces campaign to pressure the police and court system to deliver justice against the white killer
(NMP 1985:39–44). Often the campaigns affecting African Caribbean and
South Asian victims of racism in Newham were coordinated to involve
multiple communities in solidarity with each other. Through public meetings, pickets at police stations, and mass protests, NMP worked with communities who had been made vulnerable to white racial violence in order
to build up black people's political protagonism (Harnecker 2007) and
direct action participation in antiracism.

> On Saturday 27th April 1985, 3000, mainly local people marched in
> support of the Newham 7 and Justice for the Pryces campaign. The
> fact that the two campaigns linked up together symbolized black
> unity, between Asians and Afro-Caribbeans, in practice, over a com-
> mon issue and a common struggle. The march started off at 2pm
> as an angry but peaceful protest, demonstrating the extent of local
> community anger. It passed off without incident until it reached
> Forest Gate police station, where in line with arrangements agreed
> previously, the march came to a temporary halt for a short protest
> rally against police inaction over racist attacks. Suddenly police
> snatch squads jumped over crash barriers, arresting demonstrators
> accused of, amongst other things "spitting and throwing weapons."
> . . . From the police's decision to break up the march, disperse the
> crowd and break all agreements made before or during the
> march—we can only deduce (and this is backed up by comments
> made by individual officers) that the police totally underestimated
> the amount of people prepared to take to the street in support of
> the Newham 7 and The Pryce Family. The police felt deeply threat-
> ened by the political unity displayed by Asians and Afro-Caribbean
> youth on that day and certainly did not want them to march unhin-
> dered through the main streets of Newham. (NMP 1985:26–27)

It was also in the 1980s that refugees, asylum seekers, unaccompanied
young refugees, and other displaced people without permanent status began

Figure 3. Protest in defense of the Newham 7, 1985.
Photo by David Hoffman.

to increasingly resettle into the borough through lucrative financial agreements with local landlords and boarding houses or B&Bs (bed and breakfast
establishments). Newham has consistently been the top borough for the British state's placement of refugees and asylum seekers in the nation. White-
majority neighborhoods in London, and especially middle- and upper-class
areas, are seldom selected by the state as spaces to place refugees and asylum
seekers in government-assisted housing. Due to this refugee and asylum-
seeker population growth, Newham is now the most populous borough in
London, with more than 300,000 inhabitants (Jivraj 2013).

The demographic composition in Newham is far more complex than
that of Southall in West London or of Brixton in South London. Southall
and Brixton were symbolically associated with Sikh/Punjabi cultures and
Jamaican culture, respectively. But in Newham, multiple non-white communities live "cheek by jowl." No single, principal racial or ethnic minority
group is overwhelmingly identified with the locale. The borough is loosely
patterned, with multiple South Asian populations densely located in the
north, white populations in the south, and African and African Caribbean
populations slightly concentrated in the west.

Figure 4. Antiracist campaign leaflet in shop window on Green Street, 2016.
Photo by the author.

When I was doing fieldwork in 2005 and 2006, around a third of the population was white, of which the overwhelming majority was white British (London Borough of Newham 2007:26). There were very small white Irish and white Traveller communities as well (Jivraj 2013:1).[3] The white British presence in Newham, however, has since declined. In the last census of the population taken in 2011, the figures showed that the white British population was still the largest ethnoracial group in the borough, but it accounted for only 17 percent of the overall population (Jivraj 2013). The exodus of the white population has been going on for decades. There has been significant white flight to the outer and less crowded suburbs of Essex and Ilford, driven by the increasing social mobility of sections of the white working classes, many of whom were working in the imperial dockyards. They could afford to move out of the borough due to assistance from the government in accessing a number of housing programs.

At the time of my fieldwork, approximately 36.3 percent of the population of Newham was South Asian, or "Asian," mainly comprising Indians (12.3 percent), Pakistanis (9.8 percent), and Bangladeshis (9.7 percent). Approximately 25 percent of the population was of African or Caribbean descent: African (15.0 percent) and Caribbean (7.1 percent). In addition, 5.5 percent of the population was Chinese. The borough has the second highest percentage of South Asians and the second highest percentage of Africans in London (London Borough of Newham 2007). About a third of Newham's population were recent immigrants who arrived between 2007 and 2011 (Jivraj 2013). Overall, Newham's racial and ethnic minority population increased by 128 percent between 1991 and 2011 (Jivraj 2013).

These official boxes of racial, ethnic, and national identities, however, belie the complexity hidden within each census categorization. African Caribbean people may identify with a "Black British" identity, as well as with particular Caribbean island identifications; likewise, people of a specific South Asian nationality might also identify themselves by intranational regional origins. Mr. Azlan, for example, was a Gujarati Muslim from a northwestern state in India. There are many other determinants of identities among communities of color in Newham, including ethnicity, religion, caste, gender, sexuality, and skin color. It is notable then that, despite increased ethnic diversity, an increasing number of people in Newham self-identify with a "British" or "English" identity alongside a particular ethnic or heritage group (Jivraj 2013:4).

The complex overlays of racial, religious, national, and ethnic identities are evident on Newham's various main streets. Green Street, for example, is noted for its specific North Indian and Pakistani-style wedding and jewelry stores, grocery shops, and restaurants. This specificity, however, is often lost to the outside world and grossly represented in mainstream depictions. In the blockbuster film *Bend It Like Beckham* (2002), the street simply signified a generic "Little India" or "Asian ethnic" backdrop. In another mainstream film, *Green Street Hooligans* (2005), which dealt with issues of football hooliganism, the rich ethnic and racial diversity of the area was completely erased. West Ham Football Club, whose stadium was located at the southern end of Green Street, became representative of a deracinated Newham, only populated by white British people.

The owners of many of Green Street's some four hundred shops are Gujaratis or Punjabis who have origins in eastern Africa and India. In the late 1960s and 1970s the arrival of stateless East African South Asians from Uganda, Kenya, and Malawi reconstituted Newham's South Asian communities in terms of class and national origin. The arrival of multiple South Asian mercantile communities revived Green Street, which had become depressed after the borough's de-industrialization. Residents recalled only

Figure 5. Queens Supermarket and, to its right, a halal butcher, which cater to Newham's African, Caribbean, and South Asian diasporic communities, 2016. These stores are part of Queen's Market, a famous east London street market. Photo by the author.

a handful of English cafés and secondhand thrift stores as the main businesses that remained, until the advent of its commercial resurgence from the 1990s onward. For many South Asians in London and in the south of England, Green Street is also a weekend shopping destination for ethnic food, groceries, and wedding couture.

In contrast, East Ham High Street North, which is situated in the Forest Gate ward, is a center for South Indian and Sri Lankan Tamil restaurants, textiles, and shops. Business activities that are critical for these communities to maintain their important long-distance kinship ties and obligations, such as buying and selling mobile phones and calling cards, booking at travel agencies, and using wire-transfer services, are ubiquitous on this main commercial road.

African and African Caribbean beauty salons, restaurants, bakeries, and churches are dispersed amid these multiethnic South Asian businesses, coinhabiting the high street life of the inner city. In recent years, new immigrants, including Somalis and Eastern Europeans, have also opened delis and grocery stores and brought coffee culture into the inner city. The 2004 and 2007 accession of Eastern European countries into the European Union

Figure 6. Daily shopping on Green Street, 2016. Photo by the author.

Figure 7. African Caribbean hair salon and Indian candy store ("sweet centre") on Green Street, 2013. Photo by the author.

Figure 8. East Ham High Street caters to South Indian and Sri Lankan community businesses and religious life, 2006. Photo by the author.

and its resulting immigration, especially from Poland, added to what some call "super-diversity" in Newham (Vertovec 2007).

From an electoral perspective, Newham is a Labour Party stronghold and has its own municipal government and mayor. The city council provides social services such as housing and schools and, among numerous statutory duties, is also responsible for enforcing the racial harassment eviction clause within public housing tenancy contracts. It also has a statutory duty to monitor racial discrimination, to promote nondiscriminatory relations between police and the local community, and to provide equitable social services that fund youth work, elder care, refugee services, as well as many other programs that cater to its multiethnic, multilingual, and multiracial citizenry. However, the implementation and enforcement of these duties have often been uneven and ineffectual due to the way the state becomes aligned with dominant white British perspectives and everyday racial power interests. As I will document, the superior social and political power of local white British people to influence routine liberal juridical processes relative to the interests of Newham's racial, religious, and ethnic minorities is structurally embedded. And this made the work of a locally based antiracist group like NMP indispensable to victims of racial and state violence who sought remedies and justice from these state institutions and processes.

CHAPTER 1

"There Is Nothing Nice to See Here, Sir. You Go to Central London"

The Colonial-Racial Zone of East London

On one of my first visits to the borough of Newham, I headed out from central London on the District Line and went eastward to the East Ham subway stop. Family members living in London had told me about a significant Sri Lankan Tamil community there. When I got out of the subway station, I immediately knew I was in the right place when I saw sign after sign advertising Sri Lankan food and the Tamil writing script on a number of shop fronts. Over the last three decades, East Ham had become one of the ethnic minority–dominated wards within the borough of Newham and there was a significant ethnic Sri Lankan Tamil community, primarily comprising people who, having arrived as refugees and asylum seekers, had resettled there in the late 1980s and 1990s.

As I gazed up and down East Ham High Street, I noticed how different the shopping atmosphere was in contrast to the high-end and chain-store tourist enclaves of Oxford Street, a globally famous shopping area in central London. Here in east London, the majority of the people on the streets were non-white. Stores sold fine Kanchipuram silk saris, and bookstores carried religious Islamic texts and dress. Mosques jostled with Hindu temples and abandoned Christian churches that had been converted into community centers. Cell phone stores abounded, as did Internet cafés, pubs, and, of course, South Asian restaurants.

As I walked about, I saw a small half-shop with three tables inside. The establishment was called the Indo-Ceylon Café and I decided to have lunch there. The place was friendly. My initial conversation was with the two people who were in the restaurant. One was an old gentleman wearing a worn blue suit. He was clearly taking a cigarette break from work and the owners of the restaurant let him alone. I discovered later that the eatery ran a sort of luncheon subscription program, where workers in the area could pay a flat monthly fee to come in for regular meals and hang out.

The unrushed atmosphere seemed like a good place for an anthropologist to begin "deep hanging out" (Clifford 1997) and strike up a conversation. The man in the blue suit, though, did not speak much English and left as soon as I ordered a cup of milk tea and a lamb samosa. Another person entered and he appeared to be some sort of security guard. He looked like he was of South Asian descent. I explained to him that I had recently arrived in London and asked him if there was anything interesting to see in Newham.

"There is nothing nice to see here, sir. You go to central London."

Soon, another South Asian–looking woman walked in with a young boy who was fairly light-skinned and appeared to be her son, followed closely by an elderly white gentleman. They joined in the conversation.

The woman's name was Anne, and I started to laugh when I saw that her son was wearing a cap with the Malaysian flag on it. How fitting to make my first trip to Newham and discover fellow Malaysians, I thought. The place started to feel very much like home. A conversation about the cap opened up a sense of the familiar and we exchanged the usual Malaysian pleasantries.

Anne was a nurse who had migrated from Malaysia in the 1980s and the elderly white east Londoner was her father-in-law, Albert. Very quickly the Indo-Ceylon Café became a lively place of conversation as the security guard, Anne, Albert, and I started to discuss the state of the borough.

"Sir, be very careful about this place," the security guard warned. "There are many thieves and thugs here."

"Yes, this area is known for pickpockets and snatchers," Anne added. "You didn't bring your passport, did you?" she asked with sincere concern.

"No," I replied. All of them told me that passports were a big draw for thieves in the area since there were so many undocumented immigrants about, hungry for documentation.

"They found a body of a guy, abducted and dumped in a plastic bag, just a few blocks from here. Cut up to pieces," the security guard said.

"Did they know why it happened?" I asked. As he answered I almost choked on my food.

"This place is terrible. You know here there are many refugees, asylum seekers, from Sri Lanka—Tamils. They're bloody rude. You ask them something and they say to you, 'Watch out, I will kill you!'" the guard exclaimed.

"I don't know. It is not like in central London, where people are . . ." the guard gestured toward himself and mimicked wearing a suit. "They are civilized," he finished.

At this comment, Albert started to join in the conversation. "These asylum seekers! I don't know what the government is doing!" he groaned. "Yeah," he added, "that's why I am for the identity cards. If you don't have anything to fear, then it's okay, innit?"

"Sir, we have 90,000 asylum seekers, refugees, coming into U.K.! And all coming into Newham! I don't know what the government is doing at the airport. Letting them all through," the guard excitedly elaborated, buoyed by the support he sensed was forthcoming from Albert.

"They say they are refugees, but after a few years, they are driving a Mercedes Benz. But you cannot say anything, it's racist," the guard continued, very agitated, and, as he grew more vitriolic, he appeared to encourage Albert to speak up.

"Yeah! These refugees don't look too scared to me, yeah!" Albert added.

"I've been here seven years," the South Asian guard started up again. "I have to bloody queue up at the DSS, and these refugees—they're treated first!" he started to shout.[1]

"Where are you from?" I asked.

"I'm from here, U.K.!" he boasted. "I've been here seven years; if I cannot get things, how these people get everything. They have big house, big car. I have an English friend . . ."

"But isn't everybody who is black from somewhere?" I pushed on, hoping to discover more of his mode of identification and the reason why he did not seem to identify with his fellow South Asians in Newham.

At this, the guard retorted, "I not talking about immigrants. Here refugees, illegal immigrants!"

And then, almost on cue, Albert chimed in. "Yeah, it used to be secure around here. Now, look at it. Back in my day we could play around here, and if we got into trouble, by the time we got back our parents would know. We were poor, but it was secure. Now!"

The conversation was becoming tense and Anne tried to pacify the atmosphere.

"Well, everybody has their opinions. These are some of the problems of the inner city. The government never gives money here. You look at Stratford, it used to be like East Ham," she said.

Anne went on to explain the NIMBY (not-in-my-backyard) policies she attributed to the government. She seemed very well read on current affairs and had a critical analysis of the media hype on refugees. Funds had been allocated to impoverished wards such as East Ham in Newham to facilitate the resettlement of refugees and asylum seekers and, thereby, in her view, to protect the middle class and white boroughs from receiving a similar burden. And Stratford had been developed not out of concern for the interests of the people who already lived there, but to facilitate a moneymaking bonanza for corporations that had nothing to do with Newham.

"Now it looks fine. But whenever the government gives money, it is always with a hidden purpose," she reasoned, pointing to the agendas behind the gentrification of Stratford.

This conversation revealed some of the everyday talk that these Newham residents constructed about life in their borough. There were considerable anti-refugee sentiments raging in the public discourse in the early 2000s, driven especially by anti-immigration campaigns produced by popular tabloid newspapers. The arrival of non-white and non-western refugees and asylum seekers caused a hysteria that was totally unsubstantiated by the refugees' relatively modest numbers or by any other objective criteria. But these contemporary anti-refugee and anti–asylum seeker antipathies had discursively absorbed much of the anti-black immigration debates of the 1960s and 1970s.

My conversation in the restaurant, and the story of Mr. Azlan's arrival and his death as "Paki Ali" in Britain, are inseparable from the political history of the British Empire and its colonial entanglements, underpinned by racism and white supremacist politics.[2] The loss of the empire's expansive territory in the twentieth century unleashed a crisis of imperial white identity in Britain. The successes of anticolonial movements in Africa, Asia, and the Caribbean, and the return of Hong Kong to China in 1997, invalidated the aura of an overt, white racial manifest destiny that would spread Anglo-American civilization globally—as described in Rudyard Kipling's ([1899] 1993:82) poem "The White Man's Burden."[3]

Take up the White Man's burden—
Send forth the best ye breed—

Go, bind your sons to exile
To serve your captives' need;
To wait in heavy harness
On fluttered folk and wild—
Your new-caught, sullen peoples,
Half-devil and half-child.

Following the advent of the War on Terror, one *New York Times* reviewer recalled this poem to re-authorize a redemptive western imperialism: "The notion of 'White Man's burden' once again seems peculiarly relevant in thinking about the war in Afghanistan. What are the goals of the Western powers as the region is transformed? What good can be expected and how can it be achieved?" (Rothstein 2002). The political imaginary of western geopolitical domination, and universalism, as Barnor Hesse (2014:295) argues, consists of "self-assembled Europeanness (metaphorically coded white) economically administering, culturally regulating and politically legislating an externally assembled non-Europeanness (metaphorically coded non-white, black, red, yellow etc.)."

The advent of mass settlement of British Empire subjects from the Caribbean, Africa, and South Asia, however, brought to the domestic front the question of imperial racial domination in everyday social terms. The arch-imperialist Winston Churchill, who never wanted to relinquish Britain's Asian, African, and Caribbean colonies, also imagined that the empire's black subjects, many of whom possessed citizenship rights under the 1948 British Nationality Act,[4] could never belong in Britain itself. They belonged outside in the colonized zones, but not at "home," in the white colonizer's space. In affirming biologically racist and Anglo-Saxon supremacist views that were common among British elites, Churchill argued against mass "colored" immigration, arguing that such immigration patterns would threaten Britain with the prospect of racial defilement, or what he termed "a magpie society" (Jones 2012). In the 1960s, the Conservative Member of Parliament (MP) and onetime aspirant for the position of the Viceroy of India, Enoch Powell ([1968] 2007), made his famous "Rivers of Blood" speech where he reported that his white British constituents were developing "the sense of being a persecuted minority" in the face of unchecked immigration.

Margaret Thatcher's anti-immigration discourse in the 1970s built upon Powell's rhetorical strategies and also absorbed far-right discourses with

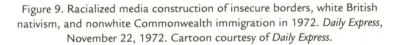

"My father was a Congolese head-hunter who married an Indo-Australian missionary domiciled in Uganda, and I was born in a B.O.A.C. aircraft on charter to Bolivian Air Lines. Which gate please?"

Figure 9. Racialized media construction of insecure borders, white British nativism, and nonwhite Commonwealth immigration in 1972. *Daily Express,* November 22, 1972. Cartoon courtesy of *Daily Express.*

regards to representing "colored" immigration as a threat to the interests of white Britons and public order.[5] Her discourse shifted the register of racism from Churchillian and Powellian fears of miscegenation and loss of white social power to questions of cultural incommensurability: "[If] we went on as we are then by the end of the century there would be four million people of the new Commonwealth or Pakistan here. Now, that is an awful lot and I think it means that people are really rather afraid that this country might be rather swamped by *people with a different culture* [emphasis mine] and, you know, the British character has done so much for democracy, for law and done so much throughout the world that if there is any fear that it might be swamped people are going to react and be rather hostile to those coming in" (Thatcher 1978).

The intertwined tropes of cultural incompatibility, fears of a dwindling white majority, and reemergent ideas about white British superiority continue to shape current political debates on controlled immigration, refugee policy, social services, social cohesion, and national security.[6] The Conservative Party that won power in 2015, for example, continued to successfully dog-whistle the anti-black immigration framework established in earlier decades by recollecting resonant fears: "When immigration is out of control, it puts pressure on schools, hospitals and transport; and it can cause social pressures if communities find it hard to integrate" (Conservative Party 2015).

Racial nativism (Pérez Huber 2010) and presumptions of white British cultural normalcy shaped the post–World War II social science paradigm on how good "race relations" were to be socially engineered. Good race relations were to be achieved by limiting the black presence to levels that would be tolerable to a putative white British majority. The race relations problem was conceptualized by political and academic elites as a societal collision between two kinds of illiberalism: immigrant illiberal culture, and white working-class illiberal prejudice (Banton 1967). Accordingly, intellectuals developed a dual strategy, adopted and announced by the state, to resolve race problems: the simultaneous integration of "colored" immigrants, and a campaign against the "intolerance" of prejudiced whites. The first was to be achieved by pathologizing the cultural practices of colored immigrants at variance with the "normal class identities" of Britain, and the second was to be pursued through antidiscrimination legislation (Little 1969). Furthermore, after the 1964 General Election, the Labour Party withdrew its political opposition to immigration control against Commonwealth nationals (ex-colonials from South Asia, Africa, and the Caribbean). A white-centric social consensus was established then that immigration as a whole must be restricted in order to preserve good race relations and social order.

The collective onus, though, fell on immigrant communities. The anthropologist and leading Fabian Socialist Kenneth Little (1969:247) argued at the time that "it is idle to expect a sympathetic reception unless some sections are prepared to accommodate themselves more deliberately to British conditions and notions of what is 'right' behavior." Similarly, when one of the pioneering pieces of research commissioned on Caribbean immigrants in Brixton appeared, the study concluded that "if accommodation and assimilation are to be achieved, the West Indian migrants must face the fact that they have to make a thorough-going and sustained effort to adapt their behaviour and values in all major spheres of life" (Patterson 1963:408).

The study's author, Sheila Patterson, had concluded that Caribbean immigrants were essentially "assimilating in character" if not in intent, due to their cultural, educational, linguistic, and religious resemblance to English society (Patterson 1963:408). She contrasted their character with that of Indian and Pakistani immigrants who were not only differentiated by color from the English, but were also culturally, linguistically, and religiously different. The literature of this period constructed this internal difference among colored immigrants by typecasting African Caribbean immigrants as desiring social acceptance and South Asian immigrants as separatists who desired only economic opportunities. This taxonomical logic of difference also informed many academic representations of South Asian and African Caribbean communities as politically disparate. Hence, even in the late 1960s and 1970s when joint African Caribbean and South Asian antiracist organizations emerged, academic arguments mediated against such solidarities. The emergence of black social movements, which cut within and across normal class politics in Britain and aimed to construct "a united black political front against both common and differential racism faced by Britain's ex-colonial peoples" (Goulbourne 1991:109), challenged in new ways the hegemony of white working-class social movements and sociological analysis alike.

The trope of the "cultural pathology of non-white communities" was apparent again in shaping the British state's "community cohesion" discourse. This new public policy was a result of a number of official inquiries (Cantle Report, Ouseley Report, Denham Report) commissioned following the Northern Town race "riots" of July 2001. These inquiries concluded that an overemphasis on multicultural policies that celebrated difference and separate social habitats had created ethnic ghettoes and, in turn, had produced the tensions that erupted into social disorder in cities such as Oldham, Bradford, and Harehills. The state concluded that it had taken a wrong turn in abandoning a strong emphasis on assimilation and integration: "Separate educational arrangements, community and voluntary bodies, employment, places of worship, language, social and cultural networks, means that many communities operate on the basis of a series of parallel lives. These lives often do not seem to touch at any point, let alone overlap and promote any meaningful interchanges" (Cantle and Independent Review Team 2001:9). Community cohesion discourse imagines liberal governance as a process of distinguishing between "good" multicultural subjects and "bad" multicultural subjects, and that the latter must be pedagogically schooled by the state in order to practice acceptable forms of ethnicized and religious identity politics.[7] The policy makes a sweeping and flattening equivalence between prejudiced and intolerant whites who "look backwards" to a monocultural British society, and bad ethnic, racial, and religious minority subjects who "alternatively look to their country of origin for some form of identity" (Cantle and Independent Review Team 2001:9). "Good" minority subjects are defined as those who visibly display interracial sociability and refuse segregation and polarization in their everyday lives.

Community cohesion discourse makes no mention of the structural impact of the racial violence and racialized state violence that constrain the agency of black communities and situate them in asymmetrical everyday power relationships with white Britons. The understanding of racial and ethnic minorities in community cohesion discourse also relies on a forgetting of the British Empire and a recasting of formerly colonized black communities as immigrants and interlopers within British history and society. Despite their *longue durée* histories of participation within the British Empire and post-empire society, black communities are still subject to racial nativism, exclusion, and violence.

The new ideology of community cohesion was quickly implemented. Within the space of a few years, programs for disadvantaged racial minority youth and other racial equality programs lost their traditional funding and had to cater their programs to the promotion of community cohesion across cultural and racial lines. During one funder's meeting on behalf of the Newham Monitoring Project (NMP), I encountered community activists who were crafting programs that would bring Muslim students to visit a church and Christian students to visit a mosque. These approaches assume that the problems of racism are to be resolved through better intercultural contact and interventions to preempt separatist tendencies.

Ironically, super-diverse inner cities such as Newham provide ample evidence that significant cross-cultural contact and cultural hybridization between ethnic minorities and whites and between ethnic minorities themselves are already banal, everyday social facts of life. In my own experience of living in the borough, where two-thirds of the population were racial and ethnic minorities, I was hard-pressed not to come into daily contact with white British people.

I had routine encounters with authorities in the Methodist Church who rented a room to me and with homeless immigrants, asylum seekers, and refugees in their church-owned boarding house. White churches owned significant property that housed community organizations and other ethnic minority spaces. As a caseworker for NMP, I dealt with numerous Newham Council officers and high-level managers, police officers, and predominantly white transport police officers. In 2006, Newham's two MPs were white, as was the borough's mayor. This was still the case in 2016. White Britons hold the highest positions of power in what is ostensibly a majority minority inner-city borough. And, as will be shown, the effect of diversifying civil service personnel in the social services of the borough does not necessarily lead to equitable or racial justice outcomes. The question that needs to be asked then is not simply whether there is cultural separatism or community cohesion in diverse neighborhoods or municipalities. Frequent interracial and intercultural encounters do not necessarily alter the tacit power imbalances that structure racialized identities within hierarchical social orders. Rather, we must ask what kinds of power relations are constituted in these spaces of diversity and interracial encounters?

The uncertain transformation of post-empire Britain has been consistently mediated by an ongoing narrative of political, cultural, and economic risks posed by racially differentiated and ethnicized identities—formerly colonized subjects, working-class immigrants, asylum seekers, and refugees —who usurp social welfare benefits and are harbingers of non-British cultural and religious practices and terrorism. In this dominant political narrative of a fragile and defensive post-empire Britain, ordinary white Britons are made to feel threatened as liberal democracy's preeminent citizenry.

Following the Brexit referendum, the popular vote in 2016 in favor of exiting European Union membership, discourses that link capitalist expansionism and racial nativistic anxieties constructed around the regulation of physical, cultural, and racial borders resemble the post–World War II panics about Britain's contradictory relationship to its former colonies. In one of his first party speeches following the success of the Brexit referendum, Foreign Secretary Boris Johnson constructed a new political narrative about the need to bolster "free market Anglo-Saxon capitalism" and waxed lyrical about how a reinvigorated and autonomous "Global Britain" would build upon its former imperial greatness of having been a "country over the last two centuries [that] has directed the invasion or conquest of 178 countries" (Johnson 2016). In 2017 state officials were strategizing how to secure Britain's post-Brexit international commerce with improbable analogies about "Empire 2.0" and returning to the old system of "imperial preference" of trading with ex-colonial Commonwealth nations (Blitz 2017). Apart from trade and empire, the neo-empire narrative also resurrected a civilizing

Figure 10. Brexit campaign poster, 2016. Photo courtesy of Al-Jazeera.

mission that Johnson termed as a "western liberal consensus on how societies should be ordered." This included achieving the "final triumph of that
conglomerate of western liberal values and ideals that unite the people in
this room, not just free markets rule of law [but] human rights, independent judiciary, habeas corpus, equalities of race and gender and sexual
orientation."

The Brexit referendum succeeded partly through the redeployment of
white British nativism in support of the vote to leave the membership of
the EU. One controversy that arose in the Brexit campaign, for example,
was a United Kingdom Independence Party campaign poster that dis-
played a photograph of a long line of Syrian and Middle Eastern refugees
with the words "Breaking Point: The EU has failed us all. We must break
free of the EU and take back control of our borders." It is important here
to note that the argument pertained to not only the migration of Europeans, but also the symbolic failure of EU membership to protect Britain
from further non-white and non-western immigration. The rhetoric of
porous national borders rendered vulnerable to racially, culturally, and
religiously different foreigners who threaten Britain is not new. It follows
in the tradition of successive racialized immigration panics initially formulated against non-white and non-western peoples whom Britain had

once sought to incorporate as subjects within the boundaries of its historical empire (Berkeley, Khan, and Ambikaipaker 2006).

Racial violence and racialized state violence in Britain cannot be examined in isolation from this recent and historical context and the reemer-
gence of political discourses that hope to reassert white-centric narratives of
immigration panics. Since the advent of anti-Commonwealth immigration
discourses and legislation in the 1960s, the two major political parties have
competed to restrict immigration in nativistic terms, while concealing the
history of the diaspora of "kith and kin" or "patrial" white British settler
colonials in different parts of the world (Australia, New Zealand, Canada,
Zimbabwe, South Africa, and the Americas) as well as ongoing emigration
to Europe and the United States. Such histories of white British emigration
are omitted in the narratives of white victimhood and multicultural backlash narratives (Hewitt 2005). More than six decades of successive racialized
panics in political life have spawned antipathies and animus against racial,
religious, and ethnic minorities, and these antipathies are intricately linked
to cycles of everyday racial violence and racialized state violence.

Racial violence in Britain has, for the most part, been erroneously conceptualized as a reified and pathological strain of deviance, for example, as
a "social ill" or, to use current British policy-speak, as antisocial behavior
(Donoghue 2010). Violent white racism is not limited to the forms of social
action and cultural behavior exhibited by "racist" working-class elements
such as "yobs," football hooligans, far-right extremists such as the English
Defence League, or even simply the "Tories," that is, the ruling Conservative Party. Such reductive theorizations of racism among the elite and middle classes tend to reify the phenomenon as something apart from the social
totality of Britishness—a Britishness that is constituted precisely through
racialized structures of liberal democratic governance and white-dominated
discourses of national identity.

However, even though a sense of Britishness is inherently if sometimes
implicitly constituted through a sense of the superiority of its western political system, long-standing issues, such as the ineffective state and social
response to white racial violence, institutional racism in the police force,
and discriminatory racial and religious profiling in the name of the War on
Terror, are not construed as urgent contradictions. The problems of racism
are peripheral in the public sphere and, while racism is powerfully linked
with strategic narratives in the formal political arena, the overcoming of

racism and the critique of the structures of white British racism do not register as a sustained cultural-political agenda, nor do they drive electoral outcomes in white-majority Britain. As the poet Benjamin Zephaniah (2001:20–21) wrote in commemoration of Stephen Lawrence, a young African Caribbean teenager knifed to death while waiting at a bus stop,

> The death of Stephen Lawrence
> Has taught us
> That we cannot let the illusion of freedom
> Endow us with a false sense of security as we walk the streets
> The whole world can now watch
> The academics and the super cops
> Struggling to define institutionalized racism
> As we continue to die in custody
> As we continue emptying our pockets on the pavements
> And we continue to ask ourselves
> Why is it so official
> That black people are so often killed
> Without killers?

This normalization of racial violence, and the normalization of the failure of Britain's liberal juridical system to mediate that racism, is a hard yet realistic starting point for a critical analysis of the western liberal social order in Britain. Western political liberalism as a tradition follows the hegemony of the rule of law, abstract legal proceduralisms that are ideally held to be color-blind, individual-based rights and access to the remedies of processual justice (Rawls 2005). In Britain, these principles of justice are seen as having emerged from the exceptional fountainhead of something often referred to as Britishness. In 2005, a former Labour prime minister, Gordon Brown, for example, stated in a speech in Tanzania that Britain should stop apologizing for empire. He asserted that it was time for Britons to celebrate the "British values that are enduring, because they stand for some of the greatest ideas in history: tolerance, liberty, civic duty, that grew in Britain and influenced the rest of the world." He added that the "strong traditions of fair play, of openness, of internationalism, these are great British values" (Brogan 2005).[8]

The idealized discourse of imperial and universal British values is certainly blind to Mr. Azlan's lived experienced of its liberal social order. And this is no less true for the other stories that will follow.

Therefore, how do we begin to understand the long-standing weakness and failures of antiracism in a liberal, political-juridical social order? Why do western nation-states such as Britain continue to experience racial, ethnic, and religious polarization and violence in the twenty-first century, despite the demise of overt white supremacist ideologies of empire, a retreat from the purported ills of state multiculturalism, and a return to what the Conservative Prime Minister David Cameron (2011) termed "muscular liberalism"?

To examine these questions, I utilize a critical race theory and postcolonial/decolonial theory framework that acknowledges the phenomena of racialization and white British political domination as constitutive features of British state and society (Gillborn 2008). White political domination in Britain is not a historically limited "geographical and temporal entity," confined to the classical period of the British Empire, but rather it is "now everywhere; in structures and in minds" (Nandy 2010:xi). Constant political work by whites, including the deployments of racial and state violence, is required to establish and reestablish the asymmetrical power that is granted to superordinate white British identities and to stabilize hierarchical power relations between other bodies, identities, epistemologies, and cultural lifeways. The subordinate positioning of people of African Caribbean, South Asian, and other non-white British groups within the domestic racial hierarchy is historically continuous with the entanglements of what Anibal Quijano (2000:533) terms "coloniality of power," where the "racial axis has a colonial origin and character, but it has proven to be more durable and stable than the colonialism in whose matrix it was established."

Uday Mehta (1999) has argued that the historical development of British liberal democratic thinking, entangled as it was within the project of a conquering and globalizing empire, constructed a social imaginary of a putative white British *Herrenvolk* in relation to multiple dark and black others who were included as objects of empire's rule but excluded from attributes such as self-determination, reason, and freedom. The distinction between imperial white Britons and subject races institutionalized a "politically exclusionary impulse," which, as Mehta elaborates, relies on a "thicker set of social credentials that constitute the real basis of political inclusion" (Mehta 1999: 61; see also Mills 1997, 2008).[9] As Catherine Hall (2011) notes, the emergence of a British modern identity was constituted through the very logics of establishing and maintaining an imperial and racialized political and social hierarchy.

Hence, I locate and identify the meaning of the social acts of racial violence and racialized state violence not as aberrations in British everyday life, but as continuous with the politics of maintaining a "possessive investment in whiteness" (Lipsitz 2006). Racial hate crimes and police violence, for example, do not lie simply with individual psychological prejudice or singular deviant elements in society (Bonilla-Silva 2014). Rather, these events are interlinked with a micropolitical process that I conceptualize as "everyday political whiteness." Everyday political whiteness means the socially agentive work done by whites (and white-aligned minorities) to block the pursuit and obtainment of racial justice and equality by subordinated racial, religious, and ethnic minority groups. It encompasses shared epistemic perspectives, co-identifications, and casual alliances among whites that coalesce when black people seek remedies from institutional discrimination, racial violence, and racialized state violence. Whites of all classes, including the perpetrators of racial violence, bystanders, and institutional state actors (whites and white-aligned officers) who are charged with performing the state's duties, engage in this racial-political work. Everyday political whiteness in Britain, overtly or tacitly, endorses the preeminence of white British identities and works to align the state and its liberal juridical processes in its favor.

When I was conducting extended fieldwork in 2006, NMP was one of the few politically black anti–racial violence and police monitoring organizations remaining not only in London, but also in the entire nation. African Caribbean and South Asian community organizers who lived and worked in the borough as well as white antiracist educators and activists founded the organization in 1980. The catalyst for the formation of NMP was the murder, in that same year, of Akhtar Ali Baig, a young Pakistani student. A group of white friends, drinking at the Duke of Edinburgh pub on East Ham High Street, made a monstrous five-pound bet that one of them could kill a "Paki." The racially motivated murder of Akhtar Ali Baig was not the only one in east London during this period. Outside the Whitechapel train station lies Altab Ali Park. This small park is named after a twenty-five-year-old Bangladeshi clothing worker whom three teenage white boys murdered in 1978. The era also saw the now long-forgotten racist murders of Ishaque Ali in 1978, Kayimarz Anklesaria in 1979, Satnam Singh Gill in 1981, and Peter Burns in 1984. It saw the killing of Shamira Kassim, who was pregnant and who died with her three other children in a fire-bomb attack on their home, and the deaths by a fire bomb of the Khan family (a mother and three young children) in an attack also on their home (Thompson 1988).

NMP's political development was indelibly influenced not only by these local and national contexts and events, but also by the international milieu of third world decolonization and national independence movements that had preceded its founding. A diasporic postcolonial consciousness began to grow in the mid-twentieth century that broke from the white British liberal and radical left-wing groups that often purported to represent racial and ethnic minority issues and interests, but in effect sidelined and subordinated them. As Marion Glean,[10] the Trinidadian academic, pacifist, and antiracist activist, argued,

> The immediate pre- and post-independence generation were West Indian; they were not Englishmen who happened to be black, and because of the nature of West Indian history they were likely to be concerned about Africa certainly and in the case of Trinidadians also concerned about the Indian sub-continent. Nor were Indians anything like the docile passive mystical people they were made out to be. . . . [T]he lack of knowledge of the modern immigrant was to complicate an anti-racist front, since British liberals were working within a framework that had been undone . . . by a shift in at least psychological relationships: a questioning of history and a new security of culture which were the products of independence. (Glean 1973:13)

It was this postcolonial context that influenced Glean and others to construct "immigrant group solidarity" organizations to challenge the exclusions of liberal individualist and white-dominated British politics (1973:14). She stated, "I had in 1964, one aim: to ensure that immigrants, West Indians, Indians, Pakistanis and Africans could themselves decide their own strategies, decide on their own priorities, found their own organizations, and in doing those things break the circle of dependency" (13). Glean would go on to organize the momentous visit of Martin Luther King, Jr. to the United Kingdom, and she cofounded the Campaign Against Racial Discrimination (CARD), which emerged from that meeting (Wild 2008).

Especially in its early years, NMP was strongly committed to similar principles that centered black peoples' political autonomy to act on their own behalf, rather than to be represented by liberal or leftist whites as passive victims: "At the end of the day, we believe that racism can only be altered by *community self-organisation* [emphasis mine] and action. As a practical result of community action and campaigns, institutions and agencies have been forced to respond to racism and racist attacks in . . . serious, non-tokenistic ways" (NMP 1985:4).

At the heart of this politics was an unwavering commitment to a racial analysis of British liberal governance. This politics was initially alien both to mainstream political parties and to the white-led, class-based social movements in Britain that frequently appropriated and subordinated the issues of race and racism in favor of more "objective" class relations and the primacy of industrial working-class struggles. In the late 1960s and 1970s, insurgent black consciousness movements also played a role in the struggle against apartheid in South Africa, antineocolonial struggles in the Caribbean, and Black Power movements in the United States, the United Kingdom, and elsewhere. These global social movements further influenced the radical political thought of Britain's African, African Caribbean, and South Asian communities. As Steve Biko, the South African antiapartheid activist and one of the leading 1970s theoreticians of a political rather than ethnological definition of black consciousness, explained,

> We have in our policy manifesto defined as blacks as those who are by law or tradition politically, economically and socially discriminated against as a group in the South African society and identifying themselves as a unit of struggle. . . . [T]he term black is not necessarily all-inclusive, i.e. the fact that we are all not white does not necessarily mean that we are all black. Non-whites do exist and will continue to exist for quite a long time. If one's aspiration is whiteness but his pigmentation makes attainment of this impossible, then that person is a non-white. Any man who calls a white man "baas," any man who serves in the police force or security branch is ipso facto a non-white. Black people—real black people—are those who can manage to hold their heads high in defiance rather than willingly surrender their souls to the white man. (Biko [1978] 2002:48)

Echoes of Biko's analysis of the structural anti-black character of state institutions, such as the police, were common sense among NMP antiracist activists, as illustrated in NMP's principles and strategies. For example, the

WHAT YOU CAN DO

NEWHAM MONITORING PROJECT

NMP is here to
● **help you** if
  - ☐ you have been racially attacked – on the street, at school, at home – or racially abused
● **help you** if
  - ☐ you have been harassed by the police on racial grounds
  - ☐ you have been unjustly arrested and need legal advice and representation
  - ☐ you think your rights have been abused by the police
  - ☐ you have been racially abused or assaulted by the police or unnecessarily detained without charge

We can also
● help you to make a complaint or take out civil/criminal action against the police if your rights have been abused.

HELP CAN BE OBTAINED 24 HOURS 7 DAYS A WEEK BY RINGING 555 8151

NMP
● *has full-time workers who can help and advise you if you have been racially attacked or face police harassment*
● *runs a 24-hour emergency service, 7 days a week, which can give you legal help, moral support, medical help and other necessary assistance if you have been racially attacked or arrested or have been arrested and need legal representation.*

(Image in leaflet: hands holding map of NEWHAM with text "FIGHTING RACIST ATTACKS", "FIGHTING POLICE HARASSMENT", "24 HOUR EMERGENCY SERVICE", "HELP AND SUPPORT", "LEGAL ADVICE", logo "NMP")

WHAT YOU CAN DO

● Inform us of any racist attack (including graffiti, abuse, damage or other incidents) you know of or any attack you think has a racist motive ·by doing this we will be better able to monitor such attacks more accurately.

● Inform us of anyone you feel has been harassed by police on racial grounds, have had their rights abused, or unnecessarily detained without charge. If charged, ask them to come to see us. Let us know of any policing tactic in the borough that you feel needs drawing attention to. We will then place pressure on the police to account for their action.

● Bring to our attention anyone who feels that the police have acted improperly in any way and wish to make a complaint. We will assist people in making their complaint.

● Advertise our 24-hour Emergency Service. We need more volunteers to join the service and encourage others to participate. You are generally required for at least one evening a month. Not too much to ask in the struggle!

● Invite us to talk about our work at a meeting of your trade union branch or any community group/political party you may belong to. This should stimulate discussion and debate, which is one of the opening shots for effective anti-racist work.

● Affiliate to Newham Monitoring Project, come to our meetings (details from the Project), and publicise our activities in whatever way you can. Keep an eye out for our activities, meetings and demonstrations, and help us to support you.

● If you have been the victim of any form of racism, and have any contact with the police, always keep a note of the names and numbers of any officers you speak to, even on the phone. The greater the number of participants, the more reflective we are of those we represent.

اگر آپ کسی بھی ناصرت سے ہوسیاں بی- یا پلیس سے
تک بین- تربیہ مہربانی کالوں مشاورت اور دیگر
ضرورت کے لیے ہم سے رابطہ قائم کریں- ہماری خیرات-
منت ہونگی- ہمارا رابطہ کنٹ حاضر ہونگی۔

જો તમને વર્ણભેદ અથવા પોલીસની ગેરવર્તનીનો ભોગ બનવું પડ્યું હોય તો અમને અમે નાખે હોન કરો. અમારો પોલીસ ભાઇઓનો ઈમરજન્સી ફોન નંબર નીચે બનેલ છે.

ਜੇ ਕਰ ਤੁਸੀਂ ਨਸਲਵਾਦੀਆਂ ਜਾਂ ਪੁਲੀਸ ਅੰਤ੍ਰ ਘੱਤਾਰਤ ਤੋਂ ਤੰਗ ਹੁੰਦੇ ਕਰਨੇ ਲਈ ਨਾਲ ਸੰਪਰਕ ਪੈਦਾ ਕਰੋ ਅਸੀਂ ਤੁਹਾਨੂੰ 24 ਘੰਟੇ ਮੁਫਤ ਕਾਨੂੰਨੀ ਸਲਾਹ ਅਤੇ ਹੋਰ ਜ਼ਰੂਰੀ ਸਹਾਇਤਾ ਦੇ ਸਕਦੇ ਹਾਂ।

24 ਘੰਟੇ ਐਮਰਜੈਂਸੀ ਮਦਦ ਲਈ ਫੋਨ ਕਰੋ:-
555-8151

REMEMBER YOU CANNOT SUBSTITUTE COMMUNITY INVOLVEMENT AND ACTION WITH WORKERS AND IDEAS

JOIN THE FIGHT NOW

Figure 11. Newham Monitoring Project's community involvement leaflet, 1988. Image courtesy of Newham Monitoring Project.

organization refused to participate in frameworks such as improving "community relations" with the local borough police, diversifying ethnic representation within the police force, or fostering community collaboration with the state's counterterrorism programs. Such discourses, NMP argued, help make invisible the liberal state's own role in constructing racial domination and subordination. Critically, the NMP focused on confronting the state's structures and policies that produced anti-black outcomes and harm, such as vulnerability to racial violence and racial and religious profiling.

With regard to the local racial, religious, and ethnic minority communities and their leaders, however, NMP would often work with a wide range of community organizations and leaders, not all of whom necessarily shared the organization's politics. As Britain's state institutions, especially at the local municipal levels, began to diversify their personnel and multiculturalize their rhetoric during the 1980s and 1990s, NMP critiqued the arguments of a "linked fate" (Dawson 1995; Forman 2017) between different class segments of oppressed communities.

NMP viewed critically the elite "symbolic representatives" (Marable 2016, chap. 16) or community leaders and organizations that preferred to collaborate with the state in advancing its agendas, rather than to hold it accountable to marginalized communities. NMP perceived that these representatives were less likely to politically support people accused of crime or terrorism and that they had a stake in seeing Britain's antiracist struggle fragment into its different ethnicized and religious components. In this way, the political blackness exemplified by NMP differed from the race and ethnicity categories utilized by the state's official system of recognizing and tracking "16 + 1" different ethno-racial classifications. Among the sixteen official racial categories, for example, are Asian British-Indian, Black British-Caribbean, Mixed-White and Black African, White-British, White-Irish, and one "Not Stated" option.

As NMP put it, "Whilst celebrating our differences, we need to be united in our opposition to racial harassment. For that reason we reject the obsession with ethnicity and the way it is used to divide us, an obsession borne of the emerging black middle class. The fight for culture can be a fight against racism, but it is not automatically so, and does not speak to the condition of the poor, working-class black communities for whom fighting against racism often means fighting for their lives" (NMP n.d.b:2–3).

The range of people included in this formation has been fluid and often contested. In observing the formations of political blackness in Britain, I

STOP & SEARCH: THE FACTS

People from black communities are EIGHT times more likely to be stopped and searched

Photo: Ray Smith

Over the last year the police in London have stopped and searched 40% more Asians and 30% more African-Caribbeans but 8% less white people...

ruа TARGET ?

NEWHAM MONITORING PROJECT · PO Box 273 · LONDON E7

STOP & SEARCH INCIDENT RECORD

YOUR NAME _____   CONTACT NUMBER _____

TIME / DATE OF INCIDENT	WHERE STOPPED?	BRIEF SUMMARY	OFFICERS' NAME & BADGE NUMBER

Newham Monitoring Project (NMP) is an independent east London organisation that has supported people facing racial harassment and civil injustice for over 21 years. We are highlighting the unjust and unfair use of stop & search by the police in Newham, Tower Hamlets & Hackney.

- There is evidence that young black people in east London feel they are unfairly targeted. One person who sought help from NMP had been stopped over 5 times in one day for no reason
- "we are clear that the perception and experience of the minority communities that discrimination is a major element in the stop and search problem is correct" The Stephen Lawrence Inquiry
- Stop and search does NOT work. It results in few arrests and fewer convictions. It is a complete waste of police time and resources

Tell us your experiences. Use this form or call us on **0800 169 3111**

(calls are free and confidential)

Figure 12. Newham Monitoring Project's leaflet addressing stop-and-search, distributed to multiple black communities, 2006. Leaflet courtesy of Newham Monitoring Project.

have seen people included from African Caribbean, South Asian, and Middle Eastern communities, as well as other racial, religious, and ethnic minorities who encounter and experience violence at the hands of white Britons and the British state. The terms of inclusion, however, have often been determined not through an ethnological or ethnocultural sense of belonging, but as a result of people's direct experiences with racial violence and state violence. For example, NMP took on the campaign to seek justice for the family of Jean Charles de Menezes, who was shot dead by antiterror police in 2005 following the London bombings. De Menezes was a Latin American immigrant from Brazil who was erroneously identified as a "Muslim-looking" (Volpp 2002; Ahmad 2004) terror suspect and was executed while going to work on the London subway.

I decided to carry out fieldwork in Newham partly because I was drawn to its dynamic, cosmopolitan character. Starting in 2003, with the consent of NMP, I began participant observation research into the work of the group for three months and followed this up with further research at the end of 2005 with extended fieldwork that lasted fourteen months.[11] The majority of my daily antiracist, activist-oriented participant observation research with NMP was not centered on high-profile antiracist campaigns around periodic incidents of racism; rather, it unfolded in a workaday world that was engaged in both meeting new victims of racial violence and grappling with state violence and surveillance.

As an NMP-affiliated activist and caseworker who daily engaged the liberal juridical structures of the British state, I spent many work hours advocating for victims of racial attacks and police abuse and injustices abetted by the discourses of Islamophobia that underlie the state's antiterrorism and prevention of terrorism policies and practices. In the course of my daily work, I wrote numerous letters of complaint that addressed levels of police and social service inaction or institutional racism. This was a pressure politics method of casework: in this mode, the state's antiracist and antidiscrimination duties were monitored by partisan activists who called and left messages for supervising detective superintendents, investigating detective inspectors, beat-patrol constables, housing officers, ASBO officers, city council–appointed solicitors and barristers, elected councilors, and MPs. The goal was to push an individual victim's case forward within a weak antiracist and white, British-aligned institutional structure.

My fieldwork emerged from both my activist-oriented positionality with NMP and my everyday experience as a long-term resident of Newham. These realities led me to focus my ethnographic work on how racist attacks on the street and racial profiling, discrimination, and violence by the state (especially the police) represented a continuum of racism that was inter-linked in the lived experiences of Newham's black residents. Material for this study is the product of a combination of overlapping ethnographic methods that all aim to establish collaborative social change politics between the researcher and the researched community. The decision to become an advocate for victims of racial and state violence, as well as a researcher of these social processes, was informed by critical debates in the field of ethnographic research that call for moving beyond traditional, Eurocentric conceptions of ethnography as a value-free methodology intent on the creation of omniscient narratives and dispassionate forms of analysis (Campbell and Gregor 2002; Naples 2003; Mutua and Swadener 2004; Foley and Valenzuela 2005; Hale 2006; Smith 2012). For example, the question of the degree of racism that a U.K. police force exhibits cannot simply be determined by quantitatively measuring the preponderance of anti-black prejudices of individual police officers within the context of gathering for-mal interview data. Such an approach privileges the interview performance of white police officers in determining, regulating, and adjudicating whether institutional racism exists or not in a social structure. The center-ing of this procedure of statistically "studying up" (Gusterson 1997), in order to achieve an "objective" social balance, privileges perpetrator pretext and motivation and frames the understanding of the concept of institu-tional racism as essentially an aberrational phenomenon carried out by "bad" social actors.

I gathered information through a combination of critically engaged and partisan observant participation, and also through oral historical research and auto-ethnographic self-reflections. I conceptualized my own personal, collective memories and experiences as a person from the former British Empire as an archive and a contemporary field site for examining how racism and white supremacy have structured the trajectories, histories, and identities of fellow postcolonial people in Britain today. In other words, I did not come to this research in Britain as a traditional white male anthro-pologist, traveling to subordinate colonial or exotic outposts in order to carry out participant observation among "native" inhabitants. Instead, I struggled as a non-white researcher and Commonwealth citizen to gain entry and retain residence in Britain, as it became the United States' partner in the twenty-first-century War on Terror. The global political atmosphere of this war makes border crossings for non-white and non-western bodies a hostile and dangerous affair. At the most literal and tangible points of access, such as at airports, I battled against immigration authorities and increasing counterterrorism profiling as both a national from Malaysia and a person of Sri Lankan Tamil descent. As one immigration officer asked me in response to my statement that I would be staying with friends, "What? English friends? How do you know them?" Such racist presumptions are normalized through collective historical erasures and are undergirded by a selective forgetting of the many connections forged by the empire between the colonizer and colonized.

My personal postcolonial connections to Malaysia, Sri Lanka, and Britain are deeply rooted in the colonial racial policies of the empire itself. Hence, it was not by mere chance that I ended up with diasporically scattered family members in Britain who had arrived from many different countries, through higher education routes or through asylum-seeking and refugee routes.

My grandparents had been British colonial subjects in Malaya and possessed citizenship under the 1948 British Nationality Act, which was later rescinded as a growing number of Commonwealth immigrants exercised their right to reside in Britain in the 1950s and 1960s (Hall 2002). One uncle came from Malaya to Britain to study law at Cambridge in the early twentieth century. He married a white English woman in 1920 and they had twin daughters. He was forced to abandon his family (but never severed his relationship to them) and returned to Malaysia because he was not able to profitably practice law as a black barrister in Britain at the time. Furthermore, whites-only laws and antimiscegenation or "white prestige" regulations of social spaces in the empire made it difficult for him to take his wife and mixed-race children back to Malaya. Aunts, uncles, and cousins in my extended family from Jaffna, Sri Lanka, started to arrive in Britain from 1983 to 2009 as asylum seekers following the civil war between the Sinhalese-dominated Sri Lankan state and the Tamil Tigers, a war that ended brutally in 2009 with the genocide of thousands and thousands of civilians.

In fact, one of NMP's campaigns for justice was the joint community mobilization and demonstrations organized after the killing of Panchadcharam Sahitharan in 1991. Sahitharan was one of the fleeing asylum seekers who came out of the civil war in Sri Lanka and had resettled from Jaffna into Newham's Manor Park neighborhood in 1990. On December 29, 1991, as he was making his way home from the East Ham subway station, Sahitharan was set upon by a gang of racist white youths armed with baseball bats and sticks. He was savagely beaten and left with serious head injuries. This particular gang had not made an isolated attack on Sahitharan; that day, they had carried out a number of attacks on black people.

Sahitharan managed to remain conscious after his beatings and fled to his sister's home where he is reported to have said, "Look what has happened. I never wanted to leave Sri Lanka. Now look what has happened. I am going to die here" (NMP 1992:38). Days after this beating, Sahitharan succumbed to irreversible brain injuries and died at the Royal London Hospital in Whitechapel.

NMP undertook a massive mobilization to encourage witnesses to come forward. Two white men were found, arrested, and accused and charged with the murder. However, the state's response to the crime was perfunctory and did not give serious attention to its racist dimension. The charged men were allowed bail and the Crown Prosecution Service (CPS), the prosecuting arm of the state, had only lackadaisical interest in pursuing the case, despite the gravity of the crime and the public's interest. In this atmosphere of official neglect, the CPS eventually dropped the case for lack of evidence (NMP 1992:48).

Two years later in 1993, Stephen Lawrence, an African Caribbean teenager, was stabbed to death by a group of white men in southeast London. Again, the investigating police and prosecuting state discharged their duties poorly, which initially resulted in the acquittal of the five men charged in Lawrence's murder. It took another fifteen years to finally bring Stephen Lawrence's murderers to justice.

As a result of these failings, the Macpherson Royal Commission of Inquiry was formed in 1997. The setting up of the commission was due to political pressure brought about through a six-year campaign by the Lawrence family and the many antiracist groups that supported them, including NMP. In 1999, this commission entered the term "institutional racism" into British law in order to describe the collective behavior of London's Metropolitan Police in the Lawrence case. Institutional racism henceforth was legally defined as "the collective failure of an organization to provide an appropriate and professional service to people because of their colour, culture, or ethnic origin. It can be seen or detected in processes, attitudes

and behaviour which amount to discrimination through unwitting prejudice, ignorance, thoughtlessness and racist stereotyping which disadvantage
minority ethnic people" (Macpherson 1999).

The cases of Stephen Lawrence and Panchadcharam Sahitharan illustrate the benefit of adopting a politically black approach to addressing white
racial violence and the state's institutional racism. In other words, their
cases are not ethnoracially disparate, but structurally related. As NMP has
persistently argued since its founding, "Each racist attack, each assault or
insult is not isolated but connected" (Open Face Films 1986). This
approach also alerted me to the importance of resisting racial, religious,
and ethnic reification when writing this ethnography.

Fifteen years after Sahitharan's murder, during the course of my fieldwork in 2006, I tried to physically trace members of my own extended
family who had become refugees in Britain. I initially felt this project was
separate from my work with NMP and my investigations into antiracist
resistance toward white British racism. I was successful in getting in touch
with a branch of my family that had been displaced by the war in Sri Lanka,
and this reconnection resulted in invitations to participate in my extended
family's social events. After one of these joyful occasions, members of my
family were racially attacked as they exited a community hall. They were
set upon by a group of drunken white pub goers intent on "Paki-bashing."
Racist violence, which I had been regarding through the still-distant lens of
participant observation, only grew more salient as my fieldwork and residence in London progressed. This is from my fieldnotes:

> I woke up this morning after a night of dancing and revelry at the
> family's engagement party for cousin Dev. It was wonderful to be
> reunited with family I did not know I had. But last night as the party
> dispersed, Kumar had been set upon by a group of white pub goers
> outside Greenford Town Hall. He had tried to help his friend who
> was having an altercation with a white guy from the pub, when five
> and then ten of his mates from the pub came out with pipes and
> batons in hand, yelling, "fucking Pakis!" and beat the shit out of
> them.
>
> When the police arrived, a white policewoman told Kumar that
> he has to have witnesses to go to court, or else the case was a waste
> of police time.
>
> "This is not Africa!" she retorted.

Why is Africa symbolized as the primordial opposite of Britain? Once again the racist mobilization draws on tropes of blackness, and especially African-ness, as a sign of the obverse of civilization, even though racist violence is savagely wrought upon a "native" body.

The police refuse to entertain racial motivation; they advised Kumar to let them pursue the matter as aggravated assault.

I therefore did not find the project of researching racism in Britain to be viable as an abstract or a politically neutral enterprise. In this research process I did not encounter myself as different from other black people who were similarly struggling to make social meaning and achieve political resolution about their collective and intergenerational struggles with British racism.

CHAPTER 2

"They Do Not Look Like People Who Would Do This"

Amina's Struggle Against Everyday Political Whiteness

In Britain, ethnic minority communities are ambiguously positioned in relation to Britishness, and they are racialized as different from white Britons. A large body of research has shown that white violence against racial, religious, and ethnic minorities has occurred and continues to occur across the British Isles. White violence and racism are not limited to urban England, where there are large concentrations of ethnic and religious minority communities, but also occur in the contexts of Scotland, Wales, Northern Ireland, and in rural areas where there are sparse ethnic minority populations (Armstrong 1989; Arshad 2003; Hopkins 2004; Neal 2009; Connolly and Khaoury 2010; Chakraborti and Garland 2011). Many ethnographic research studies have confirmed that non-white phenotypical differentiation, anti-immigration discourses, and nonwestern cultural and religious differences are still grounds for racialized dynamics that impact ethnic, racial, and religious minorities even within intimate and mixed-race family contexts (Nayak 2004; Brown 2005; Twine 2011). In other words, raciology (the ascription of hierarchical social meaning and status to phenotypical and ethnicized differences) saturates everyday social life and civil society in twenty-first-century Britain.

The afterlife of British Empire discourses, including reworked tenets of imperial white supremacy, influences everyday white British perspectives. Symbolic wounds often catalyze reassertions of white supremacy and allegiance to an imagined sense of a monocultural British identity—an identity that the immigration of formerly colonized subjects into Britain presumably disrupts (Wemyss 2009). Racialization in Britain for South Asians in this respect interlocks with African and African Caribbean experiences. The racialized construction of antipathies to "colored immigration" from "New Commonwealth" countries in the 1950s and 1960s was an emergent mobilizational strategy in British electoral politics (Carter, Harris, and Joshi 1987) and, in 2006, it was discursively revived through immigration-control debates, especially surrounding "non-EU" immigration, which at the time was a focus of political opprobrium. This occurred even as European immigration was favored due to the EU expansion of membership to include Eastern European countries. This particular dynamic, however, changed with the Brexit referendum that occurred in 2016 when European immigration and global refugee obligations, particularly to those from the Middle East, also became subject to a nativist backlash. Up to the present moment in 2017, the backlash against non-European refugees has been especially disproportionate since the numbers that Britain actually accepts are very small. For example, Britain had only accepted some one thousand Syrian asylum seekers during the height of the refugee crisis in 2015 (Mason 2015).

The political mobilization of white British nativist anxiety around immigration, however, continues to shape the everyday racisms that racial and ethnic minorities experience, regardless of their citizenship or visa status. Perpetual anxieties around immigration control—one of the key planks of the Brexit vote—help to reproduce and maintain the identity and self-representation of white Britons as the proper subjects of national sovereignty and security. As such, the discourse that white Britons are under siege from ex-colonial Commonwealth immigrants, refugees, asylum seekers, and continental European migrants helps to constitute and assert post-empire, white British identity as singularly autochthonous and defensive.

The recent discursive turn against European migrants, about 49 percent of total non-British inflows in 2015 (Vargas-Silva and Markaki 2016), needs to be understood against the backdrop of the previous half-century, during which time white British nativism was defined by politicians and government policy in relation to a "hyperconsciousness of race" (Vargas 2004). João Costa Vargas argues that even when race is not explicitly the object of discourse or attack, it is nonetheless the axis along which whites "think about/repress, interrogate/passively accept, and justify/ignore social hierarchies" (Vargas 2004:444).

These practices in raciological thinking, however, become enacted in ordinary social interactions and on many everyday levels: from face-to-face interactions on the street, to encounters with the workings and processes of bureaucracies and state agencies, to laws and public policy. When enacted by whites against non-whites, racialized "couplings of power and difference" (Gilmore 2002:15) have also taken the form of low-level harassment and violence, as well as direct physical attacks.

The British state has criminalized racial harassment as a "hate crime" and as antisocial behavior. These criminological offenses are legally defined to include verbal harassment, physical assaults, and, at the extreme end of the scale, racially motivated killings. In British criminal justice, the 1986 Public Order Act, the 1994 and 1998 Criminal Justice and Public Order Acts, and the 2006 Racial and Religious Hatred Act govern the regulation of hate speech and violent acts toward racial, religious, and sexual minorities (Jeremy 2007). Before these enactments, and even since their passage, police officers often miscode racial harassment offenses in color-blind terms as public order offenses or disturbances such as private or neighborly disputes. After a long period of grassroots, antiracist activism against police reluctance to recognize and record the racial character of crime, the Crime and Disorder Act of 1998 institutionalized the concept of enhancing punishments for "racially aggravated" offenses (such as assault and harassment) into British law. The 2006 Racial and Religious Hatred Act introduced new substantive laws and categories of hate crime offenses to include incitements to hatred based on religious grounds. The embrace by the liberal state of the criminalization of hate speech is one of the pillars by which the British state ostensibly enforces de jure racial justice.

But racial harassment and attacks are not merely irrational, discrete, and hate-based actions easily redressed by hate crime laws. The settlement of black immigrants from Africa, the Caribbean, and South Asia into white working-class neighborhoods such as Newham is marked by a history of hostile white reception and the use of violence to expel the newcomers. Everyday racial harassment and attacks are not merely irrational and psychologically driven phenomena. The acts that constitute harassment may range from the mundane to serious bodily harm, but the continuum of racial harassment is politically purposeful in that it enacts, on a direct everyday level, a possessive, white nationalist, and territorial logic (Hesse et al. 1992; Back 1996; Chahal 2003):

Unprovoked assaults including common assault, actual bodily harm and grievous bodily harm, damage to property, the daubing of slogans and/or graffiti of a racial nature, arson or attempted arson, the insertion of rags, paper, rubbish and/or any material which can be and/or has been set alight [into houses], the insertion of excrement, eggs, paint, faeces, rubbish and/or other noxious and/or offensive substances through an opening in the house concerned or within its perimeter, the sending of threatening and/or abusive correspondence of a racial nature, the making of threatening and/or abusive telephone calls of a racial nature, verbal racial abuse, demanding money accompanied by verbal racial abuse, repeated vandalism of a property belonging to the person concerned or any member of his/her household, threatening and abusive behaviour including spitting, participation in any activity which is calculated to deter the person from occupying a particular property and attempted murder or murder. (The Monitoring Group 2011)

These low-level racial harassment offenses, through the patterns of perpetrator escalation, can culminate into more and more extreme "hate crimes." In my own experience with racial harassment cases, mild forms of hate speech may involve simple verbal abuse and nonphysical assaults, but white perpetrators of hate crimes are prone to escalate the violence of racial harassment to assaults and physical attacks (Bowling 2001). Racial harassment, especially of closely located neighbors or fellow housing block dwellers, often becomes repeated and assumes the character of a sustained campaign, rather than as a one-off incident (Bowling and Phillips 2001). And even when harassment does not turn into actual physical attacks, the long-term impact of persistent racial abuse engenders its own trauma on victims.

During my fieldwork, I appeared in the capacity of a Newham Monitoring Project (NMP) caseworker at the Bow County Court at a hearing to review a restraining injunction filed on behalf of Amina, the woman who was facing racial harassment in her public housing block. The small space of the low-rise apartment complex provided many opportunities for chance encounters and new incidents of abuse from hostile neighbors, because residents shared common flights of stairs and courtyards where washing was hung up to dry.

Amina, the single mother of an eleven-year-old son, Adil, was born and raised in east London. Her father, Mr. Azlan, had emigrated from India and had since passed away (to recall, his tragic story was introduced in the

Prelude). Amina had suffered two years of repeated verbal abuse, threats, intimidation, and physical attacks from her white neighbors, Thomas Smith and Brian Robson. These two men began their harassment with deliberate late-night noise and drunken partying, and these activities slowly escalated to incidents of racist name-calling, the scrawling in blood of racist graffiti on Amina's front door, and constant verbal threats of racial and sexual violence as she entered and exited the housing complex.

Amina was also subjected to frequent verbal abuse. At various times, she had been called a "black cunt," a "Paki-whore," "wog's meat," and "black wog" by Smith and Robson. The term "wog" is a slang slur word (of unclear etymology, an acronym for the colonial stereotype of the "western-ized oriental gentleman," or a popular Victorian-era blackface doll) and is applied to both South Asian and African-descended peoples within the United Kingdom (Stokoe and Edwards 2007). These racist terms, which are now legally recognized in Britain as criminal utterances and therefore no longer protected by individual free speech rights, illustrate how South Asians are associated discursively with blackness.

The historical, established idioms of anti-black hate speech by whites in Britain, unlike in the United States, include South Asians. This has occurred since the late 1980s even though South Asians have contested or rejected self-identifying with the term "black" in favor of newer self-identifications such as "British Asian," which began to emerge in the 1990s, or "British Muslim," which arose in the 2000s. Regardless of these newer identities and self-making, whites in twenty-first-century Britain still formulate and express an anti-black animus against South Asians.

Amina's brother-in-law, himself a police officer, recommended that she contact NMP about her ordeal. She had had very little success when she tried on her own to get the Newham police and the city council to respond to her situation. One day in July she called NMP's twenty-four-hour Emergency Service helpline, and I answered the phone.

"I don't even know where to begin and I don't know if all this is even believable," she said.

I urged her to tell her story. In the short time since I had begun working as a caseworker at NMP I had come to understand that victims of racial harassment often felt an acute sense of self-doubt and uncertainty about others' acceptance of the credibility of their stories. Many people would keep silent about their situation and, as repeat victimizations occurred and the circumstances of the abuse and attacks grew more complex, they would paradoxically feel even less empowered to name and address their problem. For many people—and, certainly, within the assumptions of the liberal state's antiracist "hate crime" laws—racism is understood as a onetime incident or event and not as prolonged campaigns of abuse and harassment.

When victims seek assistance from the police and relevant state authorities, their confusion and sense of helplessness are exacerbated by routine responses of racism denial. As a result, the fear of not being believed that many victims of racist violence anticipate is a product of structural-ideological power in a system where white racism is considered an aberrational feature of an otherwise race-neutral or antiracist rule of law and social order.

As Amina slowly explained over the phone, her latest experience of harassment had taken place on a Saturday night when she returned home to her flat and was putting Adil to bed. She had recently separated from her husband, a white British man from Hoxton who had converted to Islam, and she was now a single parent, living on her own. She had a close friend, Harry, a white gay man who lived across the corridor and who also occasionally experienced harassment from Smith and Robson.

After tucking Adil into bed, she answered a phone call but suddenly heard odd noises coming from outside her flat. The noises grew closer and she went to look through the door's peephole. There she saw her neighbor, Thomas Smith, standing outside her door. He was drunk.

"Get out of here, you Paki! Go home to your own country, you wogs! All of you black bastards are the same!" he shouted. It wasn't the first time that Smith had come to Amina's door and created a scene. He then shouted that he would bite her the next time she dared to come out. He claimed that he was HIV positive. "I'll have you! You better watch your back," Smith continued and banged the door hard. He then also threatened to harm her sexually.

Amina could see the door coming loose from all of Smith's kicking and punching. "I've infected you! I've touched your son with my wounds!" he carried on. Adil suffered from frequent outbreaks of cold sores. Smith had noticed this and had issued this threat before. He would often keep watch on Amina's comings and goings and find new opportunities to threaten and harass.

In his drunken state, Smith then made his way upstairs, where he started to kick at the door of an immigrant Sudanese man whom he had also targeted for racial abuse. Luckily the neighbor was not in that night. Amina told me that Smith had physically assaulted the man before. She had witnessed an incident where Smith had pinned him against the wall and overheard him shout, "I am talking to you as a white man to a black man!"

Finding no response upstairs, Smith then came back to Amina's landing. He proceeded to smear her door with his blood, possibly by cutting himself. Amina recalled that a couple of months earlier, the word "Paki" had been scrawled on her door. It happened right after she had witnessed another white neighbor, Brian Robson, also trying to kick her door.

Garbage repeatedly appeared on her doorstep. Her washing, including underwear that hung on the common clotheslines in the housing complex, disappeared frequently. Someone once stuffed her letterbox with McDonalds curry sauce. This was intended as a mockery of her Indian identity. Amina had telephoned the council to ask for help in removing the racist graffiti, something that the local council was legally required to do. She called a council hotline that was supposed to provide graffiti-removal service, but her request was denied.

Victims of racist vandalism, who in the past had received the city council's assistance to remove racist graffiti on their homes, were now being told that if they had exercised the "right to buy" their previously council-owned flat, they would no longer be provided this service. Encouraged by the council to buy her flat, Amina had gone into debt to do so. But as a private property owner, therefore, the graffiti on her home door was no longer considered the custodial responsibility of the state. However, it should have been possible to obtain the services, because the perpetrators in this case were still public tenants.

Failing to get any assistance from the city council, Amina then called the police. When they arrived, they ordered her to clean up the bloody graffiti on the door herself. She asked them several times if she should be doing this herself or if the police needed to take photographs. One of the attending officers told her five times to remove the blood by herself and she finally relented. She gave the rags she used to clean the blood to the police, and when she inquired what they were going to do about the incident, they brashly retorted, "What do you want us to do?"

As she gave her statement about the incident to the police, Amina tried to explain the chronic, long-term nature of the harassment she had endured and still suffered. Once again the attending police officers dismissed her fears. "Why don't you just move then?" they said.

One of the attending officers who said this to her was of African Caribbean descent. He told her in so many words that she had freely chosen to live amid people such as Smith and Robson and, by choosing to stay on, she had only herself to blame for the situation. This policeman placed the onus on the victim of racism to find a private solution to her problems. Hence, despite the numerous laws at both the national and local levels that criminalized racial harassment, the local police did not seem interested in enforcing them.

A critical component of Amina's case, though, and one that made it difficult to dismiss by the police or local council, was the fact that during Smith's harangue at her door, she had had the presence of mind to pick up a video camera that she usually used to record her son's childhood and had turned it on the peephole. Amina had captured incriminating footage on tape and she turned it over to the police as evidence.

I was alarmed when I heard that the tape had been given to the police without any backup copies. It was not uncommon to hear of video evidence going missing in police custody, especially in cases of police abuse. Street surveillance cameras, or CCTVs, that had been installed as part of the borough's crime-control measures, sometimes "failed" during incidents of police abuse.

Thankfully, this did not happen. The tape was processed properly and became the primary evidence to bring criminal charges of "racially aggravated criminal damage" against Smith, who was scheduled to appear at Snaresbrook Crown Court.

After the police left, another white neighbor, Helena, came downstairs to Amina's landing and also started to hurl racial abuse at her. She was upset that Amina had called the police on a fellow white British resident. "Pakis, all these problems is their cause. You're not even allowed to call them Pakis," she hollered at Amina. "They can call each other nigger, but if you do it, then it's something really bad and you can get arrested for it!" she added.

White racial solidarity and shared perspectives become mobilized in daily life, as Helena's comments suggest, against black attempts to assert racial equality and justice. The efforts of black people to enlist and engage the law to secure a liberal schedule of rights, such as the equal protection of personhood, elicit a backlash response when whites suddenly claim the victims' status, with the figure of the "Paki" aligned with the liberal antiracist state as the imagined perpetrators against them. This is an instance of everyday political whiteness. The phrase connotes a whiteness that is not simply an ethnological category, or an a priori, obvious, identity. Instead, as Zeus Leonardo (2004:137) has argued, "White racial supremacy revolves less around the issue of unearned advantages, or the state of being dominant, and more around *direct processes that secure domination and the privileges associated with it* [emphasis mine]." Everyday political whiteness occurs when multiple whites, socially intersecting across class lines, engage in epistemic and micropolitical solidarity in order to forestall racial justice and secure liberal juridical impunity for racism. Rather than being a result of invidious prejudice and irrationality, racism and white supremacy emerge through tacit political logics and collective calculations that aim to resume and renew the status of whites as the privileged subjects of liberal juridical rule. In Helena's case, for example, while she was not the initial perpetrator of racial harassment, her mutual identification and expressions of white racial solidarity with Smith and Robson, rather than with Amina, reveal the mutual identification processes that whites who otherwise occupy different social strata forge with one another. This coalescing of everyday political whiteness especially occurred vis-à-vis the exercise of racial harassment and attempts to mitigate the power of the local police or Newham Council's housing officers to act in alignment with black people's rights or claims of justice.

Everyday political whiteness in Britain unfolds on many levels within social life, as well as in the state and liberal juridical procedures intended to regulate and contain black responses to racism. Intra-white solidarity and the containment of racial justice claims both serve to secure and sustain white racial domination. Everyday political whiteness helps to sustain mutually enabling connections between formal and informal social action and institutional and extra-institutional racism.

Amina was repeatedly told by her neighbors "all wogs should go home to your own country!" This echoed a well-known antiforeigner sentiment that had been made popular by the Conservative politician Enoch Powell in the 1960s. Powell's germinal "Rivers of Blood" speech in 1968 was instrumental in representing the "New Commonwealth" immigrants as alien threats as distinguished from the patrial principle and "kith and kin"–based white British diasporas in the "Old Commonwealth." The latter consisted of white settler-colonial countries such as Australia, South Africa, Zimbabwe (formerly Rhodesia), and Canada. Powell had successfully fused racism and nativism, and he propagated an ahistorical discourse that defined white British people as natives in antagonistic relationship to "non-patrial" but fellow empire subjects who were entering the colonial metropole.

Powell ([1968] 2007) introduced the symbolic elements and racial dis-possession narrative that still influence the reconstruction of white British nativism:

> A week or two ago I fell into conversation with a constituent, a middle-aged, quite ordinary workingman employed in one of our nationalized industries. After a sentence or two about the weather, he suddenly said: "If I had the money to go, I wouldn't stay in this country." I made some deprecatory reply to the effect that even this government wouldn't last forever, but he took no notice, and con-tinued: "I have three children, all of them been through grammar school and two of them married now, with family. I shan't be satis-fied till I have seen them all settled overseas. In this country in 15 or 20 years' time the black man will have the whip hand over the white man."

Powell's invocation of the slave-master anxiety is telling. It reveals the colo-nial premise that underlies post-empire white victimization narratives, which also rests on what Ashis Nandy calls a "homology between sexual and political dominance" (2010:4). The anxiety of white domination, as a political-sexual anxiety, is pivotal in the discourse of white British self-fashioning.

Indeed, Powell also invoked the well-documented white supremacist idea of black male sexual threats against white British womanhood in another story from his speech. He told of an elderly white woman pen-sioner who tried to evict her unruly "Negro" tenants, only to find that new race relations laws rendered her a criminal for trying to do so. In the Powellian framework, white British supremacy was in crisis because such anti–racial discrimination reforms were antidemocratic: they oppressed the white working-class commoner, who is constructed also as the symbol of British sovereignty. In Powell's world, antiracism laws and the changing racial composition of British society represented threats to the historical status habitually enjoyed by white Britons.

Powell's proposed solution to the anti-black immigration narrative that he himself developed was to call for racialized border control: "The answers to the simple and rational question are equally simple and rational: by stopping, or virtually stopping further inflow, and by promoting the maxi-mum outflow," he reasoned. In nearly a half-century since Powell made his speech, this racialized immigration-control logic is a touchstone for white British democratic demands. All major political parties today compete to unveil proposals for restricting "non–European Union" migration flows, whether through economic or asylum-seeking and refugee routes.[1] In 2015, in the midst of the Mediterranean refugee crisis, David Cameron, then prime minister, repeated Powell's trope when he described refugees fleeing for Europe as a "swarm of people" coming to take advantage of British jobs and the good life (Elgot and Taylor 2015).

The anti-"wog" immigration politics of the 1960s included the themes of immigration restriction, eviction, and repatriation. These populist narratives and political imaginaries are found at the grassroots of neighborhoods and the streets as well as indirectly through state policy. Everyday attacks and harassment against racial, religious, and ethnic minority people who enter previously all-white spaces and neighborhoods reprise the historical-political logic of white possessiveness. In fact, a majority of Newham Council's socially housed tenants in 2006 were still white (60 percent), in a borough that contained almost two-thirds black and ethnic minority communities (Harriss 2006:12).

Racial harassment and attacks at the street level are therefore not only exercises in individual bigotry, or isolated "hate crimes" by aberrant, non-conforming actors in the liberal state. They also are enactments of a white political logic, with its own historical salience, of excluding racial, religious, and ethnic minorities from social spaces in the liberal juridical order. Racial harassment in this sense follows the Powellian logic of seeking to enact repatriation, or the "maximum outflow" of black people, from putatively white spaces such as social housing, schools, and neighborhoods. As Patricia Hill Collins (1998) has argued, the real purpose of hate acts is to accomplish a political will to racial domination.

This politicized reading of racial harassment and hate speech counters theories that rationalize white racial politics as non-elite forms of cultural resistance against state neglect or, alternately, as isolated cultural pathologies arising out of poverty and its deprivations.[2] These counterclaims—paternalistic, elite interpretations of working-class white racism that discount the logics of everyday political whiteness—are quite prevalent in Britain. Following Powell's framework, many white-centric sociologists in Britain have argued that the British state's codification of antiracist laws and multicultural policies victimizes and disproportionately regulates white working-class behavior. In turn, this kindles an "unfairness to whites" sentiment within non-elite white British communities (Hewitt 2005:77–78; Dench, Gavron, and Young 2006). The narratives of white backlash against antiracism, especially white victimization in the criminalization of hate speech and racial harassment, galvanize notions of exclusive and possessive white citizenship. Its logic is pitted against the reformist agendas of anti-racist liberal rule in Britain. Among other sites, then, everyday political whiteness is worked out in contestations over the state's criminalization of racial harassment and hate speech.

Everyday political whiteness is a form of civic agency that aims to repro-duce and renew the structural privileges and the cultural-epistemological primacy of whiteness in British liberal democracy. In Amina's experience, for example, the constant referencing of her racial and sexualized difference as a "wog" or "wog's meat" in verbal abuse and the threats by her white male neighbors to violate her as a "black cunt" reveal white fantasies of penetrating and violating black women's bodies. Such fantasies are located historically also in the "idea of colonial rule as a manly or husbandly or lordly prerogative" (Nandy 2010:5), which corresponds symbolically to white British heterosexual, patriarchal political domination.

Amina noticed that her hostile neighbors began using racist and sexual insults following the departure of her white husband. The neighbors, who one day witnessed a childhood African Caribbean friend pay a visit to Amina, concluded that she preferred having sexual liaisons with blacks instead of whites. Amina suspected that one reason that she was targeted for such harassment was that, after her divorce, she had repeatedly rebuffed sexual overtures by Robson and Smith. This was when they started to use the term "wog's meat" to catcall and harass her as she entered and exited her housing complex, often within earshot of her young son, Adil, who soon started to display depressive behavior. He became withdrawn and sel-dom spoke.

Amina's sexual inaccessibility to these white males in her apartment block was interpreted, in keeping with white male notions of entitlement, as a class affront and a racial transgression. Her resistance to sexual innu-endo and entreaty was often interpreted as proof of her black uppityness toward white, working-class males. Her rejection angered them and pro-voked rhetoric aimed at teaching her racial and gender humility.

The harassment grew to involve Amina's friend Harry, a white gay man who had worked with Amina in a central London nightclub. He'd been called a "pussy boy" and a "queer boy" by Smith and Robson, and

Harry was further victimized for his close relationship to Amina and her son.

During the course of the previous two years, Smith and Robson, along with their wives, had forged a sociability oriented around drinking within the housing block's common spaces. Their loud and public soirees seemed to exert a form of social control on the low-rise and close-quarter walk-up flats, many of whose residents were non-white, recent immigrants who had to evade the antics of this white-centered clique. Harry's preference to socialize with Amina rather than white heterosexual British men was puzzling to Robson and Smith, and they soon resorted to homophobic othering and harassment. To protect himself from potential assaults, Harry would try to closet his gay identity.

When questioned by his tormentors, "Are you queer, is that your boyfriend who comes to see you?" Harry would deny it in order to protect his own safety. "I don't feel I look gay, but people have chatted," he would say, as he shrugged off the comments.

The interactions between the Smiths, the Robsons, and Amina became especially confrontational when the Robsons were discovered to have forged Department of Social Security (welfare) claims and were prosecuted by the city council. They felt betrayed and thought that someone in the apartment block had reported them to the authorities. They fixated on Amina as both the object of their suspicion and as a gendered and exoticized sexualized object.

Throughout 2006, harassment against Amina continued periodically, both in her apartment block and on the streets. Smith's wife started to stalk Amina and follow her with a camera. A carton of apple juice was thrown at her while she was hanging up her washing. All these incidents, however, were low-level harassment and did not constitute new crimes in the eyes of the police, despite my efforts as her caseworker to report them as such.

It was even difficult to get the police to connect these low-level harassment incidents with the existing racial charges against Smith. We were told that the new incidents did not meet a sufficient "evidence base" to bring new charges. I kept hearing the refrain that it was "not enough of a crime." Racial harassment frequently takes the form of perpetrators engaging in long-term campaigns of low-intensity intimidation. But within the existing policing and criminal justice framework, remedies are sought only for each individual, discrete instance of crime.

Unable to secure criminal policing responses, I started to explore the option of seeking a restraining order against Smith. I worked with a Newham Homes officer, Stewart, an African Caribbean career civil servant, who had extensive experience in antidiscrimination work at the local government level. Another antisocial behavior officer I had initially starting working with quit his job in the middle of the process and the entire evidence-gathering and affidavit process had to be repeated from scratch with Stewart.

Stewart was the first and only officer from the council whom I dealt with who perceived the seriousness of Amina's situation and responded with a sense of urgency and concern. During the laborious process of working with him I was able to learn how he too confronted an acute lack of interest in racial harassment issues from those who worked within the housing service offices of Newham Council.

Amina and I had encountered evidence of this institutional culture of disinterest among other council officers who blatantly discouraged her from pursuing any course of action. For example, she had lodged an initial complaint with the community housing officer who was assigned to her complex. The officer was a recent immigrant of Nigerian background and Amina was hopeful that "being of color, being a black woman," the officer would be predisposed to respond to her situation with empathy and urgency.

However, it became apparent that the officer was not dealing with Amina's case effectively and, in fact, seemed to be taking the perpetrators' side. The officer frequently complained to Amina that "she did not know who to believe" because there was a spate of allegations and counter-allegations. Yet, despite the counter-allegations, there was never any documented evidence presented against Amina and, unlike Smith, she had never been charged for any wrongdoing. Despite the disparity, the officer claimed that she could not make a judgment or act to protect Amina from further harassment. She felt that the case was a bother and distraction from her proper duties. As a result, Amina explained, the officer "fobbed it off to other people."

After failing to get much cooperation or help from this particular officer, I decided to complain to her supervisors. The process of researching how to go up the chain of command was incredibly exhausting, as the new private-public assemblages in social services made for a confusing maze. At one point in Amina's struggle, an extragovernmental entity outside of the local council, a conflict-resolution company called Conflict and Change, was contracted by the council to mediate between Amina and her neighbors. The organization sent two white female mediators to investigate the dispute and to engage in listening to both sides of what they construed as a neighbor conflict, or a tenant dispute.

A stated aim of Conflict and Change is to bring together the parties in dispute for a face-to-face reconciliation. The appeal of such models is based on the assumption that racism is somehow devoid of asymmetrical racial power relations and the logic of domination that characterizes everyday political whiteness. Instead, the model presumes two equal sides are engaged in a dispute rather than in the dynamics of racial oppression and subordination. The model also assumes that both parties are equally culpable and implicated in that they are vying for "power over" one another. Hence, the solution is imagined as a process where both parties could be brought to a state of ahistorical social equanimity, where they would "share power" with each other.

In Amina's experience, she felt like she was "being used" by Conflict and Change when she initially consented to go through the mediation experience. The mediation process, contrary to its intended purpose, provided additional opportunities for Smith and Robson to racially abuse Amina. During the visit of the two mediators to Amina's housing complex, she was subjected to more racial insults.

"Well, at least my son is not half and half. He is at least of one color, all white!" Robson told the mediators. The mediators listened patiently to his "side" of the conflict and allowed the racist comment to be repeatedly expressed within Amina's earshot. She had to listen and wait her turn to express herself.

Approaches such as the one provided by Conflict and Change are appealing to local municipalities because they appear to provide an idealistic and "cost-effective" service to meet the current British public policy priority of securing "community cohesion" (Cantle 2008). This "remedy" is consistent with liberal concepts of conflict-resolution, antiracism, and social negotiation. Yet efficient case disposal and conflict-resolution aims and the approach of treating each incident as one discrete act or crime belie the lived experience of people suffering racial harassment. The experience of racial harassment is often repetitive, chronic, complicated, and prolonged, and it is geared toward the implicit yet highly political objectives of ejecting the black person from what is construed possessively as a white living space. This neoliberal shift toward quick disposal, cost-effective procedures, and soft communitarian approaches fundamentally misrecognizes the logic of everyday political whiteness—a logic that is oriented around assertions of territorial and border control, and the maintenance of white supremacist forms of social relations. In situations of such asymmetry, conflict mediation premised on equal and symmetrical "sides" offers no remedy and can revictimize the victim by subjecting him or her to yet another face-to-face encounter with harassment and hate speech.

Over the course of several months, Stewart and I worked together to laboriously accumulate a large documentary dossier of repeated incidences of racial abuse and harassment against Amina. We identified witnesses and compiled pages and pages of affidavits that attested to numerous incidents of harassment. This large quantity of data was then presented to a local magistrate, which resulted in the obtainment of an interim restraining order against Amina's neighbors. Robson and Smith and their families were not to approach Amina, and they were restricted from accessing the second-floor landing of her flat. Stewart had managed to persuade Newham Council to appoint a barrister to further prosecute the offenders for repeated antisocial behavior offenses, against Harry as well as Amina. The matter was brought before the hearing at Bow County Court in front of a white judge.

Amina's council-appointed barrister was a young, ambitious, and up-and-coming white British councilman from Southwark. One of his first comments to me about the case was that he was shocked that such hate speech and harassment were still social problems in Newham. He opined that such crude racism was far more characteristic of a bygone era when the National Front, a far-right political party, often organized street gangs and mobs to attack black people. As a councilman in a neighboring inner-city borough, he said he had no knowledge of the extent of racial harassment and attacks in London overall. Despite the massive evidentiary base of multiple incidents of harassment, it strangely appeared as if our own barrister was half-hearted about Amina's case.

I also began to detect an odd alignment of sympathy between Amina's barrister and the perpetrators, Smith and Robson. During the court hearing I witnessed the barrister interact more with them than he did with his own client. Smith and Robson appeared in court with their spouses, but they had not engaged any legal representation, despite having been approved for legal aid. Our barrister was sympathetic to their unfamiliarity with court processes and would frequently guide them in court. He appeared to be paying greater attention to their discomfort than to communicating with Amina. The presiding judge also appeared to be annoyed by the case. He opened the day's proceedings by proclaiming irately, "I take issue with these allegations."

It was not clear to me why he found Amina's claims to be personally objectionable, since his job was to arbitrate between two adversarial parties in court. The comments were hard to interpret initially, but it slowly became clear that the judge took offense on behalf of what he believed to be overblown charges and an overreaction that had unduly restricted the rights and freedom of the defendants.

"What exactly is the charge?" the white judge demanded and then, in a dismissive scoff and eye-roll, retorted, "Criminal damage?" "Yes," our barrister replied quickly, to which I reacted in frustration and spoke out too loudly to remind him of the important "racially aggravated" qualification. The judge scowled at my outburst. Our barrister, seemingly out of courteous deference, did not want to press on and failed completely to argue the racial aggravation point.

The judge proceeded, "I have read the opinion of the previous judge, and I don't think that the defendants have experience with these hearings. Are they willing to comment? Do you want to say anything?" Robson spoke first: "Since we got the injunction, we have been too frightened to go back home. We've moved out. It is Christmas and we have had no way to put up Christmas decorations for our son. I was not involved in Mr. Smith's case and I live above them. I have nowhere else to go."

Then Thomas Smith spoke. "Sir, first of all I am on four hundred pounds a week and have no reason to break my bail. I am a prisoner in my own home. I cannot go out. If I broke my bail, why don't they phone the police and have me arrested?" he argued.

Smith was on bail because he was facing criminal charges for the attack on Amina, which had been caught on video. That case was soon to be heard in the Snaresbrook Crown Court and eventually he would be found guilty of the charge. And yet, at the time of our hearing, he had been charged and released without any bail conditions. A normal bail condition would have been to restrict contact with the alleged victim until the case was settled, but it had been not enforced. The lax bail condition was surprising in the context of the racially aggravated nature of the alleged offenses and the supposed hardline on crime and antisocial behavior that the national government was pursuing at the time.

In support of our injunction, the barrister responded by saying that injunctive relief was appropriate for the matter and had served its purpose of prohibiting further contact between Smith and Amina. And because the standard of proof in criminal charges was higher than in a civil issue, the barrister argued that, upon a "balance of convenience test,"[3] the injunction served to preserve the status quo, which was to provide a measure of safety for Amina and Harry, until Smith's forthcoming trial was concluded.

By then, all the state's evidence against Smith would have been presented to the Crown Court and a final judgment delivered. The barrister went on to clarify that the current injunction only prohibited contact, but did not require the Smith or Robson families to move out. Hence, the granting of the injunction against the harassment was reiterated as a proportionate and temporary remedy.

The judge listened and responded, "I have to deal with this as a matter of impression. I have doubts about whether the balance of convenience test has been met. There is something to be said about giving the Smiths and the Robsons the opportunity to show that they will not behave in an antisocial way. The claimants, meanwhile, are not particularly disadvantaged." He added, "There is nothing to prevent the claimants from coming to court again."

It had taken five whole months for us to build our case for the injunction through applying unrelenting pressure on the relevant local state agencies and officers responsible for dealing with racial and homophobic harassment. We had compiled detailed evidence and made numerous complaints against errant housing officers and police detectives who were not taking the case seriously. I couldn't count the times I had rushed to Amina's and Harry's flats with fellow NMP caseworkers in order to calm their fears when some danger of attack seemed imminent. Stewart and I had spent hours conducting interviews to construct affidavits in support of the protective order.

The interim injunction by the lower court judge had been granted a mere three weeks ago. These three weeks were the first time that both Amina and Harry had felt free from the daily harassment of their neighbors. No harassment incidents had been recorded during this period. None of this seemed to matter. The judge was not persuaded that the temporary

restriction on Smith's and Robson's freedom of movement within the housing complex—a small redaction of their full liberal individual schedule of
rights—was warranted. He had decided this on "a matter of impression"
that was derived from his purported objective assessment of the moral
comportment of the white perpetrators.

Our own barrister also betrayed complete ignorance about the enormous amount of work it had taken to secure a very minor antiracist remedy
through the liberal legal antiracist framework. Most people suffering racist
harassment in Britain do not have access to the level of expertise and
resources that NMP was able to marshal, and yet despite the evidentiary
base assembled, the judge summarily dismissed the protective injunction
on the singular basis of visual impression. The judge also did not think
that the disproportionate legal burdens placed on ordinary victims of racial
harassment to have to prove their claims were particularly disadvantageous.
It appeared as if we were all living in different worlds.

"Let's give all the parties every opportunity to live in harmony" was
the judge's final equivocating opinion. Implicit in this seemingly objective
posture was the construction of equivalence between Amina's and Harry's
claims of pain and suffering and the criminal actions of Robson and Smith.
At no point had there been allegations made against Amina or Harry of
counter-harassing Smith or Robson, but the judge interpreted the confrontation in terms of a "two-sided" dispute, devoid of the damage and harm
that sustained racist and homophobic harassment inflicts over time, let
alone the possibilities of escalation.

"If worse comes to worst we can reinstate the injunction," he added,
noticing for the first time Amina's and Harry's defeated looks. The judge
then granted a stay to the injunction we had fought so hard and long to
obtain. He reserved costs for all parties and finished by turning to the
defendants and focused his remarks on them.

He did not attempt to look again at Amina and Harry, but rather proceeded to give the Smiths and Robsons friendly advice. "It is important
that all four defendants keep in touch with their solicitors," he said with
equanimity. And with that, the hearing came to an end.

Our team exited the courtroom sunk in despair and frustration and the
following conversation ensued with our barrister. "It looks like it came
down to their word against ours," Amina said to the barrister. She started
to break down. "What can I do about *that*?" the barrister retorted, suddenly
becoming angry with her. And then seeing her tearful state, he backed up

and tried his hand at consolation. He repeated the judge's opinion that if there were any repeat behavior on the part of the perpetrators, we could submit yet another application to renew the injunction. As he left us in the courthouse, he added, "To be honest with you, Mr. Smith and Mr. Robson do not come across as thugs!"

My experiences as Amina's caseworker enabled me to perceive how the legal and extra-legal politics of everyday political whiteness coalesce through the very liberal juridical processes of hate crime and racial harassment that seek to remediate these crimes. The emergent alignment of the authoritative voices of elite whites with non-elite working-class whites helped to structure political exclusions—ironically, within the very juridical procedures of liberal state antiracism. The callous modus operandi of the white barrister who represented Amina and Harry, and the white judge's extemporaneous deliberation process were the most puzzling aspects of the experience. Why would a barrister, whose professional job was to advance his adversarial role in court on behalf of his client, espouse views aligned to white perpetrators of racism? Why would a judge, whose professional job was to adjudicate cases based on the norms of evidence and abstract proceduralism, announce a decision based on his speculative impressions of character? What was it that was so impressive about the visages of the Smiths and Robsons that almost effortlessly enabled them to realign the court's sympathy toward their liberal individual rights and against Amina's needs for an effective protection against racial violence? Because of these dynamics, another attempt at seeking racial justice was met with official antiracist failure.

In reading these ethnographic vignettes against a backdrop of everyday political whiteness, Amina's summation at the end of the proceedings provides an important framework of interpretation: "it came down to their word against ours." Her interpretation grasped the significance of the ways in which, in the eyes of the law, racial credibility appeared to hinge upon the racial-moral perception of elite whites rather than any evidentiary base. The obvious racial co-identification of the judge and Amina's own barrister with the white perpetrators summoned a powerful racial "structure of feeling" (Williams 1978) that seemed to exclude any consideration of black pain and suffering, even when the liberal juridical concerns for "pain and suffering" were supported by extensive documentation, and even when attention to such pain and suffering had been codified in hate crime law.

Also privileged by the judge was the cultural normativity of white Britons, as well as the ethical weight accorded to the pleas of unfairness against marginalized working-class whites. White perpetrators appear to intuit and sense these sympathies, and they mobilized their heartfelt emotional appeal through references to their thwarted Christmas celebrations, something that they would share in common with their racial and religious peers in court.

As such, a clear sympathetic asymmetry emerged in the court proceedings that turned the case in favor of the white perpetrators. Because Smith and Robson, who came to court well dressed, did not look "thuggish," the allegations of racial and homophobic harassment were characterized as without credence. The white judge echoed the current British state's response to racism and white supremacy as a matter of harmonizing race relations between white and black, or promoting community cohesion and integration. Such national political discourses appear to have trickled down to mean an emphasis on quieting and disciplining antiracist enforcement that could impinge on white liberal individual freedoms or stoke white electoral or social discontent.

In this example, the strategies of everyday political whiteness involved the creation of mutual identifications and interests between the white parties in the courtroom. This was true for the white judge and, ironically, for Amina's own barrister as well. Instead of fighting for his client, Amina's barrister found himself persuaded to disbelief over the likelihood of Amina's claim, and he was won over by the improbability that ordinary-looking white British people could be racist.

While working on Amina's case, I also had the opportunity to attend the 2006 Race Hate Conference organized by Newham Council's race-equality unit, Racial Equality in Newham (REIN). The event was advertised as a chance to identify best practices and improvements in tackling racial violence in the borough. The keynote speaker was Assistant Commissioner Tarique Ghaffur, who at the time was the highest-ranking black officer in the Metropolitan Police (Met).

During the Q&A session, I pressed Ghaffur to explain the Met's poor investigation record of race hate crimes, and especially racial harassment cases—those that did not result in grievous bodily injury or death. Less than a third of the reported racist incidents against racial and ethnic minorities throughout London achieved a "clear-up" or resulted in a "sanctioned detection"—where an offender was brought to charge (Martineau, Brown, and Faulkner 2007). In my own observations as a caseworker, I had often witnessed the police try to rapidly achieve a quick clear-up or disposal rate with respect to racial incidents through not recording the racist elements in a case or by disavowing the criminal nature of a racial incident by categorizing it as a neighborly dispute. This pattern of racism denial was later also confirmed in the *Report on Metropolitan Police Service Handling of Complaints Alleging Racial Discrimination* by the Independent Police Complaints Commission (IPCC), where an in-depth study of a selected twenty police cases revealed that "in 13 out of 20 cases the investigating officer made no effort to obtain additional evidence that could have supported the allegation of racism" (IPCC 2013a:5).

During the conference, Ghaffur did not address the Met's record on race hate crimes at all. Instead, he changed course and delivered a non sequitur: he used the occasion to outline his presumptive role in organizing counterterrorism security for the recently awarded Olympic Games to be held in London in 2012. While he addressed a largely racial and minority ethnic audience concerned with the problems of racial violence, he mused about the particular security concerns of Newham as the designated site of the future Olympic Stadium and Olympic Park. A speech on national security and counterterrorism was thus cast as the state's contribution to the local community's conference on racial violence.

Ghaffur was blunt in his response to my criticisms and question. The lack of serious, sustained attention on such cases was a result, he said, of the way in which the professional "performance indicators" for the police were structured. He argued that the public at large did not view investigation of racial harassment cases as a policing priority. He stated that the main indicators for police performance were the clear-up rates in two principal areas: car theft and burglary cases.

Ghaffur's comments revealed an inner police worldview and the day-to-day operational priorities and professionalized norms of police work. In the ostensibly color-blind features of police work itself we can observe a subordination of the ongoing problems of racial violence to a focus on national security, property crimes, and the hierarchical valuation of elite subjects (property owners) as the preeminent candidates for state protection. Operational performance indicators that are unmarked by race exist in a hidden tension with newer antiracist legislation, reforms, and positive duties that aim to address the persistent problem of institutional racism within the police. Such tensions, however, effectively keep black and minority ethnic communities subordinate, along with their historical social struggles to secure citizenship rights and equal protection from the British state.

After answering my question, Ghaffur then strenuously argued for consultative cooperation by grassroots groups with the police and directed me to the largely ineffectual Police-Community Consultation Group. He also derided and cautioned against the use of "ideological" and "aggressive" pressure methods, presumably in reference to groups such as NMP, and perhaps also in reference to my very question. The police ideology of subsuming community-based oversight into consultative approaches was heavily promoted in Newham.

In dealing with the police on many cases of racial harassment in Newham, I had to regularly engage a number of senior detective superintendents (DSs) and detective inspectors (DIs), and I got to know many of them. As a result, during the course of the year, a senior DI I knew called me to request that I participate in a new initiative. He asked if I would help the Newham police filter and sort out the multiple reported incidents of racial harassment in the borough. The argument was that this was necessary in order to provide greater efficiency so that the police could concentrate on "genuine" cases that constituted real "crimes." Once an incident was defined as noncriminal, it no longer became the police's responsibility and they were therefore not held accountable for pursuing a hate crime investigation.

What was surprising about this request was the implicit assumption that some of the reported cases of racial harassment were frivolous and therefore needed to be weeded out of the system. It appeared as if the police were looking for a community partner who would both help them do this and help legitimate the process.

In exploring this informal proposal, I found that it entailed having REIN function as a third-party mediator between grassroots groups like NMP and the police. If I were to agree to this system, the result would be the creation of yet another gatekeeping mechanism that would reclassify the majority of racial incidents reported to the police as non-serious incidents and non-crimes. I would thereby deny those suffering racial harassment any recourse to police attention. And the fewer the crimes reported, the better the statistics looked for REIN, which was also charged with ensuring the council's urban gentrification goal of making "Newham a place where people want to live, work and stay" for more middle-class people who commuted to central London for work. A decrease in the number of officially recorded racial harassment cases in the borough would help bolster its image.

In many racial harassment cases that I dealt with, this "gate-keeping" tactic against racial harassment (Bowling 2001) also trickled down to the front-line officers: the police constables (PCs) and detective constables (DCs). Some DCs even openly confided to me that they thought that many people who reported racial incidents were merely playing the "race card," and so they wanted some mechanism to filter out the borough's large number of reported racial harassment incidents.

It is important to understand that racism in policing is articulated not only in terms of unwitting or explicitly prejudicial forms, but also often through the very discourses least explicitly marked by racism, such as professionalism. The construction of police officer identities and the metrics of their professional success rarely focused on racial justice imperatives. In fact, some of the DCs I encountered told me that working on racial harassment cases was not in line with what they termed high-level, serious "police work." For these officers, racial harassment cases did not also fit with the "law and order" identity of policing. They felt that it was more appropriate to view racial harassment as a community-relations problem. In fact, many officers with whom I forged relationships while working at NMP appeared reluctant to work on racial harassment cases at all.

If attending DCs were not eager to pursue cases robustly, I would often file official complaints about their quality of work. On one rare occasion, I was successful in assembling a body of evidence to support getting a DC removed from a case and a new DC assigned. The supervising DI proclaimed that the new DC was one of the brightest in the borough of Newham, and one of his best officers. He told me that the new officer was very promising and ambitious to make further career progress, and therefore his good performance on the case would serve his own self-interest. Through this strategy the DI sought to assure me of his broad sympathy with my antiracist work. "I am not one of *those* guys," he assured me.

Amina's struggles to protect and free herself from racial harassment within the British liberal juridical system, where such offenses were ostensibly legislated against as criminal acts, were significantly compromised in the complex mix of acts of everyday political whiteness that effectively block racial justice. Gatekeeping policing strategies and a relative lack of priority and urgency on issues of racial harassment in police work contributed to Amina's frustrations, as did the confederated and unsympathetic perceptions of white barristers and judges.

In addition to these issues, Amina's experiences occurred when the British state was effecting a neoliberal reduction in funds for directly delivered social services. The postwar British social consensus on the social welfare state had been effectively contested through new free-market and privatization policies in both the Conservative and New Labour governments. The state, at all levels and across political party divisions, was implementing several projects to retrench and limit entitlements to social services. This downsizing and cost-cutting ethos in government was vastly reducing municipality-run social services, including social housing provisions and antiracist services, along with racial harassment victim-support projects, tenancy eviction, and graffiti-removal services. Newham Council's municipal services increasingly operated within a contracting environment involving third-party vendors, like Conflict and Change and other organizations, rather than through internally controlled state-based agencies.

The neoliberal state logic that contracted out the responsibility for tackling racial harassment further weakened the context for obtaining racial justice or official antiracist remedies on the criminal and civil levels. The local branch of London's Metropolitan Police in Newham investigated racial incidents on a criminal basis and local municipal councils such as Newham Council traditionally had been involved in antiracism through the enforcement of anti-harassment clauses in tenancy agreements.

Social housing tenancy agreements introduced explicit anti–racist harassment clauses in the late 1980s, a legal remedy necessitated by African Caribbean and South Asian people's settlement into what were perceived as white "host" areas and incidents of white working-class territorialism in social housing projects and neighborhoods in London (Hesse et al. 1992). After years of community activism in Newham, the passage of the racial harassment clause in social housing provided a civil (as opposed to criminal) statutory avenue for South Asian and African Caribbean victims of racial harassment to seek remedies against white perpetrators who were often their fellow neighbors.

The local council's racial harassment system comprised the housing and the Anti-Social Behavior (ASB) departments. The ASB department could engage the council's legal team to pursue civil action against perpetrators of racial harassment; these actions included evictions and restraining orders. Both the police and local government also ostensibly supplied ancillary support services through the Witness Support program, or by providing support workers employed by the council. Taken together, these institutions were supposed to form the basis of what is known as a "multi-agency" approach.

The police investigated racial incidents on a criminal basis and the council typically became involved through the monitoring of tenant behavior. As part of the move to retrench the social welfare state obligations following the coming to power of the New Labour government in 1997, a shift occurred at the local state levels on responsibility for responding to racial harassment cases. After the restructuring of the local council in 2005, housing services were contracted to Newham Homes—a private at-arm's-length property management organization (ALMO). This new entity was now responsible for providing the council's housing services, which were previously the purview of the local government. Racial harassment was no longer directly monitored by Newham Council's housing department, which itself had been largely privatized. The selling off of social housing and the local state's retrenchment in delivering municipal antiracist services had confused and rendered irrelevant the tenancy protections of a previous era.

Racial harassment cases involving public housing reverted to individual community housing officers within Newham Homes, and racial harassment was lumped together with an assortment of other antisocial behaviors that included "violence, harassment, graffiti, vandalism, fly tipping (illegal dumping of waste), noise nuisance and abandoned vehicles." The shift in conceptualizing racial harassment and hate crimes from a problem of racial power dynamics to the color-blind and universalizing frame of antisocial behavior formed part of the way that neoliberal logics of local governance created a false equivalence between racism and a broad range of social ills. Individual officers within the retrenched housing departments were also subjected to a de-skilling process, as the jurisdiction for dealing with racial harassment in social housing became blurred. Flats supervised by particular officers may have remained under their purview or become excluded through private property ownership.

Newham Council dutifully published a periodic Race Equality Scheme that detailed how it aimed to meet its positive statutory responsibilities required under new race relations laws. However, actual instances of the housing department thoroughly investigating and pursuing with full force its powers against racial harassment were rare.

Under neoliberal reforms, the incentive to provide such services in the face of other priorities, such as cost cutting in local government, did not tend toward the delivery of racial justice, which can be an expensive process. The cost of pursuing a single eviction case against a perpetrator of racial harassment could cost the council anywhere from thirty thousand to eighty thousand pounds. According to more experienced caseworkers at NMP, it may take up to ten years of court action to actually evict somebody, and during that time the legal costs will have to be borne by the government. The lengthy process of court action as such is clearly incompatible with the quest for small government.

Nonetheless, in Amina's case I continued to pursue the most extensive course of action available. I had learned to take a political blackness approach in casework advocacy through guidance from more experienced NMP activists who were familiar with how to put pressure on the local council and police. Political blackness in casework meant that you did not trust social services, state institutions, or the judicial process to objectively favor the oppression of black people, and that the caseworker advocate had to operate militantly through deploying official critiques and complaints and by applying constant political pressure on behalf of a victim. Over thirty-five years of experience by NMP in working with these processes had shown the necessity of these militant methods.

Along with working with Stewart to obtain the injunction against Smith and Robson, I also tried to get the police to install a panic alarm in Amina's home (which would be connected to the police station) and for the council to install CCTVs in order to have further evidence-gathering opportunities, since there had been continuous, albeit low-level, incidents of harassment. These technological fixes are often touted as great crime-solving or crime-deterring measures, but, when victims of racial harassment try to obtain them, their cost is always presented as a barrier.

I often engaged in heated exchanges with officers in the Community Safety Unit of the police department who insisted that panic alarms would only be installed in "life-threatening" situations. Amina's case, they felt, did not merit such a treatment. They further complained that I was very "demanding." After much conflict with the police concerning my insistence on installing the panic alarm, the police told me that they would provide Amina with a handheld "personal attack alarm," which was cheaper. They graciously also provided her with an "educational booklet" on how to take personal measures in order to be safe from crime.

It would have been a dereliction of my duties as a caseworker to be satisfied with these tokenistic measures. The only reason that I did not make further complaints about police inaction at this juncture was that the strategy of pressure politics on the police had started to yield some significant responses that I thought were useful to Amina. One of the concrete measures the police agreed to undertake was to create a "mid-stream comment" on the computer-aided dispatch system that monitored the emergency phone line for the police. Amina's number would now be flagged for urgent response. The police argued that this would be as good as having a panic alarm, and we decided to give it a try. They also stated that they would contact the beat-level police in their Safer Neighborhood Team and ask them to make regular visits to Amina's flat. Given these two measures, it actually did seem to indicate that the persistent pressure on the police was resulting, finally, in substantial protective responses.

The end result of the state's privatization and the retrenchment of social services was that people who were victims of racial harassment by racist white neighbors were shocked to discover that there wasn't much of an enforceable environment for asserting their rights or accessing remedies, especially in cases that do not result in major crimes such as physical assault or death. The multiplying and overlapping hodgepodge of public and private bodies obscures the path to justice. No one takes responsibility or becomes accountable for addressing these kinds of everyday situations, in spite of the presence of very real and persistent problems of racial violence in social housing.

These dynamics produce a weak racial justice rule of law that in turn empowers the perpetrators of racial harassment. Furthmore, ordinary victims of harassment are not equipped to navigate these complicated and confusing public-private partnerships in order to receive an adequate response to their racial troubles. The neoliberal retrenchment of antiracist social services, and the advent of a small government ethos, ultimately freed the state from having to demonstrate effective racial justice outcomes.[4]

CHAPTER 3

=====

"Would They Do This
to Tony Blair's Daughter?"

Gillian's Struggle Against
Intersectional Racial Violence

African Caribbean women's experiences of racial and state violence have rarely been recognized as a mainstream political issue or as an actually existing contradiction in Britain's purportedly color-blind and gender-blind liberal juridical social order. Silence in the British public sphere, and even within antiracist social movements, about black women's specific struggles against racial violence exacerbates conditions that make black women vulnerable, socially marginalized, and invisible within social and political spaces.[1] Black British feminism is both a grassroots social movement and an academic field that has challenged this "normative absence/pathologizing presence dynamic of racialization" that has abetted the subordination of racialized and ethnicized women (Mirza 1997, 2014:128; Reynolds 2002; Samantrai 2002). Historically, black British feminist thinkers and grassroots activists have critiqued how antiracist social movements have overlooked the intersectional dynamics of co-ethnic gender subordination and violence with the British state's own racialized discrimination, violence, and domination (Siddiqui 2000; Gupta 2003). As Hannana Siddiqui has argued, "The new British civil rights movement, the antiracist, as well as the left more generally, demands racial justice, which is often at the expense of black women's rights—silencing those who criticize the community itself" (Siddiqui 2000:95).

In 2017, there was a greater disproportionality of African- and African Caribbean–descended prisoners in the United Kingdom than in the United

States.[2] Racial and ethnic minority women are 19 percent of adult women prisoners, while they make up 14 percent of the general population (Prison Reform Trust 2017). Even as the total number of women prisoners in Britain has decreased, African- and African Caribbean–descended women, however, "made up 10% of the women's prison population—three times higher than the 3% they comprise of the general women's population" (Cox and Sacks-Jones 2017; Prison Reform Trust 2017:4).[3]

Julia Sudbury (2016) argues that these discrepancies are a result of widely circulating racist, gendered representations of African Caribbean women as members of unruly communities who possess strong, deviant characteristics that necessitate the state's repressive control rather than its equal protection of safety and personhood. Despite these long-standing critiques that have emerged out of decades of black British feminist work, issues around state-based racial violence in particular are still primarily oriented around male victims and their experiences. The situation is parallel to that of the United States, where the #BlackLivesMatter movement now has a corollary, #SayHerName, in order to draw attention to the invisibility both in the media and within African American antiracist social movements of women who have been killed by police violence. As Andrea Ritchie (2006:142) points out, in the U.S. context, state violence against women of color is usually seen as a secondary issue to men of color's experience of police abuse. Mainstream white feminist movements have also been reluctant to center and "imagine women as subjects of state violence in public spaces." In this regard, black women's lived experiences of policing in Britain similarly challenge "mainstream police accountability and antiviolence organizations" that ignore black women's oppression with regard to state-based racism (Ritchie 2006:140).[4]

Generally, black women's historical and contemporary experiences with state violence are discursively excluded from national political debates about Britishness and British values. Important matters of race in the public sphere typically draw on discourses of immigration control and community cohesion, the integration of alien non-western cultures and religions, as well as national security. Even so, black women have long experienced what the pioneering work of Ruth Hall (1985:48) and the activist group Women Against Rape in Britain have called "racist sexual violence" at the hands of the British state.

Incidences of sexualized assault against black women by state agents such as police officers subvert and contradict the ideal of liberal democratic governance. However, they are quite continuous with the "coloniality of power" (Quijano 2000) that grants political sanction and impunity to white male sexual violence that occurs under the cover of law and order. These structural tendencies are continuous with colonial history. Black women in Britain have experienced racialized state violence in ways that are both gendered and sexualized: "Black women's experiences of racism are not the same as those experienced by black men, for they are uniquely gendered. Thus the subjection of Asian women to 'virginity tests' by immigration officials in London was an integral part of their racialized objectification and abuse. Similarly rape, sexual abuse and commodification of their reproductive functions were integral to African women's oppression under slavery and continue to shape modern day representations" (Sudbury 1998:38–39). There is a long and sustained history of racist sexual violence against black women, particularly against African Caribbean women, by the British state. And there is an equally long history of that state violence being ignored and occluded.

The names of Esme Baker and Jackie Berkeley are rarely remembered in contemporary Britain, but these African Caribbean women were the first black women who dared to make official complaints of sexual abuse, rape, and assault against the British police. These were milestone cases in the 1980s that broke the silence and invisibility of black women's experiences with policing. Ruth Chigwada-Bailey's (1991, 2003) classic studies on black women and policing in Britain presented four key reasons why black women are likely to come into contact with and receive maltreatment from the police. First, there is the perception that black women, as part of the poor and black community in general, are likely to be engaged in criminally suspicious behavior. Second, it is due to the high rates of criminalization of black male youth that black mothers are also linked as potential accomplices. Third, their non-white racial difference sets them apart as potential targets for immigration checks and harassment. Fourth, black women are targeted by police who assert their powers of removal for persons deemed to be exhibiting behavior linked to mental disorders. These key areas that Chigwada-Bailey identifies generate representations of African and African Caribbean women as morally suspect, potentially aggressive, and devoid of the respectable qualities of genteel middle-class white femininity. These images continue to inform mainstream public perception and are simply recognized as common sense for inner-city policing purposes. A 1989 story uncovered by Chigwada-Bailey illustrates the horrific convergence of sexualized police violations of black women and a white-aligned and heteropatriarchal state judiciary. The case involved a white policeman in Surrey who had been convicted of raping a young black woman in his patrol car. He was sentenced to seven years in prison. However, upon appeal, his sentence was overturned on the grounds that the judge in the original trial had failed to direct the jury to consider the good character of the police officer (see Chigwada-Bailey 1991:141–45).

The outbreak of the famous Brixton uprising on 28 September 1985 (rendered as "riots" in the dominant discourse) and the mass protests at Broadwater Farm a week later were also events precipitated by incidents that involved the violent policing of black women in London. In the first instance, Cherry Groce was shot and paralyzed during a raid of her home and, in the second instance, Cynthia Jarrett suffered a heart attack following a police assault that also occurred in her home. Notably, in both cases, police aggressively broke into these women's homes to investigate alleged criminal behavior perpetrated by their sons.

In 1993, Joy Gardner, a Jamaican woman, was accused of an immigration infraction—she had overstayed her Commonwealth visitor's visa. Joy's mother had immigrated to Britain in the 1960s and had become a citizen. However, due to anti-black immigration politics and changes effected by the 1981 British Nationality Act, she could no longer sponsor her adult daughter, who now also had a five-year-old British-born son. At an earlier time, both women would have been considered British subjects or Commonwealth citizens, with rights to reside in Britain, but successive legislation had narrowed the conditions for eligibility. Joy was also enrolled as a student in media studies at London Metropolitan University when the police raided her home to execute an immediate deportation order after her judicial appeals had failed. A newspaper report recounts what happened: "It was early morning when five men and women burst into five-year-old Graeme Burke's home. They cornered and grabbed his mother, crashing through the furniture, forcing her face down on to the floor. They sat on her body, they bound her hands to her side with a leather belt and manacles, they strapped her legs together and wound yards of surgical tape round her head. At some stage, one officer took the boy into another room—but he could still hear his mother's cries. He never saw her alive again" (Mills 1999). Three police officers from the Alien Deportation Group were tried for manslaughter. They were acquitted after telling a jury that Joy Gardner was the most violent woman they had ever dealt with and that the treatment she received was standard practice (Amnesty International 1995).

Brutal policing violence has continued, even as African Caribbean women have contributed greatly to educational social movements and have broken the glass ceiling in public life (Mirza 1992, 2009). There are now several high-profile politicians. Baroness Valerie Amos, a former black British feminist academic, was the head of the House of Lords of Britain and a prominent U.N. diplomat. Diane Abbott, the long-standing east London MP, is also a high-profile figure in Labour Party politics. These success stories, however, have not changed or abolished the negative stereotyping and violent protocols of how the British police appear to treat African Caribbean women and, in particular, working-class African Caribbean women.[5]

In 2007, Toni Comer, a nineteen-year-old African Caribbean woman with a history of epileptic seizures, was thrown out of a nightclub in Sheffield. As she attempted to return inside through a back door, police officers confronted her. One of them proceeded to punch her repeatedly until she was unconscious. Then they dragged her, with her trousers down, into custody. The chilling brutality was inadvertently captured by the nightclub's closed-circuit television and was discussed widely in the British media as reminiscent of the beatings of Rodney King in Los Angeles or characteristic of racism in the U.S. deep South. The incident prompted a black journalist, Hannah Pool (2007), to comment that "you cannot separate who Toni Comer is from what happened to her. Very little is ever said about the relationship black women have with the police force. When the debate turns to police and ethnic minorities, it is almost always about white men versus black men. You would be forgiven for thinking that the only time black women and policemen came into contact with each other was at the Notting Hill Carnival." In spite of this long historical record, the invisibility of police violence against African Caribbean women in the twenty-first century leaves them continually vulnerable to racist sexual violence by state actors and leads to routine antiracist failures in liberal governance.

This context helps to make clear what happened to Gillian, an African Caribbean east Londoner who has spent decades fighting against police abuse in Newham. I was her caseworker in 2006 and worked with her on an incident that was not her first or last experience with racist sexual violence at the hands of white police officers. In fact, Gillian had been at the center of the Newham Monitoring Project (NMP) "Stop Police Harassment of Black Women in Newham" campaign in the 1990s that addressed issues from "police trivializing violence against women to the criminalizing of black women" and attendant racial disparities in women's incarceration (NMP 1993:38–41).

Gillian Smith was born on the island of St. Lucia when it was still a colony, and she arrived in Britain in 1969 at the age of five when her mother married a white Englishman and emigrated. They settled in her stepfather's residence in Hastings, a predominantly white seaside community in East Sussex. Gillian often recalled her childhood in idyllic terms and drew on her memories of southeast England's picturesque natural beauty as an inspiration for her own urban gardening.

"We came from good stock," she would say, "and didn't want for anything," referring to her stepfather's middle-class status as a self-employed owner of a gas station. She took great pride in her flawless elocution, a prized southeastern English accent, that to her was proof of the private-school polish she had been privileged to receive, and her integration into respectable middle-class British society. Gillian recalled her childhood in Hastings as her "happiest days," full of a quintessential seashore town "quiet life," something she felt to be the provenance of those lucky enough to be born white in Britain, and basically beyond the reach of most black people who lacked kinship connections to rural England.

"People usually think that black people have accents, but they hear me speak on the phone, and they don't think I am black," she told me. She remembered that her stepfather would always correct her if she got too Cockney and began to drop her o's and h's. She did recall however, switching into "a bit of Cockney" now and then, mostly in order to fit in to east London and not to appear as if she were putting on airs.

"I've always gotten into trouble for the way I speak," she said. "People are thinking, who the hell does she think she is? You've got other black people coming along and speaking with accents so they don't know what to do with me," Gillian continued, mocking a pseudo-African accent to express her antipathy toward new African immigrants in Newham.[6]

Gillian's stereotyping and resentment were situated in the context of the recent influx of highly educated, professional migrants, principally from Nigeria. Gillian encountered many of these immigrants as the new front-line social and housing service officers of the borough. This shift in who was employed for these positions was one of the major changes that had taken place at the local municipal level in the past two decades. However, the diversification of personnel with front-line civil servants did not alter the fundamental structural logic of anti-blackness and anti-immigrant treatment that the new, diverse group of employees was expected to carry out.

The relationship was often tense between older and settled working-class African Caribbean and South Asian communities and the new civil servants who mediated the state and municipal government policies. As had been the case with Amina's community housing worker, Gillian encountered few ethnic and racial minority state agents who were sympathetic to her plight. Lower-level local police officers and Housing and Homeless Persons Unit officers occupy a colonial-esque intermediary role between the state's law and order and austerity-based social services agenda and the working-class black communities they help to govern.

In spite of this downgraded treatment by the first-generation immigrant housing officers, Gillian asserted herself as superior in social status to the new arrivals. She mainly took pride in her tenure. She socialized widely with white British people and boasted of living a racially integrated everyday life. Gillian's long-term partner was a Jamaican man, James. Her brother had married a white British woman, and Gillian added that her son, Mark, primarily liked to date white girls. "He likes the white side of things," Gillian declared about Mark. At present, he was dating a light-skinned, mixed-race girl. In her way of thinking, this life corresponded with what the British state had come to valorize as "good" civic behavior, or community cohesion, as opposed to the "bad" behavior of new immigrant groups who are perceived to self-segregate into separate ethnocultural enclaves and lives.

In the beginning I was a little uncertain about Gillian's self-presentation as a fully assimilated English and British person. I wondered about things such as internalized self-hatred and her lack of a strong racial consciousness. Before knowing the full details of Gillian's story, I hastened to judge her remarks as ideological expressions of an uncritical colonial Anglophilia. In conversation I raised this matter with her one day.

"Yes, black is beautiful. And I am a strong black woman. Very black. But sometimes you see what you go through. And you ask God, why is it that they have nice hair and I have to put things in mine. Why do they have a quiet life and are not bothered?" Gillian said.

Then, noticing my quizzical looks, Gillian started to relate experiences that stemmed from her childhood in Hastings. She told me a story that took place when she was ten years old. A white schoolmate named Kevin had been singling her out for racist name-calling and bullying. He would call her a "black this and that," Gillian told me.

One day when she was walking home from school, Kevin waylaid her and pummeled her with his fists. He left her unconscious and abandoned by the side of the road. "He left me there for dead," she said.

Because Gillian was the lone black girl in her East Sussex town, a passerby quickly recognized her and took her home. Outraged at what had happened to her daughter, Gillian's mother went to the boy's home to confront his parents. Kevin's parents, however, did not seem interested in disciplining or admonishing their child for what he had done.

The following day, Gillian took heed of the advice her mother had given her. Her mother had told her to defend herself by any means necessary. When, predictably, Kevin attempted to taunt and harass Gillian again, she grabbed his "willie" and squeezed hard. Yelping in pain, he ran off and that was the last time he bothered her walk to or from school.

As she continued to grow up in Hastings, Gillian's own relationship with her white stepfather became increasingly strained as his marriage to her mother broke down. "It was fine when the love was there. When love was not there . . . there was lots of racism between them," she observed of her parents' interracial marriage. Gillian's relationship with her stepfather was irreparably damaged when she became embroiled with the police as a young adult. By this time, she had moved to Newham and was living an independent life.

The incident occurred when she had been out shopping on Woodgrange Road near the Forest Gate train station, in a quiet residential neighborhood in Newham. She had run into an old friend there, and an unsettled misunderstanding between them turned into a heated argument. Gillian admitted that they were quarreling, perhaps a little loudly, but that it had not been a fight.

As she and her friend argued near the train station, officers from the Area 2 Territorial Support Group who were patrolling the area in a riot van stopped to investigate. An archived NMP report details what happened next:

On seeing the two women Gill and Ms. C arguing, two officers got out of the van and approached the women. One officer moved towards the back of the pavement, grabbing her hand and saying, "if you're not quiet, you're nicked." Gill explained that she was quiet and began to move to leave, but the officer blocked her path and forced her arm behind her back. The second officer returned after having spoken to Ms. C who had told him that there was no problem between the two women. The first officer said to his colleague, "we've got her on a Section 4" and forced Gill onto the floor. The two officers then handcuffed Gill, began to drag her towards the barrier at the edge of the pavement, and forced her over the barrier causing injuries to her stomach. At this point, Ms. C, witnessing the attack, began shouting to the officers to let Gill go and stop hurting her. The officers ignored her protestations and dragged Gill towards the van where she was lifted up by her arms and legs and thrown onto the floor of the van. As she struggled to get up off the van floor, the officers began racially abusing her, saying, "You black dog, get on the floor" and "You bitch, get down, get down." One officer then grabbed Gill by the back of the neck and tried to push her to the ground. The other officer began to stomp on her legs and her back. During this ordeal, Gill suffered injuries to her body, had her jacket ripped and her jewelry snatched off. Gill was then taken to Forest Gate police station still lying on the floor of the van whilst the officers continued to abuse her racially and laugh at her discomfort. (1993:39)

The overwhelming use of force to quell a petty public disturbance was, at best, disproportionate. It was "for nothing, for nothing," Gillian said.

Unfortunately, Gillian's ordeal did not end in the police van. When she finally arrived at the police station she was subjected to a strip search while the officers who had assaulted her watched from a distance and made lewd, sexual comments. Gillian turned to the white female officer who was carrying out the search and asked that the search be stopped.

"Why are you doing this? You're a woman as well," she asked. The question seemed to have some effect and at this point the officer discontinued the search and brought Gillian to a cell. Four hours later she was released, after having been charged with threatening behavior and charged with interfering with the police in the course of their duties.

NMP launched a public mobilization and campaign for justice in response to the use of random excessive force and frivolous charges in Gillian's case. Such campaigns against the police are fraught with danger for victims of the abuse, who fear that the police will retaliate against them.

This concern would later turn out to be very real, as the local police began to target Gillian's young son through their use of the stop and search tactic.

Gillian was aware of these dangerous possibilities but nonetheless decided to turn her individual experience into a broader community and political touchstone about the policing of African Caribbean and black women as a whole. When Gillian arrived at One Love Centre on December 2, 1992, over a hundred people had gathered to hear her give her first-ever public speech. This public meeting in support of Gillian was the result of the work of an alliance of local activist organizations that had jointly mobilized around her case. Activists from NMP, the East London Black Women's Organization, Newham Asian Women's Project, and the Defend the Deane Family campaign galvanized community-wide support.[7]

Though the immediate objective of the campaign was to get Gillian individual justice through the police's internal disciplinary system and the liberal juridical framework that regulated excessive force, the larger political goal was to bring attention to the "gendered racism" (Sudbury 1998) that characterizes the state's routine, violent policing of working-class, black women's bodies. As NMP (1993:40–41) stated at the time, Gillian's case "clearly demonstrates that it is not only young black men who suffer police racism and brutality."

Gillian delivered the following speech to the community of activists and concerned residents who had gathered around her case at One Love. She was nervous and told me, "That was my first-ever public speech. I must admit it was very nerve-wracking":

Thank you for coming to support the campaign. My name is Gill as you all know. For legal reasons I personally cannot talk about the details of my case. I can say that on the 9th of October 1992 I found out what being black meant in accordance to what the police did to me. The fear, the embarrassment, and the shame they made me feel on that day will stay with me forever.

No woman should have to suffer such degrading treatment. After all, we are the women of today and fighting for the women of the future.

Show Respect.

This happened to me, it has happened to thousands of women before me, and unless we wake up, stand up, it will happen to thousands more.

We must all remember our history and think back to how people reacted in the past to these same issues of harassment and racial harassment in our community, such as the Brixton Riots before. For as long as there have been black people in this country, whether from Asian, African, and West Indian origin, they have always had to fight for their rights and justice.

This campaign will go on not only for the men and women in this community who have suffered at the hands of the police but for our children.

I do not want my sons and daughters to be stripped naked by police officers, beaten and abused and sent to prison for being black in Britain.

This is an excellent public meeting; for every person in here there are ten more supporters outside. We are not alone.

There is a powerful organization, without any doubts in my mind, who can help fight the police in Newham. Personal respect to Hoss [Houssein] for the support and work of NMP.

No Justice, No Peace!

When Gillian's case came before the Newham East Magistrates' Court a year later, the campaign had generated enough local interest that eighty supporters packed the public gallery—an unusual show of concern and public monitoring for what otherwise would have been a routine magistrate's court affair. When I asked Gillian what had happened, she searched through a folder of documents and produced a notepaper with her handwritten reflections on the events of that fateful day: "Finally we arrived at the Court House. We waited almost two hours for the arresting officers to arrive. Finally the police barrister stood up and asked the judge for more time. My barrister stood up and protested against the fact that this case should never have come to court. The judge stood up and said to the police barrister: 'No more time. Case is dismissed.'" In short, the arresting police officers had failed to show up to the court, packed as it was with community supporters, to present their evidence!

This victory was understood as a rare result of mobilized public interest and protest that had influenced what would otherwise have been a routine antiracist failure—a racially biased and typically pro-police court process. Borough-wide leafleting, public meetings, and mass picket signs that packed the public galleries at Gillian's trial demonstrated that courts could be made amenable for racial justice outcomes only through public mobilization and pressure politics. The strategy of an African Caribbean and South Asian black community solidarity that was mobilized in support of Gillian was a hard-won lesson on how to fight against regnant policing attitudes toward racial and ethnic minorities in Newham.

Despite this victory, Gillian's white stepfather never believed her account. He found her allegations to be incredible and preferred to retain his absolute belief in the quintessential image of fairness in the British justice system and in the upstanding character of white police officers over the claims of his own black stepdaughter. This was another moment of everyday political whiteness, whereby racism denial and mobilizations of inter-white solidarity reveal themselves when black people attempt to seek racial justice. "He had friends in the force," Gillian explained, and then added, "He always insisted that the police don't do that."

I spent many hours visiting with Gillian at her home during my fieldwork year when she would tell me her life's stories. Often we spoke in the comfort of her beautifully tended backyard garden, sharing casual conversation as we worked together on forms, witness statements, and so on. As time passed, our relationship progressed to a comfortable level of familiarity and I recorded some of Gillian's reflections concerning her initial impressions of NMP when she had first approached the organization to seek assistance with her 1992 case.

When I first came to the NMP, and you discover what it is about, you see the posters and all. I was really nervous. I saw a lot of Asian people; I met Houssein. I was nervous, you see, as I was thinking whether they would help me or not. I don't know what planet I was in, or what I thought, I thought that only black people got harassed or arrested, and then you met people who also went through what you did. It helped to hear that Houssein had been arrested for nothing: I mean they knew how it felt. Even today, hearing all of this and everybody's story it feels like I got to know people. You see that Turkish people and whites, I mean, lots of people who go through this. And you saw how people here worked your case, I mean, Hoss was great; things were moving. Many organizations claim to do the same thing that the NMP does, but nothing happens. Things happen at the NMP. The only thing I was waiting for in the four years was

the court cases, and that is out of your hands. But with the NMP
you will get action and you will "win."

Gillian provided insights into the grounded character and scope of political
blackness in Newham. Political blackness, in this context, was not simply a
question of asserting an abstract principle of unity or a homogeneous racial
identity. Political blackness, I realized, is always a practical possibility, given
the racial political realities of Britain as well as the historical track record
of joint antiracist struggles among people from multiple racialized and ethnicized communities. The identity of political blackness emerges and solidi-
fies through the forging of face-to-face solidarity in developing casework,
campaigns, and other activist actions around the social facts of racist victimization and state marginalization. In time, political blackness also
became the bedrock of the relationship between Gillian and me.

Gillian's own testimony of coming to consciousness with a political and
resistance-based concept of blackness took place in an antiracist organizational space where different communities and individuals could collaborate
and build alliances through struggles for justice. Her sense of victimization
as an African Caribbean woman in the context of a specific racial and ethnic
identity expanded as she discovered the racism experienced by other black
people, including her Iranian-British caseworker Houssein and others
whom NMP served.

She also began to overcome her doubts about NMP's concept of a
nonethnically defined and consciously assembled multiracial "community
of resistance" (Sivanandan 1990) as she started to experience the commitment and militant activism waged on behalf of her case and campaign.
These two features that characterized the political blackness approach of
NMP appeared to provide a transition from her initial doubts and fears to
her self-assured endorsement of NMP's tradition of antiracist politics. She
herself would emerge as a representative voice in Newham on the issue of
police abuse and black women's experiences in forums and workshops.

When I joined the antiracist struggle in Newham, Gillian's words were
a constant reminder to me that "we are all black here," and these words
would solidify a sense of recognition and acceptance crucial for my own
embrace of political blackness. This political sense of a common but not
homogeneous blackness kindled solidarity in my relationship with her,
despite our racial, ethnic, and gendered differences, and the obvious gap
between Gillian's seasoned experiences of antiracist resistance and my own

fledgling search for a sense of belonging and acceptance as an antiracist activist in Britain.

I had been working on Gillian's police complaint case for several months when suddenly I lost communication with her. She did not come by the office, as she often had, and her phone appeared to be out of service. But I knew where she lived and I had often popped over to her home to work on affidavits and other matters related to her case.

By now I knew a short route to her house and felt at home walking through the plane tree–lined streets of north Newham. The terrace homes, characteristic of the north borough, contrasted with the south, which was full of treeless tower blocks and dense housing projects.

I crossed Barking Road, which cut the borough into two and had once stood for a symbolic racial division between the white and non-white residential areas, although this had changed considerably with more black people slowly moving south and more whites moving on to suburbs. Nevertheless, I would not have ventured on foot too far south to places such as Canning Town, Beckton, or the Royal Docks. I had absorbed the common sense conveyed to me by other black people in Newham that these particular areas were no-go zones where the risk of racial harassment and attacks was high.[8]

As I walked, I thought of Gillian and her broken phone. Focused on my own good mood, I arrived at her home at an unfortunate hour—the family was having dinner, or "tea," as working-class people in Newham called it. But in characteristic form, Gillian extended her warm hospitality. "Join us for tea," she said. I protested that I would come later, but did not want to risk causing offense as Gillian was already fixing a steaming plate of chicken stew and rice for me. As I began to enjoy this home-cooked meal, Gillian told me that in fact it was a wonderful time for my visit because the whole family was very happy. "If you had come yesterday, you would have seen us all crying," she said. I didn't know what she was referring to, but I smiled and continued to happily dig into my food.

"Six pounds and forty-five pence," Gillian said slowly and cryptically. "That's what they're giving us now."

"What do you mean?" I asked.

"Benefits," she explained.

I was startled and somewhat incredulous. At the time I was not at all familiar with how social welfare benefits in Britain worked, but, surely, they could not be that low. Virtually a third of Newham inner-city residents depended on local council benefits (Newham Council 2010) and there was no way they could survive on such small amounts. As a fieldworker at the time, I was trying to live as cheaply as possible, but I was certainly spending more than £6.45 a week on food and groceries. This was London after all.

Slowly a story emerged. During the course of the previous twelve years, Gillian had been in and out of the welfare system and at various times received key benefits such as income support, housing, and child support. Most recently she had reentered the welfare system after she was suddenly laid off from a well-known builder's firm where she had worked as a personal assistant to the supervisor. Her supervisor, a well-known white local who owned the business, had sexually harassed her. Gillian's protests and resistance against her boss resulted in a dismissal after a short seven weeks on the job. After she was laid off, she went to the local Newham Council welfare benefits office to get herself back on the rolls and received a rude shock when she was told that she was no longer eligible.

"They said that I needed to have a passport!" Gillian explained. "They said that during the seven weeks that I got that job, the law had changed and now anyone who signs on needs to show a marriage certificate or driving license or a passport! Well, I had a passport and I am legally in this country, but it wasn't up-to-date!" she exclaimed.

"But aren't you a British citizen?" I asked.

"Yes, I am," she replied.

"So why did you need to show a passport?"

What had happened was that during that seven-week period when Gillian was off income support, the British Parliament had passed another round of new laws and directives to implement a new "right to reside" test that scrutinized access to the benefits system (O'Neill 2011). This test was ostensibly introduced over media-driven political panics that the enlargement of the European Union (EU) to include ten new countries in Eastern Europe would presumably flood the benefits system in a matter of months. The government urgently responded within a Powellian border-control mindset by introducing restrictive new eligibility requirements in order to assuage anti-immigration fears. Later, these rules were amended to allow new EU immigrants to access the benefits system after five years of residency. Under pressure from the European Union itself, twenty-six EU countries were subsequently granted exemption from the new right-to-reside rule. However, other countries from outside the EU, including all the Commonwealth countries, could not contest the new rules.[9]

With the new right-to-reside rule, black immigrants already residing in Britain were suddenly burdened with providing documentary evidence of their legal status, regardless of their prior history of settlement or citizenship. Clearly, these new rules did not take into account the history of black immigrants such as Gillian who had entered decades ago from the Caribbean and who were once British Empire citizens or subjects. In fact, the new reforms reinforced the historical amnesia of those previous colonial relationships and the immigration flows that they had enabled. Gillian now was required to show documentary proof of her right to reside, and this consisted of presenting a current passport (which cost seventy-two pounds to renew), a British birth certificate, or a Home Office certificate granting citizenship.

Gillian's situation is representative of the thousands of ex-colonial British subjects—people from former African, African Caribbean, and South Asian colonies—whose lives become repeatedly entangled with laws made in response to new anti-immigration policies. Even though Gillian was not a new immigrant, her standing as a black person in the social welfare state marked her immigration status and eligibility as suspicious. Documentary proof of residency was almost always the first line of gatekeeping before a British state agency would deign to provide a social service. During the year I worked as a caseworker at NMP, I had occasion to accompany victims of racial attacks and harassment to local agencies such as the Homeless Persons Unit, which was legally responsible for rehousing victims of racial attacks and harassment. These agencies almost always demanded documentary proof of residency, even in life-threatening situations.

Such abstract welfare benefits rules, however, are not color-blind. For example, while at these offices, I rarely observed white British people being asked about their legal residential status. They were assumed to be people who would "habitually" be residents in Britain, and hence the test was often waived (Fitzpatrick 2006). In Gillian's case, her physical appearance invariably triggered the need to prove that she was not a "person from abroad." She was repeatedly subjected to the new rules, even though Newham Council had been dealing with Gillian as an income and child benefit recipient for many years.

As we ate dinner together that evening, Gillian smiled cheerfully at me. "I made dinner for just £3.99," she said. Though I returned a small smile, I was feeling heavy inside. "One pound fifty pence for chicken legs, £1.89 without skin. You put in some allspice, tomato and stew for an hour in a good pot. If you have a pressure cooker you could do it in half an hour."

Although I expressed my appreciation for the meal in the best ways I could, I really wished that I hadn't just popped in for dinner. I imagined the small pack of chicken legs that Gillian had purchased with the benefits money and looked around at the faces of Gillian and her two daughters enjoying the meal. There was nothing left in the pot.

On the walls of the living room in Gillian's home was a smiling picture of her son, Mark, ten years old at the time and dressed in a scout's uniform. Adjacent to the picture were framed certificates that Mark earned for perfect attendance and punctuality. These certificates were a part of the efforts of inner-city schools to recognize the successes of their pupils who were apt to be labeled as "problem" students. Gillian was very proud of these certificates and proud of Mark, and yet she spoke wistfully and nostalgically about that time when her son had been "a very happy normal boy."

These memories contrasted with the last years of Mark's secondary schooling, which had been almost consumed with fighting a series of detentions and exclusions that prohibited him from attending school. He had been expelled from Eastlea Community School during his last year of high school.

The image and certificates on the wall, awarded to a bright young boy, and the image of Mark as an adolescent troublemaker that Eastlea had constructed could not have been more disparate. According to Gillian, for the longest time Mark dreamed of becoming a barrister and had done well in the arts. He had even brought his school fame through an award-winning performance in a school drama that was staged at London's prestigious Royal Arts Festival.

Mark's decline in school performance and his conflicts with school authorities started when he fell victim to an assault by a parent of one of his white friends. This friend's father worked in the canteen of a local police station, and he did not like his son hanging out with black people. One day while Mark was visiting his friend, the father punched Mark and told him to go away.

This racist attack was also taken up as a case by NMP, which sought to have the father evicted from his council flat for violating the anti–racial harassment clauses of his tenancy agreement. Mark and his family won the case and the father was expelled from the borough.

Such hard-won victories over barrages of racial and police attacks, however, did not mitigate the damage that had been done to Mark's spirit and educational morale. Following the successful eviction, Mark started to develop a reputation in school as a "troublemaker" and found himself running afoul of hostile teachers and administrators. He was frequently sentenced to disciplinary exclusions from attending school. These interruptions in his schooling wreaked havoc with his education.

Once again with the help of NMP, Gillian tried to mount appeals against the school disciplinary system. She requested other forms of interventions, for example, pastoral support services, to be used to address Mark's growing behavior issues, but she was repeatedly denied.

During the times Mark was expelled, most of his friends finished their schooling and moved on to college or the workforce. Mark, on the other hand, spent time in the local Territorial Army (Army Reserve) doing volunteer training as a way to pass the time and create some kind of structure in his life.

NMP was eventually able to overturn his school eviction and Mark was readmitted to the school system. But when he returned to school, he was placed with a different cohort of students who were younger than he was. In his final year, Mark's academic performance suffered badly. Gillian was devastated. "He's left school with no qualifications, nothing," she said.

After finishing high school, Mark immediately landed in trouble again. He was convicted of common assault and would spend a year appealing the conviction, again with the help of NMP. He did not often appear motivated to pursue his case and on many occasions threatened to derail his own chances of success by failing to appear for his hearings and missing his probation meetings.

As one of his caseworkers, I often had to scramble for doctors' notes to provide evidence that there were extenuating circumstances that justified his absence at his probation visits and to assist him in avoiding further arrests.

The long shadow of police harassment on the family, repeated encounters with racism, and Mark's failed school experiences seemed to leave him resigned and cynical about the "system." When I approached him to participate in an NMP antiracist workshop on police stop-and-search practices and the rights of people in those situations, he was barely interested. He brushed off any attempt I made to talk to him about further education options and the like. "He's given up," Gillian declared to me.

In Mark's view, the long-running battle with the police had only brought wrack and ruin on the family and had made him the target of police reprisals. Instead of developing a political, structural, and racial analysis of policing, he focused his resentment on his mother for her strongwilled challenges of police abuse at every instance. He interpreted her activism as the reason that his own personal dreams were unraveling. He even stated that he wanted to date and marry a white girl, "in order to breed the black out" of his violated life.

When Mark turned eighteen he had another run-in with the local police who had targeted him for a stop-and-search. He was profiled as racially fitting the description of a suspect in a burglary case. The police were in the process of arresting him on a street near Gillian's house, where he still lived. Neighbors ran to tell Gillian what was happening and she hurriedly came out.

As she reached the scene of Mark's arrest she saw that a number of police officers had pinned him down on the road. His hands had been cuffed and the police officers were repeatedly beating his legs. Gillian tried to reach Mark, but two white police officers blocked her way and held her back. She screamed at them not to hurt Mark, but they would not stop hitting him.

Gillian again tried to break free and approach Mark and this time a police officer delivered a frontal rugby-like tackle that flung her down the road. As she fell, another officer grabbed her sweater top with such force that it was pulled off her body. Her upper body was completely exposed. The humiliation was further compounded when, instead of attending to her exposure, the two officers held Gillian in a chokehold. Only when a black female officer arrived on the scene did the two white male officers let Gillian go. The black officer then told her to put her clothes back on.

Our police complaint pertained to excessive force used in the arrest procedure against Mark and the excessive force used against Gillian during the course of her own arrest for allegedly interfering with police work.

We later learned that the police knew all along they were not, in fact, looking for Mark. He happened to be present at an operation where three of his friends were apprehended on charges related to a knife assault, and they then extended the stop-and-search upon an alleged suspicion that Mark was involved in the other burglary case they were investigating. It had been a fabrication to justify the "reasonable" grounds for a stop-and-search.

These three neighborhood friends of Mark's were all white. While we worked on constructing Gillian's and Mark's official complaints, it was proving difficult to enlist the cooperation of these friends to assemble supportive affidavits.

The lack of support that Mark received from his friends became a disturbing issue for Gillian and reoriented her view of the cohesiveness and the depth of the community's acceptance of her racially mixed friendships and neighborhood circles. North Plaistow, where she lived, was a racially mixed area with an even distribution of white, African Caribbean, and South Asian families. Across from their terraced council home on London Road was a mammoth Newham Council tower block whose residents were also of many different racial and ethnic backgrounds.

Mark and his white friends, like many youth in the area, bonded over hip-hop culture and styled themselves accordingly, especially in terms of the music they consumed, the fashions they imitated, and the fearless streetwise masculinity they exhibited. Their cross-community interest in hip-hop easily signified common interests and integration that the state's official discourse of community cohesion desired.

But in spite of their shared locality, common youth interests, and similar run-ins with the law, the white friends and their respective families appeared to Gillian to be privileging their racial solidarity with the white police officers rather than giving support to her and Mark.

Gillian wanted Mark to appeal to the goodwill of his friends to come forward to assist with his police complaint, and she kept asking him to intervene. Mark interpreted his mother's insistence as a parental pressure to be rebelled against, and tensions continued to build between mother and son. On one occasion Mark declared, "I have to speak to them, innit? If they don't want to come, then there's not much I can do about it," and stormed off.

Gillian explained to me that Mark could not make any sense of why his white friends were not backing him up and he interpreted their unwillingness to do so as a reflection of his mother's wrong-headedness in pursuing the police complaint. He simply wanted to return to the color-blind ambit of friendship with his white neighborhood friends. The last thing that interested him was dealing with the bureaucratic struggles of lodging police complaints.

"He's so confused," Gillian explained. "He doesn't know how to deal with it. He thinks that it's just another beef on the road."

Gillian also tried appealing to the parents of the white friends herself. "Sam's mother knows what I've been through. They've seen what's happened to us. If I was in the church I'd say they were heathen!" she told me after she had tried and failed to get Sam's family to help. "If they were all black . . . but they come here all the time and say, 'Oh, I just got nicked for half an ounce' or whatever. If it was Mark, that would be it. That's when you see the colors. I'm a very black person. I know what we go through," she said. "They haven't got the understanding we have and they don't take you seriously. They're all white. I don't know if they're just saying it's another black thing. One of them, her son is in the force. People don't understand. Why you kicked off or why the police did you. If they were black or any other nationality they'd know what we're going through. So they look at you when you say that happened to you. *Huh?*" "But I'll get the job done. I'll get a bottle of wine and go down there to Sam's mom again," she said.

As the days passed, however, Gillian had as little success as Mark did. None of their white friends or neighbors wanted to come forward as witnesses. It did not seem that the workings of a nonracial British convivial culture could be easily mobilized to support black struggles against police abuse. Neighborhood community cohesion as envisioned by the state did not produce a shared understanding of police racism, nor did it facilitate organic, antiracist solidarities.

Clearly, repeated trouble with the police can fracture a person's sense of belonging within their home neighborhood and racially integrated social circles. To be marked as someone who is in trouble with the law, even if innocent, means a loss of respectability. Responses often follow dominant middle-class norms, whereby instead of critically assessing the racial and class processes of criminalization, the person is individually blamed. A common sense reasoning, "If you have not done anything wrong, then you have nothing to fear," underlay some of the suspicions that Gillian and Mark experienced.

Such thinking shifts criticism and attention away from the state's racial criminalization logic and toward an assumption of individual, criminal culpability (Cacho 2012). Racial profiling practices and racist sexual violence by the police meant that Gillian's and Mark's efforts to lead respectable lives, free from the trauma of state violence, dishonor, and humiliation, were continuously thwarted.

"Are you still going on with that, Gillian?" was an oft-heard comment as her troubles with the law continued. "She doesn't seem to be able to get out of it" was another overheard comment that Gillian reported to me. Despite their own entanglements with the local police, white working-class friends and neighbors preferred to view Gillian's and Mark's relatively more frequent and protracted troubles with the state as indicative of personal shortcomings. Gillian was seen as a failed maternal figure who could not constitute a normal family life.

Ultimately, though, a lone neighbor emerged who did step up in solidarity with Gillian and Mark, and she was willing to serve as an eyewitness to what had transpired between the police and Mark. Kiranjit was a sixth form student in East Ham College and described herself as a "childhood mate of Mark's." She was of Indian descent and she and Mark had known each other since primary school. Initially, however, Kiranjit was afraid, largely of her parents' reaction to her getting involved with any kind of police matter.

"I love Gill, she's like my mum, but I can't get involved," she told us when NMP first approached her. Gillian herself had rationalized and excused Kiranjit's fears, stating that her young friend had a strict upbringing and was going through some difficult family tensions. "They're a fantastic family but strict religion," Gillian told me later.

In Gillian's estimation, Kiranjit's struggle to come forward was somehow tied to the orthodoxy of her South Asian family's Sikh religion. "I admire Asian people," Gillian said, and then added, "They have their culture and show respect. Cover their hair. Me? I'm not showing respect," she said, once battling with her conflicted self-image.

However, what enabled Kiranjit to have the courage to come forward was some assurance that there could be a way for NMP to take her witness statement so that she would not have to submit herself to direct contact with the police. This strategy was a pioneering casework innovation by Zareena Mustapha, one of NMP's leading activists at the time, and since there was no explicit legal restriction on this method of writing up witness statements without the presence of police themselves, Internal Affairs grudgingly went along with it.

As we worked on writing up her statement, Kiranjit told us a story that helped to make meaning about why she felt it necessary to help Mark and Gillian. Kiranjit had herself been harassed by the local Newham police and routinely stopped and searched in the streets near her home.

As a young urban college student, Kiranjit preferred to dress in hooded sweatshirts—virtually a uniform for the hip-hop-obsessed youth of Newham. Youth were using hooded track tops to mask their identities from the ubiquitous CCTV surveillance cameras that had been installed in the borough as part of a crime-fighting initiative. Hooded sweatshirts also had recently become the subject of a burgeoning moral panic termed as anti-social behaviors. Anti-social Behavior Ordinances (ASBOs) had been introduced by the New Labour government and these new tools of policing enabled the British state to place civil liberty restrictions on anyone over the age of ten if they were deemed to have misbehaved in public spaces.

Offenses include drinking, vandalism, graffiti, and "playing loud music at night." An ASBO can be in effect for two years and could involve restrictions placed on movement, street activity, and fraternizing with other people known as "troublemakers." In this highly policed and surveillance-saturated environment, growing up as a hip-hop-obsessed teenager could spell trouble under the monitoring logic of the state. Kiranjit recalled that she herself used to dress up in "cool" track pants and hoodies, but this seemed to make her an instant target for a stop-and-search.

In exasperation she sought a way to hang out in the streets of Newham and yet avoid constant police harassment. She experimented with wearing traditional Indian clothes or, specifically, the *salwar kameez*, which older South Asian women regularly wore out in public in the borough. She wanted to see if this change in attire would cause the police to leave her alone. The strategy worked. Playing into the stereotype of a "traditional" and conservative Asian woman appeared to offer her protection from Newham police's surveillance and antisocial behavior agenda. White British orientalized notions about the traditional passivity of South Asian women ironically afforded Kiranjit a buffer against street-level forms of racial profiling and criminalization by the state, which was not possible for African Caribbean women.

It was this firsthand experience of police harassment and her own negotiations with the differential ways that black youth were criminalized on the streets of Newham, however, that led Kiranjit to relate to and empathize with Mark's and Gillian's travails. She told me that this was why she wanted to provide an eyewitness affidavit, even though it meant going against her parents' wishes to become involved.

After collecting Kiranjit's testimony, I went with Mark and another NMP caseworker to a local police station where Internal Affairs officers had asked to meet us in order to take down Mark's statement. During the official interview with two white female detectives, I witnessed the secondary modes of racist victimization that negatively affect the morale of black people who try to make police complaints over excessive force.

My fieldnotes from the meeting recount what took place as two officers interviewed Mark:

> I initially did not think that she was asking questions in an overtly antagonistic fashion. However, I began to get the sense that underneath the very smooth line of questioning was a police officer's logic and sympathy at work. The application of "excessive force" was weighed in with the logic of an officer's "risk assessment." At one point she remarked, "you're not a small guy" in response to Mark's description of how he was roughly handled and later was thrown into the ground and had smashed his head. Mark replied, "I wasn't big, I was not as big as I am now." He had been about two inches shorter, at 5'8?. The police officers were of equal if not slightly taller height than he was then. He was eighteen years old now, and the incident happened last year.

Mark's frustration grew as the white female detectives kept stereotyping his physical appearance as a young black male and his "big-ness" to trivialize the violence he had suffered. And this was despite the fact that the police had in their favor both the force of numbers and the legal sanction to apply violence. Under the guise of getting at the two sides of the story, the female officer was drawing on well-known racist stereotypes about the aggressiveness and hypermasculinity of black males (Jackson 2011) to guide her interpretation of Mark's testimony.

As the interview progressed, Mark narrated how the arresting officers would not heed his screams of pain when they had him in a hold and refused his pleas for them to stop hurting him. Once again the white female detective quickly countered the assertion. She suggested that Mark might have been moving his large shoulders, thereby necessitating the extra force.

Mark tried to clarify that an overwhelming number of about five to six officers had been involved in restraining him. The lead detective, however, shot back and asked if any of his friends were also present in the vicinity. Mark responded that three friends were present. The detective wrote this down in her notes. Only when I protested that this was not accurate because the friends had only arrived after the arrest was in process did she consent to strike the detail.

The subtle antagonistic behavior of the white woman detective was linguistic, epistemological, and cultural. It did not involve direct physical, racial violence. And yet the interaction between Mark and the detective was racialized and already symbolically violent. The detective was drawing on a deeply sedimented repertoire of tropes and representations about black masculinity to appraise Mark's claims of mistreatment. And they would assist her in constructing the official and legal documentary version of the event.

The detective's duty was not necessarily to take Mark's side, but it was to write down his point of view, which would later be reconciled and compared to the police officers' accounts of what happened. It was also widely known at NMP that police officers accused of misconduct would often collaborate with one another to write up their notes so as to corroborate a fellow officer's story. For numerous reasons, then, the process of gathering and verifying police complaints was stacked against Mark.

The detective also queried Mark about the veracity of the sexual assault on his mother. A basic understanding of the difficulties involved in having a teenage son describe a sexual assault on his mother should have warranted a sensitive approach to the topic. While he was in school, Mark had already experienced police interrogations and the attendant efforts to demoralize and dehumanize him. Here was yet another instance in which he learned that black males could not expect British institutions or individual state agents to acknowledge or even consider the most basic of human feelings and frailties. My fieldnotes, written right after the internal affairs interview, record what happened:

> This was the most difficult part of the interview. The sergeant kept needling him to provide a description of what had happened exactly. She wanted to know what top his mother was wearing, what color, and if the top had come off slightly, all the way, if she had been wearing a bra. Mark grew very distressed and reluctant to speak. "Can we move past this bit?" He vacillated between becoming very stiff and reticent to talk and often moved his forehead to the edge of the table. The sergeant persisted without showing any empathy for the emotional aspect of what he was going through or wanting to recognize his anguish. . . . There was no understanding or even perception of his capacity to have difficult emotions. He was not

seen as a "victim" and, in fact, had to continuously justify his allegations with clinical details. I wondered if this would have been a
reaction to a crime victim who was white and female and blonde.

The specter of gendered racism, in multiple guises, was unrelenting in both
Gillian's and Mark's lives. It took the form of police abuse and violence,
and repeatedly delivered dehumanizing assaults. As Gillian herself put it,
"Would they have done this to Tony Blair's daughter?"

Following the complete course of the internal investigation, the police
were fully cleared of any disciplinary charges—there was no case to answer.
Gillian's experiences revealed how white police officers routinely applied
excessive force upon black women's bodies, with reasonable expectations
that the state's liberal juridical processes would decide in their favor and
assign immunity. Internal Affairs police detectives colluded with abusive
beat police officers in everyday acts of political whiteness in order to limit
and constrict accountability to black people. Together, they enacted and
enforced tropes that dehumanized Gillian and Mark.

In the process of filing numerous police complaints and listening to her
life stories, I came to a deep recognition of how Gillian had been forced to
experience and endure the behavior of white police officers and other white
British males who had sexually violated and physically brutalized her over
the course of her entire life. Their collective actions helped to construct her
body as an object for the acting out of white supremacist and misogynistic
entitlements. Such a continual loss of bodily integrity and respectability
continued into Gillian's intimate family life. Due to the criminalized gaze
of the local police, and Mark's coming of age within the escalating context
of criminalization and racial profiling, police officers acquired the right to
enter and disrupt her private space at will.

But Gillian's family and home spheres were shaped not only by these
cumulative layers of racialized and gendered state violence, but also
through domestic violence. Domestic abuse mirrored police abuse—where
Gillian's body was again subjected to the loss of respect and integrity.

Mark became depressed and continued to accumulate numerous infrac-
tions with the law. He had also fallen in with what Gillian called a rough
crowd. One day he came back home in a maddened rage, trashed his room,
and physically assaulted both Gillian and one of his teenage sisters. He had
lost control and Gillian felt she had but one choice. "I called the police on

him. Do you hear what Gillian is telling you, Mohan? I called the police on him!

"Inside my body I'm calm as you like, outside I'm shaking like a leaf. James [Gillian's partner] and Mark have been abusing me for years. I've been abused in my own home. I'm not such a perfect family after all. I've been with this man for twenty-three years and I've been threatened and threatened. I've had to take so much shit for people around and from my own family." This was the first time Gillian had confided in me of the long-term abuse she had suffered at home.

"Mark is so twisted and confused," Gillian said. And glancing at her son's picture on the wall, she continued, "I've faced it for you and why have you got an element of doubt? I've got to hold it together for the girls. Thirteen years on, I'm up at six in the morning to see if the police are coming!"

Recently, Gillian had endured a home break-in. Members of a gang who were looking for Mark smashed their way in with guns, physically assaulted Gillian, and threatened her daughters. I was terrified for Gillian's safety and contacted Newham Housing Services to express the urgent need to have her rehoused to a safe address. In my limited capacity as her caseworker dealing with social services around racism and housing, this was the one concrete option for safety that I felt I could facilitate, now that I was aware of the danger that she faced from Mark's rages and embrace of criminal activity.

Ironically, when I was Mark's advocate, I had to mediate the demands of the local housing authority's urgent response team, which required that Gillian no longer house Mark, since he had by then reached an adult age. Even as a black antiracist activist, I felt that I had been pushed into carrying out a colonial intermediary role where the underlying political roots of violence and dispossession were unaddressed in favor of the state's policy proceduralisms. Mark's exclusion from living with the family was the council's condition for rehousing them to an adjacent borough. I told Gillian that these were the choices in dealing with Mark's violence and his growing criminal activities that were endangering the family. After some thought, Gillian finally agreed to the move, and she resigned herself to excluding Mark from the home in order to secure safety for herself and her daughters.

This account of the work of NMP, through which my activism intersected briefly with Gillian's and Mark's lives, shows that such forms of activism were only partial interventions in the complex and broadly lived experiences of intersectional violence and racism. The intimacy of casework and the grounded quality of working with individuals and their problems enabled me to glimpse how African Caribbean women's existence in Britain is shaped through a racism that is further elaborated by gendered and sexual vectors of power and violence. Such a complex racializing environment defies the reductive understanding of racism as event-based or issue-based phenomena. In other words, the experience of intersectional racial violence is a chronic and lifetime condition and not an episodic or discrete aberration in the lives of its victims. Multiple, interlinked forms of violence against black women do not simply emerge in episodic "racist incidents," as they are imagined within the state's liberal justice frameworks.

My relationship with Gillian was also shaped in the context of a particular police abuse complaint that I worked on. The case was one event among many others that had occurred and were simultaneously unfolding in her life. I was discovering how black women's experiences were woven through complex intersections of interpersonal violence, racial violence, and racialized state violence. These experiences produced unresolved contradictions for the activist anthropological positioning I used to identify myself as a researcher and also affected my research, which I had thought could undo the colonial dynamics of knowledge production. Rather that treating the people I worked with as "informants" or even "consultants" or "collaborators," I had aspired to refashion my role as a fellow antiracist actor and racial justice advocate, who worked with people in pursuit of struggles that emerged out of shared histories and yearnings to overcome racism and colonialism.

The political choice of doing partisan and politically engaged observant participation rather than classical participant observation research did not, however, resolve the objectifying issues of ethnographic research. It was not only that the political victories or remedies for injustice were not guaranteed, but that the experiences of racism in the life of a single person were far more multidimensional and bigger than the remit of casework or a particular issue-based activist campaign in which I could participate. Many aspects of intersecting racism in the lives of people I worked with were left untouched by the limited NMP model of fight-back and activism against the state's anti-black racism. Practical victories and clear resolutions, even in the specific aspects of racism that I did address in my apprenticeship as a caseworker, were also rarely available. And it is the reality of black life in Britain that even after a rare victory or obtained remedy, another encounter with racism is waiting just down the road.

The many forms of intersectional racial violence that Gillian and her son experienced further question the narrative that twenty-first-century British society is making progress toward a post-racial conviviality (Gilroy 2005), as well as the state's official community cohesion discourse. While they lived in integrated neighborhoods and not culturally separatist ethnic or religious "ghettoes," and while they habitually socialized across racial lines in everyday life, Gillian and Mark still confronted the emergence of everyday political whiteness when they pressed for racial justice with the police. These racialized disparities set them apart from their white working-class neighbors and friends. Additionally, the police complaints process that Gillian and Mark engaged in with the hopes of redress and justice was constrained by everyday political whiteness. White officers who investigated allegations of racism against fellow police officers mobilized racially coded tactics and lines of questioning that aimed to favor their colleagues. These maneuvers relied on tacit assumptions about the criminalized predispositions of African Caribbean people and white supremacist fantasies about the subhuman strength of African and African Caribbean bodies to withstand pain as well as presumptions concerning the sexually violable status of black women. Gillian and Mark had to prove that they were *not* what these beliefs made them out to be in order to be recognized as human. They would fail time and time again.

The police complaints process has been subjected to a number of official criticisms and reforms over the years, but even the British state's own Independent Police Complaints Commission (IPCC) has continued to assert that complaints of racial discrimination are "poorly handled" and that the internal processes of police departments in England to deal with such complaints lack basic standards (British Broadcasting Corporation 2014). In a research study undertaken by the IPCC in 2007, the odds of having a complaint upheld against the police were stated to be one in ten. Women made one-third of all complaints against the police and the study also showed that 91 percent of the complaints were made against white police officers. Significantly the IPCC deemed only a third of those complaints as needing further investigation. Most discouraging of all, only 6 percent of the nearly five thousand complaints lodged against the entire Metropolitan Police force in London at the time were eventually upheld.[10]

The life experiences of African Caribbean people such as Gillian and Mark demonstrated the true futility—or limits—of integration and assimilation. The intimate and public domination of her body and life had little to do with English or British acculturation. In fact, it rendered such an acculturation incongruous and irrelevant. Gillian's positive self-ascription as a strong black woman and as a politically black antiracist activist in her community arose as necessary acts of survival. But the "myth of the strong black woman," as Michele Wallace (2015) points out, is a harsh valorization, one that makes socially unavailable forms of genteel femininity—and their accompanying codes of respectful treatment—that are granted to privileged white women. Gillian's dogged strength to fight unrelenting police abuse also alienated her from Mark, who, swayed by unquestioned white heteronormative codes and creeping, violent hypermasculinity, wished for a more feminine and "normal" mother and a "quiet" middle-class English life—a life that was never meant for him or Gillian in the first place.

CHAPTER 4

"We Are Terrified of You!"

British Muslim Women
and Gendered Anti-Muslim Racism

In 2006, Newham was not an entertainment destination for middle-class white Londoners or tourists. Shops and restaurants on Green Street or East Ham High Street catered mainly to local communities. Vijay's Chawalla on Green Street was a popular restaurant because it served vegetarian food, and eating this food was an important religious observance for some of the borough's Hindus and Sikhs. Well known to residents north of the borough, but virtually unknown outside Newham, the *Guardian* reviewed the restaurant in 2015: "The queues snaking out of the door on a weekend are reason enough to explore this no-frills vegetarian restaurant, which sits amid the sari outfitters and Indian jewelers of *east* east London's Green Street in Forest Gate. . . . It may be too close to Essex for the hipsters to have discovered just yet, but they will surely come, drawn by the stunning spicy, crisp potato bhajia with carrot chutney, mogo chips, or the fluffy deep-fried bhatura, served with a deeply spiced chickpea curry" (Aitch and Bernhardt 2015).

I took a fellow academic colleague, a white woman lecturer teaching at one of the University of London colleges, to this restaurant. This liberal-minded friend lived in an upper middle-class neighborhood in Swiss Cottage, a district in the north London borough of Camden that was predominantly white. She had never been to Newham.

As we took our seats, my friend noticed a Muslim family enter and take their seats. She became startled at seeing a woman in the *niqāb*, a fully veiled dress that covered the whole body, with the exception of the eyes.

Figure 13. British Muslim women participating in a political protest in Newham, 2006. Photo by the author.

"Let's see how she does it. Will she take it off?" she asked, with her hands covering her mouth. She could not fathom how the woman in the niqāb would eat in public. Her reaction was a shock to me. Accustomed to seeing some Muslim women wearing a form of head or chest covering in Newham, I had not taken special notice of the woman in the niqāb.

My friend's culture shock, on the other hand, appeared to be focused on reading the Muslim woman's niqāb as a sign of absolute difference and as a sign of gendered degradation. She could not fathom how this Muslim woman wearing it could perform the most quotidian of human functions.

While observing my white British friend's reactions, I thought about an ongoing case at the Newham Monitoring Project (NMP) that involved a local Muslim woman who had been harassed and assaulted in a bank. The woman had been walking into her local bank branch on Stratford High Street when a white male customer started hurling racial expletives at her and physically pushed her out of the building. The woman quickly used her cell phone to call the police who, when they arrived, trivialized her assault by remarking, "Well, what do you expect? *Look* at you." The responding group of police officers, all of whom were white, refused to record the woman's charges of assault and racial harassment.

I then remembered another recent tension around the hijab that had arisen even within the antiracist ranks of NMP itself. As the British state's counterterrorism surveillance expanded, Muslims in Newham were subjected to frequent antiterror policing raids and a number of people had been placed under "control orders," or virtual house arrest, pending further investigations. In response to this situation, some allied white antiracist activists were to distribute "Know Your Rights" pamphlets. However, they were uncomfortable with the prospect of leafleting a local mosque. The white activists worried that they would be asked to cover their heads while carrying out the leafleting action. There had been no such demands from the mosque leadership, however, and furthermore, the plan was that the women activists would be on the sidewalks and do their leafleting on public streets outside the mosque. However, they were anxious about an improbable demand that, as a result of their mere proximity to Muslim religious spaces, they would be forced to wear the hijab.

My reflections on these sudden eruptions of white disorientations and violent animus concerning the presence of hijab-wearing Muslim women in Newham raise the question of new forms of racializing and white supremacist imaginings. How do these assorted British anxieties about the Muslim practice of the hijab complicate the gendered definitions of racism, and the scope of antiracist work or political blackness in Britain today?

The visible difference of the Muslim woman occupying public space, signified by the act of wearing the hijab, has been subject to fraught domestic political debates as the War on Terror assumes a permanent place in imperial policies and statecraft (Cornell 2004; Eisenstein 2004; Abu-Lughod 2006, 2013; Alexander 2006; Puar 2007). The hijab-wearing Muslim woman appears to conjure fears about the unraveling of a putative set of "British values" rooted in liberal individualism and a social order that normatively separates the realm of the religious from the political. White British discomfort with and hostility toward the hijab-wearing British Muslim women's presence appear linked to the assemblage of popular and state fears of a globalized and rhizomatic "theological-political" (Anidjar 2003) threat, not only to national security but also to cultural loss.[1]

These popular-state constructions of national anxieties presuppose that a domestic Muslim terror threat could arise from anywhere, and that any ethnic British Muslim or new immigrants, such as refugees from the Middle East, could at any time undergo radicalization and become activated as terrorists. In addition, the visible difference of the hijab-wearing Muslim woman appears to trigger white fears about sudden acts of terrorism as well as the crisis of "Britishness" or British values.

Foundations of the modern nation-state, such as secular liberal individualism and women's freedoms, are perceived to be potentially compromised or threatened by the figure of the "veiled" Muslim woman moving freely on the streets, entering a bank, or eating at a restaurant. At both the everyday and the state policy levels, the mark of a Muslim woman's difference elicits confusion and debate about how to cope with the presence of a religiously marked, gendered comportment. To stabilize this unsettled sense of safety and cultural stability, unveiling, either through direct force or cultural assimilation policies, appears as a social action aimed at expressing moral sanction as well as securitization.

Anti-Muslim or "Islamophobic" hate crimes have steadily increased in London, with the Metropolitan Police reporting a 70 percent rise in such crimes in 2015 from the previous year (Adesina and Marocico 2015). Even state authorities have acknowledged the scale of the problem (Linning 2015; Stupples 2015). Muslim women who wear the hijab have become particular targets for violent anti-Muslim animus on the streets of London. In 2012, Tasneem Kabir, a sixteen-year-old teenager who wore the hijab, was knocked unconscious in Plaistow, the Newham neighborhood where Gillian lived, while on her way to college. Her attacker jogged up behind her and randomly punched her in the head, sending her crashing to the pavement. Another teenager in east London, Meanha Begum, who wore the niqāb, was out walking with a friend when a woman approached her and said, "What are you doing here, we don't trust you! You need to get that off your face!" (Linning 2015). She then proceeded to tear off Meanha's niqāb before punching and kicking her.

White British identity politics and the British state's politics in the current War on Terror posit a separate "West" opposed against an essentialized Muslim "other" that is ontologically defined as prone to terrorism and cultural backwardness (Rana 2011). The dichotomy, however, did not simply arise out of post-9/11 geopolitics. It has foundational antecedents in the concept of a secular Europe that evolved through conceptualizations of the enemy as an abject religious figure, specifically in western modernity's relationship to Islam (Anidjar 2014).

Western discourses about the uniquely oppressed Muslim woman helped solidify the orientalist narratives that emerged with modernity and that have created an archive of dominant images of Muslims as locked in forms of religiosity that are dissonant with the west's secular model. This discourse serves the dual functions of obscuring the gendered inequalities within the liberal nation-state and of estranging in the western imagination the objects of their colonial forays and oppression. In short, Muslims have been constructed in modern European discourse as bearers of fanatical and despotic religiosity and illiberal politics (Kahf 1999; Mernissi 2003; Zine 2006). This "Western colonial cultural gaze" (Mohanty 2003) constructs Muslim women as trapped within monolithic, static, and oppressive Islamic cultures.

British politicians and media commentators deploy an almost continuous barrage of rhetoric that demonizes and creates moral panics around the wearing of the hijab. The practice of wearing the niqāb especially has been labeled by some national politicians as a "mark of separation" and as an "abusive walking rejection" of British freedoms (Perlez 2007). For example, Jack Straw, a former Justice Minister, went so far as to exclude women wearing the niqāb from attending his meetings with constituents unless they first unveiled themselves.

Within this current conjuncture, how do British Muslim women themselves live through these antagonisms and advance their projects of freedom? It is not easy to attempt a representation of the question of the hijab in ways that can sidestep the orientalized tropes of patriarchal oppression. As a diasporic person from the Muslim-majority country of Malaysia, I was aware of a different public debate concerning the hijab. In Malaysia the increase in adherence to the hijab has been interpreted as a form of "Arab colonialism" that erases indigenous Southeast Asian Muslim cultural dress styles such as the *sanggul, selendang,* and *baju kebaya* (Boo 2015). Historically, Malaysian Muslim cultures did not adhere to conservative Arabic forms of the hijab. However, Islamization policies by Malaysia's ruling regime have popularized the hijab (or the *tudung* as it is known in Malaysia) as a symbol of Islamized capitalist modernity and as an assertion of majority-Malay Muslim difference. In the Malaysian context, the meanings of wearing or not wearing the hijab differ greatly from western contexts, and have to do with the nexus between capitalist developmentalism, the Malaysian state's growing emphasis on Salafi-inspired Islamization policies and Malay majoritarian domination, as well as renewed grassroots resistance against the standardization of Muslim identities wrought by state-sponsored and enforced "Arabization" (Zaid 2015; Norshahril 2016).

In my conversations and dealings with British Muslim women in Newham, however, I found that the majoritarian white British and state anxiety and animus against the hijab-wearing Muslim woman provoked counterphobic reactions, which further entrenched and reified what is arguably a culturally variable and contested practice within the global Muslim world. As Fawzia Afzal-Khan states,

> [The] notion of "Muslim womanhood" as a collectively "victimized" category has been circulated effectively to perpetuate both discursive violence in the United States (and the West in general) against Islam, as well as to sanction the "War-on-Terror." . . . Violence against women in different parts of the Islamic world and within Muslim societies everywhere has also escalated in the name of a "return" to an imaginary theocratic past, posited as an identitarian necessity to ward off the evils of a Satanic West bent on destroying the "*ummah*" (believers). (2004:187)

Afzal-Khan's important work examines western, anti-Muslim anxiety and animus toward the hijab from the standpoint of Muslim women's own personal and political contestations with the cultural dynamics unleashed by the War on Terror. Muslim women's autonomy and ongoing negotiations with religious tradition and the subjugation of Muslim patriarchy have now become entangled in a dynamic that pits western imperial, military, and everyday actions against defensive, religious reifications of diasporic Muslim identity.

In this contemporary geopolitical context, there is a spectrum of positions among Muslims in western countries concerning the wearing of the hijab. For example, the Europe-wide Assembly for the Protection of Hijab, or Pro-Hijab, argues, "As Muslims we are proud of the hijab, we are not oppressed" (Dear 2004). Groups such as British Muslims for Secular Democracy, however, argue that "the veil is so steeped in subjugation . . . it's retrograde" (Perlez 2007). An interview-based study of some 1,200 Muslims in Britain also argues that "one of the most significant findings . . . was the articulation of the idea of the Hijab as a concept rather than a piece of clothing that affected both men and women . . . for the purposes of exterior social harmony and internal spiritual humility" (Ameli and Merali 2006:22). These intra-Muslim debates about the essential character of the hijab and interpretations concerning its practice, however, do not operate in a geopolitical vacuum. Under conditions of dominant western representations of and imperial militaristic actions in the Muslim world, it is arguable that the symbolic act of wearing the hijab has been made into a new cultural touchstone by British Muslims precisely because of the demonization and attacks that the practice endures.[2]

During my fieldwork in Newham I encountered multiple and varied Muslim women's voices as they related their experiences with gendered anti-Muslim racism. The religious and pious politics of Muslim women are diverse, but their experiences of racial harassment and religiously motivated hate crimes reveal the extent to which the War on Terror in Britain has come to regulate everyday Muslim women's freedoms and to increase their vulnerability to racial-religious violence.

In the inner-city borough of Newham, a quarter of the borough's population is Muslim, with about 80 percent comprising different South Asian nationalities and 20 percent comprising African nationalities such as Somalis, Nigerians, and Tanzanians (Harriss 2006). It is not uncommon to see Muslim women wearing a variety of ethnic and national styles of the hijab while walking through commercial streets and public parks. Nationally, it is estimated that approximately half of Britain's Muslim women adhere to the practice of wearing some form of head covering. Some women dress in *salwar kameez*, others wear headscarves, some the full niqāb, while others are dressed in jeans and jackets. Muslim women I encountered in Newham often spoke of wearing the hijab in terms of a shared co-Abrahamic religious practice with Christians and Jews.[3] Some Muslim high school students I met while researching the activities of the Newham Youth Parliament pointed to the presence of the veil in iconic Judeo-Christian sculptures of the Virgin Mary that were plentiful in church compounds in the borough. They complained that it was Muslims who were being unfairly targeted for conservative religious practice and drew comparisons to the orthodox Jewish community in nearby Stamford Hill in Hackney. "Nobody seems to complain about *them*," they would reason.

At most, however, only a very small percentage of that community actually adopted the wearing of the niqāb.[4] As one commentator, participating in an online discussion, noted,

I live in Newham, east London, and there are plenty of *niqābis* here who work, are very active in community projects, and so on. There is only a barrier if people make it, otherwise if you are talking to a *niqābi* on the phone you wouldn't even know would you? lol so I don't see how in office jobs, admin jobs, catering jobs, telesales, etc. it would matter if the women wore or not.

I have never seen a woman wearing a *burqa* outside of pictures of Afghanistan. Also these women in Newham manage to pick up their kids from school fine.

Believe it or not you can tell who someone is from their eyes, height, voice etc., and it is not that hard! If you meet a *niqābi* once, and then you see her again you are likely to realize it is the same person from body language voice, eyes etc! (British Broadcasting Corporation 2010)

For this Newham blogger, the ubiquity of the veil in east London does not elicit the heightened moral and political antipathies expressed in the dominant media or political spheres. Even wearing the full niqāb is not perceived as an obstacle to accessing liberal, individualist notions of middle-class women's empowerment, for example, through work outside of the home.[5]

Dominant British cultural narratives, however, do not typically reference or include these kinds of self-representations from British Muslim women. The question of veiling or unveiling the Muslim woman draws instead on an archive of colonial tropes about backward Muslim cultures that lack individual rights. The emancipation of Muslim women through liberalism's regime of rights contributes to the justification and legitimization of the War on Terror itself (Eisenstein 2004; Bhattacharyya 2008). The military intervention in Afghanistan and Iraq was also supported by a number of white imperial feminist groups that include Feminist Majority in the United States who, along with the U.S. state, argued that military attacks and the waging of war to save Muslim women from Muslim patriarchy and the Taliban in particular were necessary and just (Abu-Lughod 2013). As Gargi Bhattacharyya has argued, "The present 'War-on-Terror' constructs the abuse of women and the denial of their public rights as a marker of eastern barbarism and as an indication of societal sickness, a sickness requiring military intervention" (2008:18).

There is furthermore a discursive assemblage that links dominant white feminist humanitarianism, orientalized media stereotypes about non-modern Muslim cultures, and state militarism in the West (Puar 2007). For example, the cover of *Time* magazine's August 9, 2010, issue depicts a young, mutilated Afghan woman, with the stark caption "What happens if we leave Afghanistan," referring to the prospect of total U.S. troop withdrawal in 2014. This gendered and sexualized ideological assemblage appears to be gaining currency as the War on Terror becomes reauthorized as an urgent project of liberating the Muslim world from horrific violence against women (Asad 2015). Omitted, paradoxically, from these western humanitarian discourses about the oppressed Muslim woman in countries abroad is the rise of anti-Muslim violence in the form of racial attacks or hate crimes within the domestic realm. Ironically, the narrative of rescuing women from Muslim extremism seems unable to think through the productive links between growing Islamophobia, militarism in Muslim countries abroad, and gendered anti-Muslim violence inside the jurisdiction of western liberal democracies.

According to research by the National Union of Students/Black Students' Campaign (2011), 72 percent of Muslim women in Britain have been the target of verbal abuse and publicly threatening behavior related to their appearance. Alana Lentin argues that "visual signifiers of racialized difference (skin color, dress, etc.) are intimately linked with the process of naturalization. In the case of the Muslim headscarf-wearing woman or the black skinned person, they become reduced to that single aspect of their outward appearance" (2008:38). The visual markers of racial and religious difference are highly correlated with acts of aggression and violence that Muslim women in Britain and Europe experience (Jawad and Benn 2003). The emerging views of Newham's Muslim women who live in this climate of oppression require us to rethink what it means to be progressive, feminist, and antiracist in Britain today.

The patriarchal regulation of women's bodies is not a new issue in Britain. The anxieties provoked for traditional patriarchal systems by women's free movement in public Britain have been well documented. Elizabeth Wilson (1991), in her pioneering study of women's mobility in Victorian London, argues that the city was, from its earliest history, a contradictory space for expressing women's personal freedoms. Paradoxically, it was a place that allowed for the deregulation of women's sexuality and simultaneously for the recontainment of that sexuality. Contrary to mythologies of sexually free western societies, Patrick Joyce argues that liberal rule is predi-cated upon contradictory articulations of freedom and regulation:

> Liberalism was shy of too much governing, and it confronted itself with realities—markets, civil society, families, and . . . cities—in which these subjects could be identified. These realities had their own internal logics that had to be respected. Liberalism therefore depended upon cultivating a certain sort of self, one that was reflex-ive and self-watching. Yet this self also watched liberalism, in the sense that liberal governmentality depended upon persons who could, and can, practise freedom by constantly questioning its lim-its. In liberalism, rule is ceded to a self that must constantly monitor the very civil society and political power that are at once the guaran-tee of freedom and its threat. (2003:8)

In western liberalism's colonial gaze, Muslim women who wear the hijab absolutely lack this ability to participate in rational discussions of freedom and its limits. The sign of the hijab or niqāb automatically signifies the Muslim woman's exclusion from the definition of the self-reflexive, liberal subject.

Interrogating the idea of urbanity as an already liberated feminist or women-empowered space is important if we want to better understand the contemporary struggles of Muslim women in Britain. In this spirit, it is possible to view the struggles of Muslim women who wear the veil as con-tinuous with a long genealogy of resistance and contestation to liberal gov-ernmentality. As Wilson (1991:8) states, "Although women, along with minorities, children, the poor, are still not full on citizens in the sense that they have never been granted full and free access to the streets . . . they have survived and flourished in the interstices of the city, negotiating the contradictions of the city in their own particular way."

As the following ethnographic encounters show, British Muslim women are also self-reflexive liberal subjects who negotiate, monitor, and mediate institutions such as the family and religion, very much as Joyce imagines and describes liberal individual governance. However, they exercise these agencies at the intersection of violent, racialized anti-Muslim politics and communal and state-based heteropatriarchal gender regulation.

Muslim women's struggles against patriarchy in a diasporic context transcend the boundaries of the nation-state. Reforming Islamic sharia law and its gendered codifications are key issues for global Muslim women's movements (Zainah 2015). These debates unfold within Islamic jurisprudence itself and are not simply determined by or derived from the western cultural or state influence (Mahmood 2005). For example, the debate over the heteropatriarchal construction of the duty of obedience in the home (*ta'ah*) by the wife is one critical site of struggle. As the legal scholar Azizah Y. al-Hibri (2000:224–6) argues, this code seeks to enforce "the duty not to leave the home without the husband's permission." Muslim women in communities who have adhered to this practice have challenged these edicts in both everyday life and in law. They struggle over their own autonomy and fundamental liberties vis-à-vis fathers, husbands, and male relatives. Debates concerning the equality of women in Islamic jurisprudence are also vigorous, centering around the work of Muslim women scholars who are reconceptualizing male-centric Quranic interpretation (Basarudin 2015; Lamrabet 2015). Such issues have coalesced into the *Musawah* global movement for equality and justice within Muslim families (Mir-Hosseini and Al-Sharmani 2015).

The everyday relevance of these issues and debates is apparent during any walk from the north to the south end of Green Street, a journey through a veritable global emporium of goods, foods, and ethnic cultural entertainment, punctured only by the West Ham Football Club's enormous stadium in the south. Shopping for daily household necessities, clothes, and wedding supplies and enjoying the pleasures of ethnic restaurants or Bollywood films at the Boleyn cinema represent some of the many activities in which Muslim women openly participate in London's inner-city urbanism. Their public presence challenges the orientalist stereotype of the sequestered Muslim woman, kept hidden from social view.

Gendered anti-Muslim violence in Newham, however, was a constant and very serious concern. It was especially prevalent around white-dominated public housing in the southern wards of Canning Town, Custom House, and the Royal Docks. I encountered a number of NMP cases where people would plead with caseworkers to help them with housing transfers to the north of the borough in order to escape the daily harassment they were subjected to in the south. But even on seemingly safe streets in the north, where co-ethnic and co-religious people were more dominant than in the southern wards, harassment and attacks on Muslim women nonetheless occurred.

One persistent pattern was the harassment of women who wear the hijab that took place every time there was a West Ham Football Club (FC)

Figure 14. Reading in West Ham Park, 2006. Photo by the author.

Figure 15. Everyday life on Green Street in Newham, 2006.
Photo by the author.

home game. West Ham FC is a major English premier league soccer club and, at the time, its stadium was located at the south end of Green Street, adjacent to a Catholic church and around the corner from the Boleyn Bollywood cinema. During the soccer season's home games, thousands of white West Ham fans traveled from neighboring boroughs to watch the games.[6]

In the 1970s and 1980s West Ham fans fashioned spikes out of pennies and hurled them at South Asian and African Caribbean people who came to watch a game. Many second-generation African Caribbean and South Asian east Londoners told me that their parents forbade them to attend West Ham games and to avoid going out in public during game days. As a result of such memories, open support for West Ham FC is rare in Newham. However, in the adjacent white-flight suburbs of Essex, where white working-class families from Newham migrated in response to ethnic minority settlement, long-distance support for West Ham FC is a part of the local patriotic identity. In a great number of homes in Barking and Dagenham, where the far-right British National Party has succeeded electorally, it is common to see displays of West Ham flags alongside the English flag of St. George. The phenomenon, however, is rarely seen in the non-white neighborhoods in West Ham FC's own backyard where South Asian and African Caribbean people predominate. Local Muslim women who wear the veil experience harassment and attacks on game day as crowds disperse and white fans traverse their way back to subway stations and bus stops. Women complain of being taunted and report having to fight off attempts by people to pull off their hijabs.

It was in this context of the harassment of Muslim women who wore the hijab that I helped to organize an NMP community outreach effort. We held a workshop in a room at the Citizen's Development Centre on Katherine Road. The meeting was the result of months of coordination and discussion over the phone with the center's director, Rohima Rahman. Rohima would later win the city council seat for Green Street East in the May 2006 elections on a Labour Party ticket, securing one of the largest majorities of the elections and becoming one of three Muslim women councilors from the borough who wore the hijab. (There were other Muslim women councilors who did not wear the hijab.) Originally from Bangladesh, Rohima had started the organization from her house only two years earlier.

The center offered classes on sewing, dress making, health information, and welfare benefits advice for single and married women, most of whom were in their twenties and thirties. The women who attended classes or sought information at the center represented a range of South Asian ethnic groups, among them a large number of Urdu- and Bengali-speaking women, as well as second-generation British Asians who were, for the most part, fluent in English. I started the workshop with Estelle, a white NMP activist, and we were rather disappointed with the turnout. We later discovered that a rumor had spread that we were somehow associated with the local police.

Attendees told us that there was a great deal of fear and insecurity about approaching the police. The women explained how they feared their own criminalization as potential terrorists due to stereotypical representations linking them to the July 7, 2005, bombings in London. They were all dressed in a range of the hijab, from simple headscarves to a full niqāb. As women who wear the veil, they discussed being the targets of continuous street-level taunts and jeers. These encounters sometimes turned into attacks, as the women recounted being knocked off sidewalks and, in one incident, a man tried to throw a bottle of milk on a woman in order to "whiten" her. They often reported use of the word "Ninja!" as an insult, and they described how these slurs were accompanied by gestures that tried to simulate threatening kung-fu moves.

I noted the detailed way the women talked about and analyzed their victimization, spatial restrictions, and their chagrin at the matter-of-fact way they related the lack of remedies and protection from the liberal British state. They vehemently agreed that racial harassment and violent antipathies against the hijab severely restricted their mobility and equal rights. Ironically, while dominant tropes posit the hijab as almost inherently a gross restriction on women's rights and mobility, the salient restriction on mobility as these women reported it came from the violence that they experienced, and feared, for wearing the hijab—a violence perpetrated by white Britons and indirectly from the state's aversion to the hijab and its designation as a fixed signifier of oppression.

This was particularly the case when the women traveled into central London. They characterized "the city," as central London is known, as a space of casual racist verbal abuse and negative commentary on Muslim women's dress. The women both laughed and became angry at recounting negative comments openly hurled at them when they had been in central London or on subways going into the city. "Oh my God! You must be boiling!" "No one told me it was fancy dress party!" Due to repeated experiences of harassment, the women imposed restrictions on themselves as far as venturing out of the community bounds of the inner city.

Figure 16. Newham Monitoring Project's outreach workshop on racial
harassment at the community development center, 2006.
Photo by the author.

Although women talked of a distinction between the unsafe space of central London and the more comfortable refuge of home in Newham, it became
clear as their stories unfolded that they were somewhat idealizing their safety
within their own neighborhood. "Home" was not free of racist harassment
either. The women in the workshop told numerous stories of harassment and
attacks that took place on streets such as Katherine Road and Romford Road
that lie in the very heart of the predominantly non-white neighborhoods of
north Newham. Another key frustration was the racism they faced on buses.
The women all recalled waiting for buses, only to have them pass without
stopping to pick them up, and even on the occasion that they were able to
board the bus, they inevitably confronted harassment.

The women also normalized their discrimination at the hands of the
police, agreeing that their issues would be of no interest to the authorities.
They were further discouraged from seeking help from the police, not only
by the long and tedious process of making a report, but also because most

of them were afraid to enter police stations in the first place. They were largely unaware of the antiracist laws that, at least on paper, protected them or that racist verbal abuse was against the various Race Relations Acts and, as such, a serious offense that the police had a duty to investigate.

The British state-based subordination of Muslim women was compounded by the ways that their own families and communities responded to their gendered experiences of anti-Muslim racism. During the workshop, participants revealed that their attempts to speak to their families and communities about the experiences of racist harassment were usually met by paternalistic criticisms of their exercise of independence.

One of the women, Sukaynah, reported during the workshop, "My father would say, 'Why are you going out on your own? Why do you need to go out?'" Her fellow participants strongly identified with her story. Sukaynah then qualified her decisions by stating, "When it is dark, no way I'd go out on my own." And at the same time she was insistent that the need and right to go out was important to her in terms of maintaining her autonomy and independent status within the family: "I don't want to ask my brother or somebody to go get my food for me," she said.

The act of going out was a critical freedom issue for local Muslim women who aspired to exercise autonomy from domestic patriarchal supervisions; occupying public spaces such as a neighborhood or a street was not an apolitical act. Although their visibility marked their presence in public, it risked the gendered anti-Muslim violence of the streets and rejection of equal protection through the routine antiracist failures of the police, which then rebounded to reinforce patriarchal control and protection at home.

One characteristic of colonial social relationships and power dynamics is the entanglement of western and Muslim discourses concerning gender norms. Frantz Fanon (1965) argued that it is through the process of colonialism that the hijab, as a marker of exotic, abject, and radical racial difference, comes to occupy "maximum psychological attention" for the west. His observations of the colonizer-colonized relationship in Algeria revealed how the French subjugation of the hijab practice was critical to the success of its colonial project. Fanon argued that colonial rule's legitimation, always a tenuous and anxious matter, was projected upon "the veil" as a signifier of native recalcitrance, and an over-determined symbol of white-native conflict. The campaign to unveil the Muslim woman, to force her into a sphere of cultural control, became a critical measure of the masculine colonial state's power to maintain its social command of non-European subjects.

Every rejected veil disclosed to the eyes of the colonialist's horizons until then forbidden, and revealed to them, piece by piece, the flesh of Algeria laid bare. The occupier's aggressiveness, and hence his hopes, multiplied ten-fold each time a new face was uncovered. Every new Algerian woman unveiled announced to the occupier an Algerian society whose systems of defense were in the process of dislocation, open and breached. Every veil that fell, everybody that become liberated from the traditional embrace of the *haïk*, every face that offered itself to the bold and impatient glance of the occu- pier, was a negative expression of the fact that Algeria was beginning to deny herself and was accepting the rape of the colonizer. Algerian society with every abandoned veil seemed to express its willingness to attend the master's school and to decide to change its habits under the occupier's direction and patronage. (Fanon 1965:42–43)

Fanon further observed how such colonizing compulsions gave rise to a politics of cultural reappropriation by the colonized in their own proc- esses of self-making. He noted two tendencies in the Muslim women's political responses. First, there was a defensive cultural-nationalist move toward counter-assimilation that reemphasized the pre-Islamic practice of wearing the hijab. Taking up the hijab was not simply a matter of cultural fidelity; it was also now imbued as an act of anticolonial political resistance. Muslim women reappropriated the practice of the hijab in defiance of white colonial authority, and by doing so they became figures of resistance. Fanon noted another tendency toward the seemingly compliant act of unveiling by armed Muslim women revolutionaries. These women ventured from Muslim quarters toward the segregated European parts of North African cities in their capacity as infiltrators and subversives, disguised by their very appearance as "good" unveiled and native women subjects.

The white desire for colonial forms of power, and the consequent politi- cization of the hijab, in turn catalyzed many symbolic reappropriations. This strategic and symbolic geopolitical character of regulating Muslim women's bodies within western contexts is important for deciphering the politics around the hijab in the contemporary moment.

The antipathy against the hijab continues the tradition of the British state's anxiety over gendered non-western and non-white bodies, for exam- ple during the 1970s panics about "shambolic" arranged marriages and immigration from South Asia. As part of its effort to stem Commonwealth immigration and particularly the family reunification and spousal routes to immigration, the British state carried out "virginity testing" of immigrant South Asian fiancées. These "examinations" took place at airports and overseas embassies as part of its immigration-control regime. Evan Smith and Marinella Marmo's (2011) archival work within the recently declassified documents of these "medical examination" practices has yielded evidence of the state's descriptions about its gendered practices of immigration and racial control: "Penetration of about half an inch made it apparent that she had an intact hymen and no other internal examination was made. The doctor then examined her chest with a stethoscope, but she was not asked to remove her blouse or bra for this. The only time she was bare chested was for the X-ray examination. . . . The doctor told the immigration officer verbally that the lady had not had children and she was then given conditional leave to enter for 3 months as a fianceé" (Smith and Marmo 2011:147).

The colonial and post-empire British state's relationship to colonized women's bodies and its desire to exercise violence over these bodies help to align the state with white racial nativist demands of racial population control as well as demands for cultural and national security. Then, as now, the British state and popular imaginings worked in tandem to construct the immigrant and black woman's body as a nervous sign and as a danger to popular white sovereignty and the national body politic. These narratives then also authorize and empower aggressive forms of social and state regulation.

The discriminatory treatment of Muslim women in public spaces, particularly those who wore the hijab, combined with their utter lack of police protection were primary concerns of mine when I attended a meeting of the Newham Police and Community Forum (PCF) on April 20, 2006. The PCF was a community-relations panel established to bolster police-community relations in London's inner cities. This forum was promoted in the aftermath of the so-called Brixton "race riots" of the 1980s and following the recommendations of the Scarman Inquiry into the disorder. PCFs are part of the "community policing" concept in which the strategy of "winning the hearts and minds" of residents is a way to entrench police legitimacy and to channel ongoing police-community tensions around discriminatory treatment and abuse. The emphasis on facilitating functional police-constituent relations is also arguably a strategy to bypass more radical demands for community or civilian control and oversight of the police.

The meeting I attended was the forum's annual general meeting. Following the elections of officers, many of whom were drawn from civic and ethnic cultural organizations in Newham, the Newham Youth Parliament made a theater presentation. The Youth Parliament was a city council program that promoted civics education for fourteen- to nineteen-year-olds by engaging them through mock elections and theater activities. For this event, the youths were tasked with creating skits to publicly communicate what they perceived as their most important issues.

The students presented two skits. The first revealed how African Caribbean and South Asian males were constantly stopped and searched by Newham's police, on suspicion of committing petty crimes such as stealing cell phones. The group staged its dissent against this form of police harassment. The students tried to enlighten the audience by drawing a distinction between "young people's groups" that hung out in places like Stratford Mall or the parks and "real" criminal "gangs." They felt this difference was lost on the police, who tended to lump together and criminalize all inner-city youth.

The second skit introduced a true story that took place on the #262 bus that crosses Newham from the white-dominant area of Beckon to the main transport hub in Stratford Station. A young African Caribbean student played the role of the bus driver. He sat on a chair and mimed the motions of driving a bus. As his bus approached a stop, he spotted two young Muslim women wearing headscarves who wanted to board. As the driver approached these waiting passengers, his happy demeanor changed and he acted like a person who was afraid. Although the Muslim youth in their hijabs appeared to have provoked this fear, he nonetheless picked them up.

The Muslim youth played the role of teenagers concerned with "natural" teenaged topics. They were gossiping in their seats about "girlie" concerns, such as going out with boys and eventually getting married. On a more serious note, they also talked about how racism was present within the Muslim community itself, particularly when it came to questions of selecting marital partners. They alluded to prejudicial and racist contradictions within the Muslim community, or ummah, and how their parents, who were South Asians, would never consent to them marrying local Somali Muslims.

As they conversed, a tough non-Muslim South Asian teenager boarded the bus and spotted the two Muslim girls. She was a fast-talking tomboy and led a rambunctious group who boarded the bus with her. The tough girl then walked up to the two girls already seated on the bus. She donned a tracksuit, quickly pulled her "hoodie" over her eyes, and exclaimed, "Guess what I am?" "Terrorist!" her mates shouted. She then proceeded to taunt and harass the two girls for the duration of the bus ride.

The situation was brought under control when another Muslim girl, who did not wear the hijab, bravely intervened and fought off the bully. The skit ended there and the theater troupe performed a summing-up rap song that moralized against stereotyping people. They delivered one critique against the police by making clear that they should not stereotype inner-city youth as "yobs."[7] The young actors also tried to rally the entire audience to affirm that everyone, no matter their race, religion, or dress, was unquestionably British. "We are all one community!" they cried in unison. This uplifting theatrical fare by the idealistic and hopeful youngsters seemed to me to be an unobjectionable and laudatory presentation.

After the refreshments that followed the performances, the Youth Parliament performance quickly became the subject of heated exchanges for the rest of the meeting. A dam of pent-up emotions appeared to break when the newly elected chair of the PCF, an elderly white woman, rose to thank the students and allowed for an open Q&A session. Immediately a white male stood up. He was a local teacher and proceeded to angrily demand that the two Muslim girls who had acted in the skit explain why they wore the hijab. The chair then chimed in and also wanted to know what the headscarves were called. As the girls tried to explain the intricacies of their cultural practice, the chair turned to the audience and sardonically retorted, "Well, there you go!" which drew laughs from the audience, comprising mainly fellow white east Londoners.

As the girls continued to clear up some of the misconceptions surrounding the wearing of the hijab, they tried to frankly express their sense of discomfort when white people constantly stared at them. At this, the chair became impatient and turned to the girls and, addressing them in a condescending voice, admonished them not to jump to conclusions and to take a positive approach to the questions being posed to them. She proposed that the correct response that the girls should give to white people who stared at them was to politely ask a question like "Is there a question you want to ask me?"

"You could break down a lot of antagonism like that," the chair explained. She then challenged the African Caribbean and South Asian boys who had presented the first skit to "fess up" that they often talked "rudely" to the police. The youth appeared chastened and grudgingly agreed that sometimes they did talk back when they were being stopped and searched.

The chair beamed at their response and said, "Thank you for saying that and being brave!" She turned to the girls and instructed them to also heed her advice. The girls agreed that they would try the approach of asking people who stared at them if they would like to ask a question and the chair once again smiled in satisfaction.

No sooner had this exchange ended, though, than a white woman in uniform rose up. She identified herself as an officer from the British Transport Police. "We are terrified of you!" she protested to the Muslim youth, but then added, "This has nothing to do with you personally. I was part of the group of people who stopped every Asian with a backpack on 7/7," she continued, alluding to the suicide bombings that had occurred in London on July 7, 2005. "And I worked fourteen-hour shifts that week!" She started to cry and her voice became shaky.

She further expressed why she felt that racially profiling South Asians was necessary. "London has more black people!" she said defensively. And she compared the city to more serene places like Newcastle, where she was from, and where there were "not so many black people."

Finally, a middle-aged African Caribbean man, the leader of the Dominica Association, got up to protest the direction that the Q&A was taking and the backlash that the students were experiencing. He tried to reason that there were problems with "misperceptions," and that was precisely what the students had tried vainly to present. His admonitions seemed to fall on deaf ears.

Members of the audience then noticed that the Newham police's chief inspector in charge of community-public relations was in attendance, and he was summoned to share his views. The chief inspector proceeded to lower the temperature by calmly responding that he felt that the skits did challenge popular assumptions, and he added that the performance had in truth challenged his own assumptions, although he did not mention what those were. He smiled and appealed to everyone present that they could learn something from the students' valiant efforts.

During this forum, the meaning of the hijab was framed within the context of "sanctioned ignorance" (Spivak 1999:2) whereby the role assigned to the students was restricted to that of infantilized native informants, rather than critical knowledge producers or social commentators in their own right. The students were disempowered from making antiracist critiques and schooled into addressing the epistemological anxieties of whites. The meaning of the hijab assigned by white east Londoners was that of a threat to a putative sense of "Britishness" and national security. White east Londoners attending the forum associated the hijab with the risk of terror attacks perpetrated by undifferentiated "black people." Whites also interpreted the hijab as a sign of how "normal" British sociability and social organization were being erased, with some white attendees lamenting the lack of support among Newham's ethnic minority communities for the revival of patriotic celebrations such as St. George's Day.

And with this understanding, the hijab-wearing Muslim woman, or even a child, reminded whites of their political failure at maintaining a racial, religious, and monocultural Britishness. It was difficult for the Newham-born and raised youth to conduct a dialogue with older white Britons given the ways in which they were thrust into anthropological roles as native informants. Since the elders forced them into seeing their roles and the knowledge they presented as subordinate, the students were left with the message that they should feel subordinate to dominant society.

I raised the vexed question of wearing the hijab with Amina, who, I noticed, sometimes identified as British Indian and sometimes as British Muslim. Amina did not wear the veil, and her political relationship to contemporary British debates about the hijab revealed a very different logic from white colonial projections. The anthropologist Begoña Aretxaga (1995, 2003), in her study of Irish Republican women living in 1990s Belfast, argued that the notion of the "political" needs to be reconceptualized to take into account the ways in which women participants in colonized situations of oppression craft political viewpoints and lives. Aretxaga (1997) argued that women in anticolonial resistance "explicitly blend their lived experience into a political view of social relations" and this is the form of "political experience" that guides their analysis of gendered racism.

Amina's decision about whether or not to wear the hijab was but one of the many challenges that confronted her. Her everyday experience as someone who was racialized as a black person and as a Muslim by her white British neighbors created a complex field of political experience and analysis. My own work with Amina was facilitated through NMP's solidarity-based practices of political blackness, which aimed to mobilize Newham's different racial, religious, and ethnic minority communities, which suffered from racism, into a joint community of resistance. However, this was not always how people in the community viewed their own identities. I, a non-Muslim male activist from the Muslim-majority country of Malaysia, was able to engage and develop political relationships with Muslim women in Newham only through the aegis of NMP's long-standing reputation as an antiracist force. Even though political blackness in these spaces facilitated alliance building and relation-based organizing across different forms of experiences, there was never a need for the development of a homogeneous sense of identity or ideological agreement among those who engaged with NMP in addressing anti-Muslim and anti-black racism in Newham.

The following is excerpted from an interview between Amina and me in which we reflected on a year of mutual collaboration in fighting against the frequent attacks that took place in her apartment building.

> *Mohan: In the 1980s we [NMP] started with this notion that we are black communities united, not that we are all the same, but of coming together for a purpose.*
>
> Amina: I think it's a real big shame. Before, it was easier for us to stick together and fight our corner together. I think personally that Muslims are being attacked, not just because I am Muslim. I was waiting for this day to come. I knew it would. They are so scared of anybody's peoples turning to Islam because they don't want to make it any bigger than it already is, because they are fearful that it would overtake the world. They are scared that it's happening in this country now. They see more headscarves and all but they don't realize that they're pushing people to become that.
>
> I am even in a dilemma because I'm thinking to myself, my God, do I want to show people that I am not like them, that I am this other person? How would I do that? Do you understand? Because, they don't see me as different—only when they choose to. But push comes to shove I am a Muslim. That is where it would take me. If I had to fight against somebody because of my faith I would stick up for the Muslim religion and I would stick up for the Muslim people. You know, I just think that it is the television and the media that is making people—they creating race hate against people in this country, against Muslims. Muslims this. Muslims that. I think it's ridiculous. I think they're scared and they don't know anything about Islam and it's easy for them to just tar them off with the same brush.

Have you felt this pressure recently?

Yeah. Yeah. I had this friend of mine, a black person, make terrible
comments about Muslims. And I just thought, how sad. You're
grown up and you've played football with Asian Muslims, and
you have this attitude, like oh my God these bloody Muslims,
why can't they shave off their beards.

When did you start to feel the dilemma? After 9/11 or 7/7?

Well, I felt it. I got married on September 13, two days after
September 11. I felt it straight away because my husband
started praying, and where he came from, in Hoxton, it wasn't
the done thing to even change your religion, let alone go to the
mosque. And then he went to perform the hajj in Mecca and
his own mother said to me, "Oh my God, he's going to mosque
and he's involved in terrorism! Is he a terrorist?"

I mean, how sad. He's gone to pray, not to learn about
making bombs. People started being horrible to him, people
who've known him all his life. People couldn't understand that
this has just happened, 9/11, and why have you become a
Muslim? Why have you taken to that faith? Of all faiths, why
have you become a Muslim?

And I thought, oh my God, is this problem ever going to
end? If it's not one thing, it's another.

I think Muslims are the ones oppressed. I don't think they're
the ones oppressing, maybe other countries, but here, they're the
ones oppressed. If I had more guts, you know, I am me. But if
push comes to shove, Mohan, if all Muslims had to wear a
headscarf to prove a point, then I would put one on my head.

To prove what point?

If ever there was a point to prove. If it was the case that girls were
not allowed to wear headscarves in school, or that all Muslims
were asked to wear headscarves to say we're not taking our
headscarves off. We're Muslim women and we're strong as a
nation and whatnot. I would put a scarf on my head to prove
that point.

In Amina's deliberations over the political choice to transform her
bodily comportment as an everyday response to the War on Terror as a
Muslim woman, gendered colonial and racial power dynamics were intersecting considerations. Her navigation of her status as a British Muslim

woman transpired not only in the public sphere, but also within the private sphere: for example, the rejection meted out by her white husband's family. The family's reaction to his marriage and conversion to Islam did not bring about greater cohesiveness or intercultural understanding, but, rather, Amina's displacement as an outsider—an intimate expression of a broader notion that Muslims are the national enemy.

Through these political experiences in both public and private spheres, Amina came to understand that color-blind and religious-blind inclusion in liberal Britain is at best conditional and tenuous, "Because they don't see me as different—only when they choose to." This is Amina's analysis of the dialectics of white colonial recognition. As someone who is perceived to have created appropriate distance from the "bad Muslim" (Mamdani 2005) aspects of her identity, she has been included by dominant whites. As an unveiled Muslim woman who wears non-Asian clothes, speaks Cockney, and once worked at a nightclub as a dancer, her cultural behaviors are seen as the polar opposite of illiberal and incommensurable Muslim difference.

But inclusion is not a settled and unalterable state. She is only accepted as "one of us" because there exists the ulterior "them" that she is defined against—and the "them" in question is made up of nonassimilating and nonaccessible, veiled Muslim women. In short, the "real Muslims." Furthermore, Amina is simultaneously constructed as racially black in the eyes of British whites—as someone who is of an alien race and a former colonial subject. She achieves temporary or momentary inclusion at the discretion and power of whites who grant that status.

If we center the complex subjectivities of British Muslim women like Amina and their multifaceted experiences of colonizer-colonized dynamics of oppression and co-religious resistance, then we must reconceptualize Britain's participation in the War on Terror as a gendered colonial and racial domination project. Bodily comportment and religious identity have become sites of regulation and of struggle in the ongoing processes of creating separation between normative Britishness and abject Muslim identity. Amina responds to this underlying racial and religious animus by turning to the question of the hijab, which has become a reified and powerful symbol of Muslim women's resistance.

Additionally, Amina engages with NMP's solidarity-based political blackness, even though she does not entirely embrace blackness as a self-identity. Her specific reasons for disavowing political blackness, however, are important. It has been argued that the ideology of political blackness in the 1970s and 1980s rendered South Asian cultural references invisible in relation to a more dominant African Caribbean culture, and therefore constituted a harmful political choice for ethnic minority South Asian communities (Hazareesingh 1986; Modood 2005). Amina, however, takes a political position against political blackness for different reasons. First, she is reacting to experiences of rejection by African Caribbean friends in Newham who have also re-disseminated Islamophobia and anti-Muslim racism. Furthermore, she is resisting well-documented and long-standing white British racist constructions that homogenize all ex-colonials and non-Europeans as nonwhite, nonpatrials, and black.

A younger generation of Muslim women born and raised in Newham in the 1980s continues to grapple with questions of the hijab, family life, their role and position as women, activism, and political blackness. One of these young women is Zareena, a leading NMP activist and lawyer who specialized in civil liberties cases, including the defense of terror suspects. She was also the person who trained me to do antiracist casework. Her father is Palestinian, and her mother is Tanzanian-Pakistani-Gujarati. As a child growing up in Newham, Zareena lived in a block of flats behind the now-demolished West Ham FC stadium and by the age of five she repeatedly witnessed the police and state harassment of her father, an engineering graduate student at the University of East London.

Zareena's father was arrested the first time because he tried to intervene when he saw an elderly white couple arguing violently on the streets. He tried to stop this fight, which was escalating into physical violence. When the police arrived on the scene they immediately arrested Zareena's father for disorderly behavior.

The second arrest was part of an antiterror raid. The police arrested Zareena's father on the mistaken assumption that he looked like a terror suspect they were searching for. They remanded him for two nights at the infamous antiterrorism interrogation cells in Paddington Green. No evidence of his purported terrorist activities was ever substantiated and he was released.

As her family experienced the combined force of Newham police's everyday criminalization of black people as well as the British state's counterterrorism violence, ten-year-old Zareena encountered NMP, and the organization became a political lifeline. It enabled her to make meaning of what was happening to her family and resist.

Her first contact was through her mother, who was familiar with NMP's work. Her mother was a community worker at the Fellowship House, a charity organization that focused on women and domestic violence issues, and she would take Zareena along to antiracist demonstrations and marches.

As a teenager in 1996, Zareena participated in the NMP campaign to seek justice for Ibrahim Sey, a Gambian asylum seeker who had been killed at Ilford police station by CS gas sprays (a form of tear gas). Four police officers sprayed him at close range and held him down for fifteen minutes. When the ambulance arrived Ibrahim was already dead. He was still in handcuffs and face-down on the police station floor.

Zareena remembered marching down the streets of Newham chanting "Black people here to stay, here to fight!" in subsequent NMP-organized rallies and marches. Unlike Amina, she would become strongly self-identified as politically black *and* Muslim.

While these personal and local struggles against racist state violence were unfolding, international politics also contributed to Zareena's evolving local-global consciousness of antiracist struggle. The first Gulf War began when she entered sixth-form college and there were many debates among Newham's youth, many of whom were Muslim and also had connections to the Middle East. Zareena remembers many of her Newham peers who had no interest in global politics and little interest in school suddenly becoming passionate in challenging the anti-Muslim racism they felt was behind the Gulf War and then later the Chechnya war. She observed that the west's wars in Muslim countries were moving her Muslim peers in Newham to embrace their faith more closely.

"Faith is becoming really important to younger people," Zareena said. "They are more practicing and this is true particularly for Muslim male youth. I knew two boys in school who were not religious, never paid any attention in class, and then with the wars they suddenly became very religious."

Zareena herself had been observant of religious practices such as wearing the hijab. She had worn the hijab all through her law school degree, which she obtained from Queen Mary College, University of London. She no longer wears it, however.

"You want to have a debate about the veil, have a debate about the veil. But you start muddying the waters and it starts becoming about women, and it becomes about communities not integrating. They provoke their own reactions and say this is the reason why things are so crap in this country because *they* are refusing to mix, *they* are producing barriers to communication," Zareena argued.

Despite the double challenge of navigating stereotypes of the oppressed Muslim woman on the one hand, and her community's internal theological debates about the hijab and the role of women on the other, Zareena found a way to construct a role for herself as a community advocate. She credits this both to the complex views of gender and progressive political views in her own family and to the growth she experienced with the antiracist black politics of NMP.

"I really only got my freedom when I was sixteen. I lived quite a sheltered life and I felt really restricted," Zareena said. "It was the community I grew up in, there was a lot of talk about how girls should be doing things, the way that I dressed, which was like a 'tomboy' to them.

"Things are not as bad as it was and they are more progressive now. And even then, strict as it were, there was always the view that girls were to be educated. Not going to university was not an option, even if you had to stay at home while you went to uni!" she said.

"I really do appreciate the space I was given to become an activist and work at NMP. My mom also took a lot of flak from her family for me. When she would go around they would have words with her about what I was doing.

"But my three years at NMP were amazing. It was the most independent I have been," Zareena recalled. "I came to it with a political viewpoint, unlike a lot of workers who stumble into the caseworker jobs. But even then I did not want to open my mouth for the longest time. The thought of doing my worker's report at the MC (Management Committee) meeting was like an exam anxiety!"

Zareena's father's Palestinian background was critical to her firsthand historical and personal knowledge of Middle Eastern geopolitics; she also distinguished between her own analysis and that of many of her Newham peers who she felt lacked a broad historical or political analysis.

"All they needed to know was that these places were Muslim countries and they were getting their arses kicked. That was their analysis," Zareena said.

She also remembered shedding tears at television reports of when the United States had bombed a civilian shelter, alleged to be a military installation, during an aerial attack in the First Gulf War. This was the horrific bombing of the al-Amiriyah shelter that killed more than four hundred civilians. One woman lost eight children in this action. Human Rights Watch (1991) declared, "The United States' failure to give warning before proceeding with the disastrous attack on the Amiriyah shelter was a serious violation of the laws of war."

"But you can never shy away from the political though," Zareena reasoned. "It is never just about the human side. There is a wider reason for this." I asked her what exactly she meant by "the political" and how she saw her own analysis as "political" in contrast to her peers' reactions. "Don't focus on the suffering," she continued. "Hell no, can't do that. It is not about charity; this is old-fashioned colonialism and occupation. You can't separate human suffering and the politics that is behind it. That's why it is happening.

"Racism is not just about a black person getting bashed about by a white person," Zareena argued. "It is much larger than that. It is not just what happens on the street. There is something much bigger behind it. It is state-enforced. You have to understand the role the state plays, whether it is the laws that are made, or whether it is in the enforcing attitude by not doing anything for the victims of racism or when the police are arresting the victims of racism themselves!" she said.

"What do the police do? They are implementing and enforcing state laws that are racist. It's not just a few bad apples in the police force. It is an attitude that is seen throughout the institution." Zareena's critique of racism, informed by her activist experience and thinking, centered a critique of racialized rule of law in Britain.

"Somebody started talking about muggers, about how most muggers are black. That is not the point, is it? The issue is not about what these people have done. No matter how bad the crime is, you're entitled to certain rights. That's all we fight for. You're entitled to legal advice. You have the right not to have the shit kicked out of you at the back of the police van. Just because muggers somewhere tend to be black does not give you the license to go and stop and search every black kid you see who looks a bit 'dodgy,' who is wearing a hoodie. Whatever it is in his behavior. That is the point," she said.

"But is it that simple? You can't explain it to some people. People say, 'There is no smoke without fire.' Point is? Point is if these people have done anything wrong they should be charged and tried like everybody else. You can't bang them up or threaten to deport them to a country where they will be tortured or killed. I don't see what is so hard about it. I really don't.

To me it is simple, easy. I don't understand. Going back to the point about why can't you separate the politics and focus on the human suffering. I don't see where they are coming from."

As our conversation progressed I became aware that Zareena often negotiated a number of tensions between her political viewpoints and those of her community. "There have been problems with NMP being seen as a 'leftie' organization and secular," she observed as she explained these tensions. "There have been some personal falling-outs with people I have worked with."

Zareena had been the key NMP activist who began to mobilize community responses to the Forest Gate Antiterror Raid that occurred in Newham in 2006, which will be discussed in the next chapter. She had initiated the casework and campaigning work in support of the accused brothers and their families, and had organized numerous community meetings. Often she was the only Muslim woman at these meetings with local community leaders and mosques.

"I didn't really think about being amongst men. And I usually felt safe around NMP male activists," Zareena said. "But one day I went home very late after a meeting and my mom got mad. She cried, *you* were the only girl there!" Zareena was surprised at her mother's reaction, and that despite her mother's active work in the community the question of respectability was a big concern. "Remember the community you're in!" her mother said.

While family support, albeit ambivalent, enabled her to access NMP to further develop her own Muslim woman's antiracist voice, she eventually had to confront the suspicions of the British state toward her activist work, especially in relation to her legal work in defending terror suspects. Toward the end of 2006 Zareena and her family were subjected to another antiterror raid, where they were thrown out of their homes until the state completed its thorough examination in search of "radical" Islamist literature, proof of radicalization, and possible evidence that Zareena was linked to terrorism. In the end, nothing was ever found and no charges were made.

It is a consequential irony that Zareena's struggles with preserving respectability within her own ethnic and religious community as an advocate and leader so closely tracked with and resembled the surveillance and regulation that the British state also placed upon Muslim communities and Muslim exercises of political agency. For Zareena, negotiating multiple forms of racialized and religious gender regulation was part of her interactions with her own community and with the British state.

CHAPTER 5

"The War on Terror Has Become
a War on Us"

The Forest Gate Antiterror Raid
and Counterterror Citizenship

Since the events of September 11, 2001, the War on Terror has been framed in western media and public policy as a struggle against "evil" (Reese and Lewis 2009; Kellner 2016). The source of "radical evil" in this Manichean binary is typically assumed to originate outside of the west's own moral order.[1] Racialized state violence, in the form of war-making abroad or counterterrorism at home, is perceived as legitimate or necessary violence against the forces of evil, in aid of securing a greater "good" or universal humanitarianism (Asad 2015). As such, the increasingly draconian and dehumanizing practices of western counterterrorism are rationalized as consistent with new abstract legal proceduralisms that permit the derogation of civil liberties and human rights. In contrast, Muslim terrorists (and, more vaguely, Islam itself) are construed as alien to the foundational concepts of the social good and the rational in western modernity. British Muslims are crypto-western subjects. Their presence, betrayed by skin color or cultural and religious markers, is inherently a sign of a potential danger that consequently sanctions repatriation to juridical gray zones, where violations of personhood, due process, and the right to life routinely occur.

In this dichotomy, the racialized ways in which political liberalism continues to develop within and through a history of conquest, slavery, and the British Empire are elided through selective acts of historical amnesia.[2] These afterlives of racism are interpreted as self-correctible within and by the framework of contemporary British governance. For example, the Race

Relations Acts of 1965 rendered racial discrimination and the "incitement to racial hatred" as legal offenses for the first time. Similarly, the criminalization of institutional racism entered into law following the Macpherson Report (1999). The Racial and Religious Hatred Act of 2006 created new substantive law that specifically named and added religious-based hate crimes as a part of the state's antiracist duties (Maer 2009). Incidents and crimes of interpersonal and institutional racism technically should be able to find remedy within these expanded frameworks of liberal justice and equal protection.

However, as Britain continues its geopolitical and military interventions in the broader Muslim world, exacting disproportionate tolls of civilian deaths, the diasporic and ethnic Muslim minorities within its own polity exist like a nervous, anxious question. British Muslims or would-be British Muslims, like Syrian war refugees, desperate to flee to European shores, and from there gain entry into Britain, are repositioned in political discourse as subjects with dangerous, innate proclivities for threatening the social order, including its internal race relations, tolerance, or social cohesion. The presumptive and collective castigation of native-born and immigrant Muslims encodes racialized difference and panic. The answer to this manufactured suspicion is the creation of a new form of citizenship for the preeminent and normative white British subject—a counterterrorism citizenship defined in relation to the suspicious collectivity constructed as Muslims. This counterterror citizenship is rooted in the processes of everyday political whiteness and tacit reassertions of white British sovereignty that reprise and build on anti-black and racial nativism discourses.

Inherent to the new counterterrorism citizenship is the institutionalization of a visual and heuristic racial grammar. Counterterrorism is formulated by the British state as "public vigilance" and citizens are invited by the state to practice counterterrorism surveillance in daily life by being "alert" and by reporting "suspicious activity," which is "anything that seems out of place, unusual or just doesn't seem to fit in with day-to-day life" (National Counter Terrorism Security Office 2015). This grammar encompasses many aspects of everyday experience: How exactly does one see a potential act of terrorism? Who gets to see? Who is seen? What is seen? Does an Italian economist working on differential equations on a plane (Garcia 2016) or an Iraqi passenger saying "inshallah" (Revesz 2016) constitute "something" to be "seen," feared, and reported as occurred in 2016? How does an image of a Sikh man wearing a turban that is digitally altered to include a suicide vest and a Quran become repeatedly viralized as a credible image of a terrorist? (Grice 2015). What sight, and what skin color, and what behavior, is suspicious? This racial grammar of surveillance shapes British Muslim lived experiences in the twenty-first-century War on Terror.

The consequences of this pervasive climate of surveillance revealed itself during the Forest Gate Antiterror Raid in Newham. Early on Friday, June 2, 2006, 250 police officers from the armed C019 branch of the Metropolitan Police—antiterrorist officers, riot police units, and personnel from other state agencies—raided two houses on Landsdown Road, Forest Gate, London. Operation Volga was the largest domestic antiterror operation that had ever been carried out in Britain (Metropolitan Police Service 2006). The targeted homes were situated in the middle of a residential street in Newham that housed a mixed South Asian, African Caribbean, and white population. To recall, a quarter of the population in the ward is also Muslim and the area is home to a number of mosques, religious schools, and shops.

One of the homes belonged to the family of a Bangladeshi-British family. The police claimed they were acting on classified "secret" intelligence from a "credible, sensitive source who in the past had provided corroborated information" (Hayman 2006:1). This intelligence asset claimed that she or he had seen something. The source claimed that there was some kind of bomb factory located on the premises. Before daybreak, the police stormed the house with an advance squad of thirty-five officers while the inhabitants, a multigenerational family of grandparents, parents, and children, including an eight-month-old, were sound asleep.

During this raid, twenty-three-year-old Mohammed Abdul Kahar, the eldest son in the family, was shot by the police, dragged out of his home, and dumped on the sidewalk, where he lay bleeding. Later he was taken to the Royal London Hospital and kept under armed guard. When the raid began, he and his family members feared they were being attacked by armed robbers and screamed for the attackers to take everything, but to let them live. At this moment, the British Muslim family members saw themselves first as normal citizens of British liberal democracy, secure in the private domestic sphere, who were being threatened not as Muslims, but as property owners, and not by state violence, but by burglars. While the family presumed that they were victims of a violent home invasion, British state violence had constructed them as an enemy to the very liberal democratic social order to which they imagined themselves members. Here is Abdul Kahar's account of the experience:

> At about four o'clock in the morning, I was woken up by screams that I had never heard before. My younger brother was screaming, and from upstairs, from my room, I could hear him screaming, so I got out of bed. I just had my boxer shorts on and a T-shirt. It was dark and I assumed a robbery was happening. As I made the first step down the stairs, my brother was still screaming and I turned to look at the stairs. As soon as I turned around, I saw an orange spark and a big bang. I flew into the wall and I slipped down. I was on the floor. I looked to my right, on my chest, and saw blood coming down my chest and saw the hole in my chest. At that moment, I knew I was shot. The first thing I was thinking was that an armed robbery was taking place. As I went down, I saw an object flying in my face. At that moment I did not know what object it was but I now know it was the gun. He tried to hit me over the face with it. I saw the shotgun in my chest and I was begging, "Please, please I cannot breathe." He just kicked me in my face and kept on saying "Shut the fuck up." I said, "Please, please I cannot breathe." One of the officers slapped me over the face. He was saying, "Just shut the fuck up, stay there, stay there."[3]

Abdul Kahar's testimony of this near-fatal moment raises an important question about the now-normalized legitimacy of state violence extended in the name of the War on Terror. How does the jurisdiction of state violence, specifically in terms of its proliferation of endless war powers, reanimate racism and reproduce a white-centric and white-normative political order in Britain?

Six major pieces of antiterror legislation in Britain now allow for abridgments of traditional criminal rights in cases of terrorist suspicion. These now-legal restrictions include pre-charge detentions without trial, control orders that restrict the movement of terror suspects, the criminalization of terrorism-related speech, or "incitements," as well as preemptive actions against possible radicalization. In a recent case that I am familiar with, a British Muslim father was denied contact with his own children because of British security services' assessment, over and above that of child and welfare services, that he posed a potential Islamist radicalization threat to his own family.

While the liberal state aims to develop these policing powers that extraordinarily go against the principles of habeas corpus, it nonetheless maintains that such deviations from customary rights are lawful for particular subjects (Roach 2011). The state tries to "achieve the appropriate balance between the measures necessary to deal with the very real threat to national security posed by terrorism and the need to avoid diminishing the civil and human rights of the population" (House of Commons 2007).

The state requires and demands derogations of liberal rights because of the way it conceptualizes the threat it names and confronts as "terrorism." As the British state described it, "The terrorist threats we face now are more diverse than before, dispersed across a wider geographical area, and often in countries without effective governance. We therefore face an unpredictable situation" (Home Office 2015b). Western liberal democratic states construct terrorism as an anxiously diffuse "total threat" (Buck-Morss 2006) to the body politic, where both the physical and ideological security of liberal democratic hegemony is envisioned as fragile and at risk. The construction of a totalizing anxiety concerned with rhizomatic terrorist formations anywhere and at any time emboldens a permanent warlike disposition that tries to reconcile and self-valorize British liberalism's morals and ethics with state violence.

Abdul Kahar, however, was "hit by a structure" (Ahmed 2015). He was assaulted by a militarized police officer who had permission to take his life if necessary, regardless of the sanctity of liberal rights to life and personhood, regardless of due process or proof of guilt. Abdul Kahar had been cast into an indeterminate gray zone between being a terror suspect and being a citizen and for one perilous moment his life hung in suspense between the state's liberal values and its antiterrorist debasement of civil and human rights. The violence Abdul Kahar experienced is not easily explicable with reference to a "bad actor" or the ill will of the officer, or even "unwitting" forms of racial discrimination. In many ways, what occurred to Abdul Kahar defies entirely the British legal definition of aberrational individual racism, or even "institutional racism," which is defined in law as the "collective failure of an organization to provide an appropriate and professional service to people because of their color, culture, or ethnic origin" (Macpherson 1999). Instead, the antiterror officer in this scene was already positioned in a structure of war that requires state violence to secure a higher good—that of a liberal order and its ironic universal promises of personhood and rights for all. This is a new, racialized "illiberal paradox"

(Richardson 2011) of antiterror and counterterrorism laws, and the practice of traditional liberal individual rights such as due process.

Counterterror citizenship normalizes the ongoing work of pursuing and identifying potential Muslim terrorist suspects who are legally and morally subjected to the possibility of death. It shifts politics toward a politics of deciding who will die and who will live in order to secure the liberal democratic social order against a perceived existential threat (Mbembe 2003). For British Muslims, counterterror citizenship has become normalized as a new loyalty test of self-sacrificing patriotism.[4]

The work of finding terror suspects is the War on Terror's civic and national security endeavor. The national security service (MI5) and police departments have set up antiterrorism hotlines for the public to join in "total policing" and identifying suspicious activity. After the Tunisian attacks that killed some thirty Britons on holiday in 2014, a new elite, militarized police unit was formed that was to be trained in underground "kill room" bunkers built in the middle of the military's Select Air Service headquarters (Nicol 2014). The permanent blurring of wartime and peacetime, the civilian and military, is part of the forceful logics of contemporary liberal democracy in the War on Terror age.

When the antiterror police descended upon him, Abdul Kahar was made an ambiguous British subject. He was marked by racial, religious, and ethnic cultural difference and by what Muneer Ahmad describes as fungibility (Ahmad 2004; Marshall 2012):

> Both individual acts of hate violence and governmental racial profiling have helped to create a new racial construct: the "Muslim-looking" person. The logic of post–September 11 profiling turns on an equation of being Muslim with being a terrorist. For the perpetrator of post–September 11 hate violence, the error lies in assuming that because all of the September 11 terrorists were Arab and Muslim, all Arabs and Muslims must be terrorists themselves, or terrorist sympathizers. The logic of governmental profiling is only slightly more nuanced: (1) because all of the September 11 terrorists were Arab and Muslim; (2) because most Arabs are Muslims; and (3) because the terrorists claim religious motivation for their actions; (4) all Arabs and all Muslims are likely to be terrorists. . . . The profiling effected by hate violence depends upon two different assumptions of fungibility. The first associates all Muslims with the

terrorists who perpetrated the September 11 attacks. The second identifies all "Muslim-looking" people as Muslims. The end result is to view "Muslim-looking" people as stand-ins for the terrorists themselves. The "logic" of these twin fungibilities is, of course, devoid of much logic at all and appears to derive from fear, ignorance, and pre-existing racisms rather than any rational decision-making. (Ahmad 2004:1278)

Abdul Kahar's body is made into a form of life that can be expelled from liberalism's jurisdiction of traditional individual rights (Razack 2008). At the same time, British liberalism needs also to include Abdul Kahar as a part of its pluralistic body politic, in keeping with its own ideals. Expansive antiterrorism powers have produced, therefore, a liberal state that behaves paradoxically and duplicitously vis-à-vis its own regime of rights. Begoña Aretxaga (2003:397) argues, "The violence of the security apparatus can also turn into homeland policing of the state's own citizens in a paranoiac gaze that curtails civil rights and extends terror through the social field." It is clear that the British state's imaginary of the War on Terror is concerned with wars fought not only abroad but also at home, as practiced through counterterror surveillance and the militarized policing of its internal spaces and Muslim communities—the unruly "enemies within."

Caught in the contradiction of having nearly killed a clearly innocent man, Britain's antiterrorism police initially claimed that the shot that hit Abdul Kahar had been accidentally fired. The shooter was a specialist C019 officer whose sophisticated Glock 17 semiautomatic pistol was apparently triggered during the heat of the moment because the gloves that he wore were too thick. An accident like this would nicely resolve the state's own moral and legal inconsistencies and contradictions, its near-fatal exercise of force against one of its own citizens.

Public support coalesced around the police's actions and explanations, however implausible. A local newspaper columnist in the *Newham Recorder*, for example, argued that, bracketing the operational errors, the terror and violence inflicted on Abdul Kahar were permissible because, "in a *warlike situation* [emphasis mine] accidents happen and we have to learn to live with that regrettable fact" (Duncan 2006). The British cabinet at the time chimed in with similar arguments about the "police acting in *the best interests of the whole community* [emphasis mine]." During the failed raid and in its aftermath, Prime Minister Tony Blair politically backed the police's conduct, in what was now known as the Forest Gate raid, "101 percent." "The bottom line in all of this," Blair argued, "is a recognition that intelligence is not an art form where you can be 100 percent right all the time. But what you have to do is act on credible intelligence and then support those who take the decisions to act on credible intelligence" (Hills 2006).

Blair's tautological comments seemed to echo a puzzling refrain that I had heard about the logic of the state's War on Terror. It was said that the state's moral, ethical, and human rights transgressions against innocent Muslim terror suspects did not delegitimate the justness of the War on Terror, or the habitual anti-Muslim racial profiling that it feeds. This seemed to be as true for the question of weapons of mass destruction that were never found in Iraq as it was for the chemical bomb factory that was never found in Forest Gate (Falk, Gendzier, and Lifton 2006).

Between September 11, 2001, and the end of my fieldwork year in 2006, the Terrorism Act of 2000 had been utilized to authorize some 1,166 arrests that emerged out of antiterror raids (*Guardian* 2007). Of these arrests, the British government could bring about terrorism charges for less than one-fifth of those arrested. This means that, within five years, more than nine hundred lives had been subjected to counterterror operations without a legal or otherwise credible basis. There had been an evidentiary basis for successfully convicting only forty people between September 11, 2001, and the end of 2016 (*Guardian* 2007), yet the raids continued apace and an additional antiterrorism act was passed in 2006 that generated a broad new range of terrorism offenses.

This pattern of using antiterror raids summarily, or as "fishing expeditions" in order to find proof of a suspicion, however frivolous, also characterized Britain's colonial conflicts against the Irish Republican Army (IRA). Between 1974 and 1993, 7,193 people were detained under the Prevention of Terrorism Act of 1974 in relation to the armed struggle for Irish independence (Joyce 2002:172). Of those detained during that entire period, only 3 percent were ever charged with terror offenses. The prevalence and justification of these state practices had been on the decline since the end of the Irish conflict in the late 1990s, but started to rise again exponentially with respect to Muslims and Muslim-looking persons. In 2005, following the 7/7 London bombings, the state's War on Terror operations exacted its first domestic fatality. Jean Charles de Menezes, an immigrant Brazilian electrician, was mistakenly identified as a Muslim-looking suicide bomber in the aftermath of the July 7, 2005, subway bombings. Following surveillance and confrontation with armed police, and possibly specially attached military officers, he was shot seven times in the head with hollow-point bullets as he boarded a train at the Stockwell station on his way to work.

Joseph Pugliese (2006) has argued that de Menezes's killing demonstrates the logic of a "racialized regime of visuality" at work in antiterror policing and the War on Terror: "As de Menezes steps outside his flat and proceeds to walk down the street, a regime of visuality activates the stereotypical iconography of racial profiling as it re-signifies his ethnic identity from Brazilian to (South) Asian: in advance of any offence he is racially suspect." British common sense includes historically racialized ways of seeing, and these operations are crucial elements of antiterror racial profiling and policing. These regimes of visual interpretations and signifiers of racial hierarchy depend on white-centric understandings of how the universalizing greater good, undertaken by antiterrorism policing, is to be borne by particular racialized bodies, families, neighborhoods, and communities.

Under the new raison d'être, the structure of War on Terror violence against Muslims and Muslim-looking people does not register as injustice or horror, but as necessary violence. Abdul Kahar's neighbors testified to what for them was a surreal scene at daybreak, where Abul Koyair, the younger brother in the Forest Gate raid, was "dragged down the road, put down on the pavement and then plastic sheets were put on him" and he was restrained with "white overalls" (Townsend et al. 2006). The report documented that "even the grandmother of the family was led from the home in handcuffs." The momentum of state violence was uninterruptable. The police themselves later stated that, besides the wounded Abdul Kahar, "two other people went to hospital. One was a woman suffering from shock, the other a man with a head injury."

I interviewed some of the family members shortly after the raids. One of them described to me a desperate scene in which they begged the police to allow their grandmother to reach for her asthma rescue inhaler. While liberalism defines and congratulates itself for securing the safety of the private sphere and the intimate, individual realm, it is evident that in warlike conditions, these freedoms—even the simple, life-sustaining request to use an asthma inhaler—are not sacrosanct for those construed as terror suspects. Or, in other words, they are positioned to "just shut the fuck up."

Immediately after the raid, Abul Koyair was detained and held as a high-profile terrorist suspect at the Paddington Green police station, the site infamous for almost four decades of counterterror interrogations in an era of intense IRA activity. Suspects are kept within eleven-foot-square cells with no windows. Under the current rule of law inaugurated in the 2000 act, terror suspects can be held under such conditions and interrogated for up to twenty-eight days without any charges before they have to be brought forward to a court of law. Even after these twenty-eight days, detention can be renewed if adequate evidence is presented before a judge (*Guardian* 2007). There have been repeated and ongoing attempts to expand the 2000 act, including allowing for indefinite detentions, as was sought unsuccessfully in the 2001 Prevention of Terrorism Act. In 2008, a counterterrorism bill was passed to increase pre-charge detentions without trial for up to forty-two days.

In this same Forest Gate raid, authorities invaded another home. It belonged to neighbors who were also of South Asian and Muslim descent. The family was renting the adjacent terrace house from the father of the two arrested men. One of the members of this family had his head severely beaten with the butt of a rifle. The members of this family were not arrested nor were they ever under suspicion for any wrongdoing. But they too were suspicious by proximity and association, and by the notion that suspected Muslims are fungible, and were caught in the collateral damage of the War on Terror's imperatives. These neighbors were then taken by the police and held for twelve hours at the local Plaistow police station. An area that included seven neighborhood roads was cordoned off from the public for over a week and police officers had to escort all the residents who lived within this cordon to and from their homes.

Following the Forest Gate raid, the families involved, for all intents and purposes, were rendered homeless. In their media statements during the raid, police triumphantly boasted that, "if necessary, we'll take the house down brick by brick" (Edwards 2006) and they basically did just that. Abdul Kahar and Abul Koyair's father, who had worked for years as a restaurant cook, originally purchased the home in 1987 and then renovated it. Additionally, the two brothers had recently helped to further renovate the house to create a basement gym. This was the activity that some neighbors felt was misinterpreted by a police informant who reported that a bomb factory was being built by "Muslims with beards" (Goodchild and Elliot 2006). It was months before these homes, which had been virtually stripped bare in the fury of the search, were habitable again.

Figure 17. Police cordon on Landsdown Road during the Forest Gate
Antiterror Raid, which lasted several days, 2006. Neighborhood residents
were not evacuated during the search for a possible chemical bomb factory.
Photo by the author.

The end result of the Forest Gate raid and investigation was that no
chemical materials were found. The Newham Monitoring Project (NMP)
had stepped into the situation to represent the affected families and, eventually, after a week of the organization's campaigning, the two brothers
were released without charge on the evening of June 9. After Abdul Kahar
and Abul Koyair gave an internationally publicized press conference at St.
Emmanuel's Church on June 13, the Metropolitan Police issued statements
that apologized for the "hurt," "disruption," and inconvenience" it had
caused to the families concerned (*Stratford Guardian* 2006). The commissioner of the Metropolitan Police, Sir Ian Blair, concluded that the police
"had got it wrong" and that "there will be other raids, but the lesson of
Forest Gate is that we have to find new methods of engaging with the
Muslim community in particular to reassure them of the necessity and
appropriateness of police actions" (Davenport 2006).

The British state responded to irrefutable evidence of the brothers' innocence by combining illiberal rationales of collateral damage and warlike "death ethics" (Maldonado-Torres 2008) with a therapeutic, liberal discourse of sensitivity. Redress appeared in the form of the state admitting to a private injury of pain and suffering in that, after two years, the state compensated the brothers monetarily. But the violent apparatus of the War on Terror remained unshaken by the state's acknowledgment of Abdul Kahar's pain and suffering—harms that were more easily disposed of or measured. No state actors, in contrast, were found guilty of excessive use of violence under the color of law. Deborah Glass, the commissioner for the Independent Police Complaints Commission (IPCC), carried out an inquiry into the near-fatal shooting of Abdul Kahar and concluded, "I have no hesitation in concluding that the two families affected by the raid were the *victims of failed intelligence* [emphasis mine], I don't think that these are ground for disciplinary matters, but I do think they are grounds for an apology. I mean, they were—some of them were injured as a result of this, they all went through what must have been a terrifying experience" (Independent Police Complaints Commission 2006). Abdul Kahar was hit by the state apparatus of the War on Terror, one that does not admit to its own fallibility, human rights violations, or racial profiling, emboldened as it is by imperatives of national security.

Before their full exoneration, however, the state tried one last strategy to cast suspicion upon Abdul Kahar and Abul Koyair. During the investigation, the police alleged that child pornography images had been found on the hard drive of a computer seized in the raid. These new crimes were categorically different—they were of a criminal justice nature—but the timing of the potential new charges dampened the public outrage and media criticism about Abdul Kahar's and Abul Koyair's treatment. While the allegations mobilized a new cycle of news stories that returned credibility to the police for a few days, it was eventually determined that the brothers had purchased the computer in question secondhand: the child pornography matter against them was not pursued for lack of evidence.

The state also never fully retracted its claim that it had credible intelligence about the chemical bomb threat that had triggered the raid in the first place. The police continued to issue statements that argued that "the intelligence received by the police continues to be developed and we will continue to exhaust all lines of inquiry" (Shaikh 2006). Eventually, however, this particular story faded from the headlines and the country turned its attention to new panics over new terrorist plots and new anti-Muslim and Islamophobic fears.

The heart of the discourse of national security and counterterrorism is a repressive, regulatory social and state logic that regulates the bodily comportment and lifeways of Muslim subjects. Through the control of Muslim women's bodies as exemplified by the question of the hijab and neighborhood intelligence gathering and preventative militarized raids on putative Muslim terror suspects, the British state and white British racial formations are constituted in relation to what is seen as abject Muslimness.

This is in contrast to the British state of the 1990s, which governed through the discourse of multiculturalism that sought to recognize the many identities composing its pluralistic society. The multicultural state is at least formally and nominally interested in collectivized identities, and requires some recognition, often through ethnic development projects and inclusive practices that cultivate diverse representation in governance. Multiculturalism intends to de-essentialize the notion of a homogeneous citizenship body, and to positively recognize the rights of culturally different groups (Taylor 1994; Benhabib 2002). But state-based multiculturalism and its imperatives effectively ended as a result of the northern towns uprisings in the summer of 2001. South Asian (largely Pakistani and Bangladeshi Muslim) youth took to the streets to confront far-right political agitation and long-term racial discrimination and tensions between their communities and working-class, white British communities in cities like Oldham, Bradford, and Harehills (Amin 2003; Webster 2003; Bagguley and Hussain 2008). These youths were severely punished by the British state and pathologized for causing social disorder and breakdowns in community cohesion. Soon thereafter, with the events of 9/11 and the advent of the War on Terror, there has been a further demonization of ethnic minority Muslim communities as likely sources of home-grown Islamist radicalism as well as social incohesion (Kundnani 2001, 2014).

This collective and cultural pathologization of British Muslims is evident in the frequent public debates that arise over everyday Muslim practices and lifeways. The Commission for Equalities and Human Rights is the statutory body tasked with promoting social equality. But in the early 2000s, it was precisely within this state institution itself that some of the most rancid Islamophobic discourse was generated. The failure of liberal state institutions to remedy anti-Muslim racism in community cohesion and national security discourses revealed the limits of official antiracism.

The extent to which these very institutions promulgate the racism they seek to remedy was reflected at the highest levels. The former head of the commission, Trevor Phillips, was pivotal in the construction of Muslims as questionable British citizens. Phillips responded to the northern towns clashes by suggesting that the so-called "riots" were the result of the separatist tendencies of poor and marginalized communities. "Britain," he declared, "was sleepwalking its way to segregation." In a coded manner, he especially described Muslim urban areas as "fully fledged ghettoes— black holes into which no one goes without fear and trepidation, and from which no one ever escapes undamaged" (Gillan 2005). In 2006, during the Europe-wide Muslim protest about Danish cartoons that satirized the Prophet Muhammad, Phillips issued another statement on the issue of free speech and debate concerning the use of sharia laws in Britain. He proclaimed that "Muslims who wish to live under a system of *sharia* law should leave Britain. . . . I don't think that's conceivable." He added, "We have one set of laws . . . and that's the end of the story. If you want to have laws decided in another way, you have to live somewhere else" (Bowcott 2006).

The goals of protecting liberal British values against culturally incommensurable Muslim practices and protecting the nation against terrorists have become strategically interlinked. Antiterrorism (policing, surveillance, and raids on terror suspects) and preventative counterterrorism (anti-radicalization campaigns that target softer issues of community values and cultural-religious practices) are different elements of one repertoire of counterinsurgency. In many ways, the War on Terror renegotiates the post– World War II popular consensus that legitimated the British social welfare state. As the rise of free-market reforms in both the Thatcherite and New Labour periods eroded this former consensus, a new kind of citizenship that does not make social rights and welfare demands on the state was cultivated. Citizen-subjects were increasingly encouraged to be responsible for their own social needs and the risks they took (Miller and Rose 2008). But the War on Terror also refigures custodial expectations and social entitlements into a new welfarism—the provision of national security. While the neoliberal state retrenches traditional social services, it endeavors to guarantee national security through new laws and expansive counter-terrorism programs that appear to compensate for lost entitlements.

Concomitantly, the War on Terror represses Muslim identity in the cause of national security policing, yet aims to incorporate Muslim communities within a (now-repressive) multicultural governance model that seeks, if not requires, the willing compliance of the oppressed themselves. These inseparable logics—of religious repression and multiculturalism; of the neoliberal state's devotion to individual rights and its growing securitization apparatus; of the neoliberal restriction of government and its expansion of government violence and surveillance—were all on display during the Forest Gate raid.

On June 29, 2006, I attended a meeting of the Metropolitan Police Authority (MPA), a civilian oversight body convened to discuss the conduct of the police during the raid. At this meeting, Operation Volga was a major item on the agenda and Andy Hayman, an Assistant Commissioner of the Metropolitan Police and head of operations, made a presentation. He had just received an honorific award of Commander of the British Empire, despite the raging controversy over the raid's errors. Through its granting of these honorary titles, the state appeared to be sanctifying the collateral damage of antiterror policing as a norm. In 2017, Cressida Dick, the senior Metropolitan Police officer in charge of a number of police failures that led to the wrongful execution of Jean Charles de Menezes, was similarly sheltered with a "wave of impunity" and was promoted to become the first woman police commissioner (Netpol 2017).[5]

A timeline of Operation Volga, presented to the audience at the 2006 MPA meeting, detailed not only the schedule of the planning and execution of the operation, but also a "hearts and minds" campaign to secure the acquiescence and acceptance of the operation in Newham's Muslim communities.[6] As the legitimacy and the veracity of the basis for the Forest Gate raid were unraveling, the Metropolitan Police engaged in an intense campaign to multiculturalize its damage-control strategies. One key tactic to produce consensus was the inclusion of Islamic and local community institutions' expressions of support for its counterterrorism efforts.

The groups and institutions selected for engagement included all the major mosques in Newham and national ethnic media outlets such as the Muslim Safety Forum, Islam Channel, Bangla TV, and the Muslim Centre. The police stressed that the Muslim community's "partnership" in the War on Terror was a key citizenship responsibility of Muslim subjects. The police strenuously campaigned against other dissident political actions, such as non-cooperation with the police, an option that was publicly proposed by politicians from the Respect Party, a loose coalition of the Socialist Workers Party and local Muslim activists that operated in east London between 2004 and 2016. Within this group, there were several elected local councilors in Newham. At the same time, the police set in motion surveillance of dissident activity through its Cultural and Communities Resource Unit. This unit was tasked with running a hotline that would monitor Internet discourse and assuage emerging "tensions" (Metropolitan Police Service 2006). Any demonstrations against the antiterror raid gone wrong were also subject to the "Newham Demo monitoring" task force. Some one hundred and twenty community leaders and local members of Parliament met to smooth community relations with the police.

Most of the local and national Muslim groups that had been selected to become what Manning Marable (2016, chap. 16) calls the privileged "symbolic representatives" of Muslim communities in relation to the British state were extremely slow to defend the people victimized during the Forest Gate raid. Furthermore, the groups did not take up a more interrogatory, challenging stance concerning the terror suspects' human rights, due process, custodial care, or quality of legal defense. Muslim groups interested in partnering with the state did not pursue the unpopular work of developing a public interest consensus surrounding the rights of *unrespectable* members of their community, such as those represented as terror suspects. Respectability and community valorization required that symbolic representatives or community leaders, and the Muslim community at large, validate the state's counterterrorism work as demonstrations of their loyalty to new citizenship norms.

Certainly the state did not wish critical opposition and resistance from symbolic representatives in the heat of antiterror raids. Accordingly, leading Muslim groups worked to shore up the distinction between good/bad, moderate/extremist Muslims and to stress their own relevance as multicultural partners of the state. Hence, even when the brothers Abdul Kahar and Abul Koyair were eventually released without charges, representative groups did not call for accountability or for an investigation of the rights violations of British Muslim subjects. Instead, they chose to characterize the raids on Muslims in apolitical terms, such as a "tragic incident." They asked only that "appropriate lessons" be learned. Muslim groups in return agreed that "this is not a matter of apportioning blame but trying to ensure the foundations are in place to maintain trust and build a partnership between the Muslim community and the police" (Shaikh 2006).

Asad Rehman, NMP's chair, who was also involved with other Muslim organizations, such as the Muslim Human Rights Forum, critiqued the politics of the traditional British Muslim leadership. In narrating his own evolution as an activist within the ambit of political blackness, he recalled the conflicted relationships between second-generation British Muslims like himself and the religious leadership in immigrant South Asian communities:

> In terms of the elders, they were looking to their organizations and their own institutions, which were inevitably religious institutions. They were the first institutions that people wanted to build. They were always the meeting place and social place, organizing place for the community. But for the younger generations, the younger people, we also looked to ourselves, you know. "Black People, here to stay, here to fight." It bound us all together. We didn't see ourselves as being separate from the mosques. In fact the mosques were places where we got to see other people in our community, and finding other young people who were interested as well.
>
> And also having first experiences of the negative aspects of religious institutions—I remember the local imam and members of the local mosque came with the local councilor who was Muslim to tell my dad to stop hanging out with communists. We were launching a political attack on the local Muslim leadership, in terms of an attack on the one councilor because they were more interested in having tea with the police than dealing with the fact that we were being attacked. We had to fight our way to school, fight in school, and fight our way back from school and the police were doing nothing. . . . That sort of politics began us.[7]

For Asad Rehman, becoming a black political activist, meant an analysis of both the value and contradictions of ethnic and religious community institutions. At times, the hierarchical ideologies of religious leaders and their self-interest in winning ethnic or religious recognition from the state led them to distance themselves politically from criminalized and nonrespectable members of the community, namely terror suspects. Such contradictory political allegiances can also lead to political quiescence toward police abuse and state overreach.

In contrast to this accommodationist approach that was consistent with counterterror citizenship, NMP examined the impact of the raid in terms of the lived experiences of the immediate, affected community. NMP researched, wrote, and submitted a report to the MPA (Metropolitan Police Authority), an oversight body, that detailed the collateral damage suffered by the local community. NMP's main criticism of the antiterror raid was that the state focused more on public relations and media damage control than in attending to the subordination and repression of the local community.

> The Metropolitan Police say they have spoken to "community leaders" but no efforts were made to communicate with residents whose roads were suddenly closed. Whilst briefing what might be described as "opinion-formers" is important, the basis for choosing who receives information remains very much in the hands of the [police]. The Met has also consistently refused to provide a senior officer to respond publicly to local people who are not considered "important" enough to be hand-picked as community leaders. . . .
> At the Asian Friendship Centre's meeting on 8 June, residents expressed concern that the police had given no explanation of what was happening, and had responded to some residents' initial questions by simply telling them to "watch television." Other officers stated in response to residents' questions that they had undertaken diversity training, and so are aware that they are a "service" to the public—although residents felt that they were far from being answerable to the public. (NMP 2006:4)

In contrast to the state's discourse of a collaborative counterterror citizenship agenda, NMP's experience with resisting the racialized subordination of black communities led in a different direction—to the group's mobilization of its casework and campaigning resources in order to question the state's violations of its own liberal juridical duties to Abdul Kahar and Abul Koyair.

NMP's strategy was to focus insistently on the state's democratic accountability toward its own Muslim citizens and communities. One key task that was assigned to me was to document the impact of the raid on the neighborhood situated in Landsdown Road and the surrounding streets affected by the cordon the police had erected during the raid. I interviewed the immediate neighbors of Abdul Kahar and Abul Koyair's family.

For days, residents labored to enter and exit their homes, while a purported clandestine chemical bomb factory in their midst was to have been

Figure 18. Local residents are checked entering and exiting their neighborhood during the cordon that was maintained by the police during the Forest Gate Antiterror Raid, 2006. Photo by the author.

uncovered. Fortunately, one of NMP's activists, Kevin Blowe, happened to live on one of the affected streets and thereby had the right to leave and reenter the cordon. We worked as a team to interview residents in the area, to document their responses, and to see who might possibly step forward as willing witnesses.

What we found was that the state's antiterrorism practices had unleashed post-traumatic desolation in the neighborhood. I wrote the following in my field notes:

> I then went to the neighbor in No.——. Kevin had already talked to her. But she was very agitated and vocal. A dark woman who wore glasses, she reminded me of my aunties in Malaysia. She looked Tamil to me. Her name though was Mrs. Shahid.
>
> She was really beside herself and talking to Kevin was not enough. Her five or six year-old daughter was dressed in a white *kurta* and sat on the front wall listening to us.

"The boy's blood is still here, in front here!" she shouted. She pointed to a spot outside her wall on the edge with the neighbor's where the concrete was still moist and stained. "They dragged him and threw him here. And the parents," she was nearly in tears, "the mother—how she was screaming—even now I can hear in my head. How she screamed: 'My son, my son!' If I close my eyes I can see her. I was shaking, crying after that and I told my children, I'm gone, I'm gone. I'm a mother; I have children.

"They told me, 'Mummy don't, you're still our mummy.'

"They dragged all of them out—the man, the woman—with nothing, no shoes, took her and put in handcuff—she had no *dupeta*." She clutched her own *dupeta* to show me. "I'm sorry, sorry. But there's something inside me."

We started talking about what happened in the following days. "We feel like criminals," she said.

"People come knocking on our door want information," she said. "They ask, are they religious people? Yes, I said. What is wrong with that? Religious people can be Christian, Hindu. Then the dustbin man come—they see us with police. Police talking to us—they think we criminal."

By this time an uncle on the other side of the road had come to join us. He had met Kevin at the Green St. community forum meeting yesterday. They started to talk, but often both the uncle and aunty would turn to talk to me.

"This is to keep white people happy, keep America happy, go behind America," he said.

In effect, the British state's War on Terror expelled the Muslim residents of Landsdown Road from the framework of liberal individual rights. They were not the direct targets of the Forest Gate raid, but were treated as loosely fungible with those who were. For the people who lived in the vicinity of the state's operation, it was clear that the antiterror raid was meaningful not only locally and domestically, but also globally. Landsdown Road British Muslims found themselves cast as interchangeable substitutes and targets for what was presented by the state as the domestic front lines of a global War on Terror, led by a western alliance and fought by militaries in Muslim countries.

Mrs. Shahid's understanding and identification with the mother of Abdul Kahar and Abul Koyair, however, was very strong. Her empathetic feeling of annihilation during the Forest Gate raid contrasts poignantly with the state's insistence on the legitimacy of its antiterrorism violence and its demand for a popular consensus on dehumanizing terror suspects. In her affective response, Mrs. Shahid refused to accept the state's agenda of transforming some people, consigned as "bad Muslims" and terror suspects, into subhumans.

Instead, Mrs. Shahid understood herself as a culturally marked feminine subject—"I'm a mother . . . she had no *dupeta*"—whose constituted dignity was immaterial to the British state. She felt like a subject and body whose very existence was vulnerable to the political and militarized imperatives of policing in the War on Terror. Mrs. Shahid's capacity to identify with vilified terror suspects and suspicious Muslims disrupts these hegemonic tenets of counterterrorism citizenship. In spite of the danger that she might herself get ensnared in the state's violence, Mrs. Shahid cleaved to visceral and emotional ties that bound her to her maligned neighbors.

What is so rehumanizing about Mrs. Shahid's ethical responses is her ability to forge noninstrumental or self-interested identification with the War on Terror's archetypal enemy: the terror suspect. Mrs. Shahid demonstrated this identification for audiences such as her young daughter, who in this experience was made to understand that what had happened next door had also happened to her. She was fungible. Her mother's life was not the one being made safe in Britain's counterterrorism operations. In fact, their particular lives were positioned as vulnerable to state violence and even expendable in the name of a greater, universal idea of national security— from which they were excluded.

Among many other people in the community affected by the Forest Gate raid were the immediate family members of Abdul Kahar and Abul Koyair. In an interview I conducted with their sister, Sarah (a pseudonym), I further learned of the gendered impacts of the raid for immediate family members. Sarah told me that female members of the extended family were not only feeling fear, outrage, and despair—they were feeling guilt.

Initially I could not understand this. But Sarah explained that the women of the extended family felt guilty for having been spared the worst brutalities in the antiterror raid. The strong ascription of Muslim-looking men with beards as potential terrorists made the unveiled female members of the family question their own non-visibly marked Muslim identity, she said. Sarah did not wear the hijab, and she now harbored acute guilt over the possibility that she had been spared the near-death violence and state brutalities suffered by her brothers because of the lack of this Muslim signifier.

Like Amina, Sarah felt that she was alienated from the suffering and oppression of fellow Muslims because she did not visibly signify herself as Muslim. Her lack of the hijab might have privileged her in the racist, colonial white gaze of the police, and she was repulsed by the estrangement that this created with the brutalized male members of her own family, whom she identified with and loved. This incident caused her to reassess her own decisions and self-fashioning as a Muslim woman.

> When I heard my brother saying that he had been shot, and I heard noises which I know was when the police were slapping him about, telling him to shut the fuck up. That could have been us, but it wasn't us. They could have easily hit us, but why didn't they hit us, the women in the family? The only explanation that I have in my head was physically we didn't look different. Coz the men did, they had their beards. Us, the women in the house, didn't have no scarves or nothing, we didn't have our scarves. We didn't look physically different. I don't know how to explain it. To separate us and them. My brothers and my dad did. And my dad is a really old man. You've seen him. And for them to kick him in the chest, to hold him down and be kicking him. In my head I can't see how they can do that. And in fact these people are trained to kill. . . . I haven't sat down in the family and said to them, "How come they treated you guys different from us?" sort of thing, but I know in my head what it was.

In this moment in the War on Terror, we are further able to unmask the violent, gendered dynamics of anti-Muslim domination. The expulsion of the Muslim terror suspects from the liberal state's political juridical rule, and the expectation that the British Muslim communities accept this vulnerability to expulsion as fulfillment of the new terms of counterterrorism citizenship, was a form of forced belonging that Sarah and Mrs. Shahid could not politically accept.

Although her children were not harmed in the raid, Mrs. Shahid had a profound understanding of the fear, recognition of glossed-over oppressions, and determination to protect her family that she shared with the

mother of the alleged terrorists. Likewise, the strategy and support that
political blackness provides, or at least makes manifest, are the affirmation
of a denied reality that affects those who are members of communities that
have suffered oppressions at the hands of the police and others who enforce
the status quo of everyday political whiteness at their expense. They also
offer the potential to confront and change those conditions. Political blackness is not meant to erase or diminish differences, but rather to offer a
public and productive opportunity to break through much of the mistrust,
disaffection, and skepticism that keeps those who are subjected to racialized
violence divided and alienated from one another.

More formally, political blackness first tries to catalyze the political self-
affirmation and self-organization of people who are victims of racial and
state violence. Second, it works to build movements by creating broad solidarities and new communities around campaigns for justice. As a senior
NMP activist, Cilius Victor, theorized, "Part of what we do is to build
people so that people rally around other people. So if there is a family that
is being abused you don't just try to galvanize support from that particular
community, but from other communities as well to get them to see what is
happening and to see what might happen to themselves a bit further down
the line. That's the way it always works." The deliberate double strategy of
NMP was to work with and alongside victims of racism to meet their needs
for immediate remedies from the state's social services via casework, and
simultaneously to stage direct action protests and demonstrations to expose
and critique the racialized underpinnings of the British state's liberal governance. This intertwined strategy combines "practical" and "political" work
that allows racially marginalized communities to engage the procedures of
liberal justice, while also contesting the structural tendencies within those
very systems that cause antiracist measures to fail, including machinations
of everyday political whiteness that block racial justice.

NMP insisted that it was the right of Abdul Kahar and Abul Koyair to
be recipients of justice not only because they were "innocent" or because
they had dutifully performed the compliant patriotism demanded of Muslims by the state's counterterrorism definition of citizenship. In addition to
these arguments, NMP mobilized a mass protest in Newham that empha-
sized a bottom-up resistance to other issues—ethno-racial and religious
profiling, state violence, and discriminatory denials of civil liberties. This
activism helped to deploy counterhegemonic and counterphobic representations of Muslims in resistance to the routine tropes of suspicion and

nefarious presence that the British state's counterterrorism discourse promotes.

NMP first undertook practical casework in response to everyday life crises affecting individual victims and families. The raid, in effect, had rendered the family of Abdul Kahar and Abul Koyair homeless. As their house was being taken apart "brick by brick" in search of a nonexistent chemical bomb factory, NMP activists pressured the unwilling local Homeless Persons Unit (HPU) to accept the family as its charge. The HPU is a government agency statutorily obliged to provide housing for people who find themselves homeless for whatever reason. In this case the agency was initially, predictably reluctant to recognize terror suspects—who had not had the opportunity to defend themselves through due process—as citizens they were obliged to serve.

Furthermore, family members needed a doctor's slip to justify their absence from work and to avoid losing their jobs. Another consequence of the antiterror police action was that the family's cat had gone missing from the home. After an exhaustive search on the streets by NMP activists who looked in alleys and called out the cat's name, she was finally located in the home of a neighbor who was looking after her. This moment illustrates the salience of combining practical and political work. Finding the family's cat was part and parcel of political blackness: it was an act that responded to the family's own practical and political concerns and was a form of solidarity and support. By this community-centered ethic, the victims were "rehumanized," and that is a key element of political blackness. This rehumanizing went beyond the mere provision of social services. It fed into a political circuit where NMP challenged the structure of the state's laws and practices in counterterrorism that had justified these violations in the first place.

NMP also organized a casework and legal defense intervention for the two brothers. Two legal aid solicitors who had been appointed for the families concerned had to be removed. NMP knew that the quality of legal representation was critical if the brothers were to have any chance against the state's prosecutorial powers. While some firms and lawyers become invested in these terror cases strategically as a way to raise the profile of their companies, other lawyers realize that the legal acumen and experience necessary to provide the highest standard of defense in highly complex antiterror cases may be beyond the scope of legal aid solicitors and barristers who are assigned to terror suspects. In the initial days following the

Figure 19. One of the largest demonstrations in Newham's history took place
on June 18, 2006, in response to the Forest Gate Antiterror Raid.
Photo by the author.

raid, NMP watched aghast as inexperienced legal aid lawyers made blunders
that worsened the situation for the detained brothers and dimmed their
prospects for release. NMP activists worked with the families to substitute
their legal representatives to avoid a finding of guilt due to inadequate
legal representation. A seasoned barrister, Gareth Pierce, was secured as the
brothers' counsel. She had had vast experience with antiterrorism laws and
had previously defended falsely accused terror suspects, such as the Guil-
ford Four in the state's anti-Irish Republican Army (IRA) case.

Finally, NMP mobilized numerous racial, religious, and ethnic minority
groups—as well as broad local and progressive community support—to
organize a mass demonstration. Flyers and direct invitations were distributed to multiple community centers, women's centers, social clubs, unions,
mosques, gurdwaras, temples, and churches. This outreach produced an
impressive turnout of between three thousand and five thousand people
who took to the streets of Newham on June 18, 2006.

This newly constituted political community of diverse people, united behind the campaign of justice for the brothers, enabled NMP to speak back critically to the British state. Arising from this popular mobilization, NMP and the demonstration's co-organizers presented a seven-point list of political demands to the Metropolitan Police that carried out the raid:

This protest is a united demonstration of feeling, from the residents of Newham and those beyond who support them. We believe:

1. A full and unqualified apology from the Metropolitan Police to be personally issued to those who were victims of these events. The treatment of the families and neighbors of —— Landsdown Road by the Metropolitan Police on the day of the arrest was barbaric and unacceptable. The leaking of lies and misinformation after the arrest was devious and similarly unacceptable.

2. A call for an end to police privately "briefing" newspapers. The sensationalized way the arrests were reported and the exaggerated media speculation, uncritical of the leaks and briefings, heightened a sense of fear and has further advanced a demonization of the Muslim community as a suspect community.

3. Stop the politicization of the police force. The police should not allow itself to be pushed into such raids on questionable intelligence, and used as a political pawn in the government's wider policy agenda. Their job is the safety of the public and not propaganda. The reports of the directive for this raid coming from the Cabinet Office will trouble many.

4. We are not prepared to live in fear or be silenced. Despite this sense of fear in general and this demonstration, the Muslim community and others should continue to speak out against injustices, stereotyping and ill treatment, and should never be cowed into silence.

5. End to the association of Islam with Terrorism. There needs to be an end to associating religion with terror or any other breach of law. Terms such as "Islamic terrorism" are inaccurate and divisive. The questioning of those arrested—by the police and some of the media—about their association or

beliefs—be they political or religious—is deeply disturbing as it encourages a mentality of "guilt by association" or "guilt because of conscience."

6. A full apology from the Prime Minister to the families and community. Statements by the Prime Minister such as saying the government is "101%" behind the police action even when they have not bothered examining the facts of the arrest are unhelpful, and indeed only further add to the reckless manner of law enforcement.

7. The War on Terror needs to be urgently reviewed. These aggressive raids, together with the large number of innocent Muslims arrested as terrorist suspects in the last few years are inevitable and damaging costs of the so-called War on Terror. The policy needs reviewing as it is dividing communities and heightening alienation. Despite this we will not allow our communities to be divided by such events and will work to further sincere understanding between Muslims and Non-Muslims.

These demands expressed grassroots democratic visions and social imaginaries that opposed the War on Terror governance paradigm. Robin D. G. Kelley (1996:9) has argued that "politics is not separate from lived experience or the imaginary world of what is possible; to the contrary, politics is about these things. Politics comprises the many battles to roll back constraints and exercise some power over, or create some space within, the institutions and social relationships that dominate." The demands produced a powerful counter-paradigm that challenged the state's counterterrorism citizenship and the racial hierarchies that are constituted in its actual implementation.

The demands advanced a critique of the War on Terror as a state-sponsored racist marginalization of Muslims. Collective suspicion, militarized police violence, and a reckless lack of care and democratic accountability toward British Muslims structured racialized antagonisms in the conduct of the War on Terror. This paradox is not confined to how the British state suspends liberal juridical precepts and proceduralisms when it unleashes counterterrorism operations against whole Muslim communities. To underscore that multiple communities were targeted by the state's racializing logics, NMP united the justice campaigns of the Forest Gate

Figure 20. Abul Koyair, the younger brother of Abdul Kahar, joins Patricia da
Silva Armani and Alex Pereira, cousins of Jean Charles de Menezes, en route
to protest the Forest Gate Antiterror Raid, June 18, 2006.
Photo by the author.

victims with the ongoing justice campaign for Jean Charles de Menezes.
The family of de Menezes would engage in years of struggle to challenge
the impunity of his murder, including appeals to the European courts. The
family's refusal to accept the collateral damage of de Menezes's death in
Britain's War on Terror was a stark rebuttal to the state's assumption of
death-dealing prerogatives.

A very important symbolic and instructive moment in the protest
march occurred when the younger Abul Koyair, the brother who was not
shot, met en route with the de Menezes family, who were participating in
the march, and exchanged his clothes for a Brazilian World Cup jersey.
Images of Abul Koyair donning the Brazilian jersey appeared on the front
pages of both local and national papers and catapulted him to visibility in
the national and international media. It was also an important political act.
In putting on the Brazilian jersey, Abul Koyair was affiliating the oppression

Figure 21. One of the Newham neighborhoods on the route of the protest against the Forest Gate Antiterror Raid, 2006. Photo by the author.

Figure 22. British Muslim women participating in the demonstration to protest the Forest Gate Antiterror Raid, 2006. Photo by the author.

Figure 23. Benjamin Zephaniah (middle), a poet, artist, and Newham Monitoring Project patron, joins the protest against the Forest Gate Antiterror Raid, June 18, 2006. Photo by the author.

Figure 24. Between three thousand and five thousand people participated in
the street protests against the Forest Gate Antiterror Raid, June 18, 2006.
Photo by the author.

suffered by his family and community with another community of sufferers
who were non-Muslim, non–South Asian, and non-British. It shattered
commonsense constructions of Muslims as separatist and religious absolut-
ists who refuse to integrate and who are culturally incompatible with democratic values.

This symbolic action also sent a signal to the Muslim community that
there was a wider political context, and solidarity, for their suffering, and
that they were not isolated and bereft of allies in their alienation. Notably,
before the event, rumors and press sensationalism had stoked expectations
of angry and irrational Muslim mobs running amuck, but coverage of the
event itself got redirected toward a unifying rally composed primarily of
Muslims but also of Sikhs, Hindus, Africans, and African Caribbeans. The
local Sikh gurdwara, which in the past had itself been targeted for racist
attacks and vandalism, was prominent along the protest route, distributing
bottled water. The mutual mobilizations and support for the Forest Gate

protest enabled what Ruth Gilmore (2008:42) calls a "bottom-up politics of recognition in the face of threatened annihilation." The space of the public protest, created by the ethics and strategies of political blackness, enabled marginalized communities in Newham to engage in the possibilities of a "syncretic rescaling of identity" among themselves, rather than pursuing strategies of division, boundary setting, and social distance (Gilmore 2008).

NMP's work in the critique and resistance to the Forest Gate raid was an important milestone in how political blackness was rearticulated in a post War on Terror conjuncture. Rather than reifying its struggle against racism, NMP extended the methodology of solidarity based political blackness to contest the oppression of both Muslims and Muslim-looking people who were increasingly endangered by the racialized contradictions of a liberal rule of law and the institutionalization of counterterror citizenship.

CHAPTER 6

"If Political Blackness Is So Damn Difficult, Why Do You Keep It?"

Cilius's Passage to Post–War on Terror Political Blackness

The War on Terror, inaugurated with the U.S.-led response to the terror attacks of September 11, 2001, became an acute reality for British Muslims after the London bombings on July 7, 2005. The fact that the perpetrators— three British-born South Asians and one immigrant African Caribbean— had converted to Islam and had no prior record of terrorist involvement was framed widely as reasons for regarding British Muslims collectively as a suspicious community. Newham Monitoring Project (NMP) activists considered two possible options, each of which had its own rationale, for how to address the rising tide of Islamophobia and the development of state-based racial and religious profiling. On the one hand, some NMP activists thought that the best approach was to resist the growing phobia against British Muslim identities by "taking the focus off Muslim communities."[1] By this they meant that they rejected the pathologization of the racial and religious Muslim category generated by the state counterterrorism discourse. They resisted being pushed into a defensive corner where they had to vindicate the Muslim community against malicious stereotyping. A second position, and one that eventually became dominant within the organization, was to expand its practices to include a civil liberties defense of people targeted as terror suspects and to monitor the development of the state's counterterrorism practices in Newham, especially in the aftermath of the Forest Gate Antiterror Raid. NMP also developed rights awareness workshops and literature to be disseminated among the bor-ough's many ethnic South Asian and African Muslim community organi-zations.

Activists associated with NMP initially did not share a clear consensus on how to think about the new racialized antagonisms and racial hierar-chies that the globalized conjuncture of the War on Terror had catalyzed. Their positions, analyses, and strategies evolved in the context of how peo-ple in the local Newham communities approached the organization, and their changing realities and needs. Daily casework and organizing urgencies presented new questions and suggested new areas of work, such as the impact of antiterror raids and counterterrorism surveillance by the police. Historically, NMP had worked with many different minority communities that on an everyday level might espouse multiple forms of identifications and political ideologies. Zainab Kelmsley, a Nigerian-English lawyer and community activist who once served as the director of NMP, framed the emergent challenges for political blackness in the following way:

> I didn't think about black as a political umbrella until I started read-ing about politics and stuff, but in my own thinking, growing up, it was obvious that anybody non-white my age, born and brought up in the UK was going to have a similar experience. I wouldn't get caught up in what kids today do, a mixed group of kids picking on someone wearing a hijab or something. I wouldn't have been caught up in that. Because it was easy to see that it was the same experience that I was having. They were picking on her hijab, as opposed to my curly hair. It's the same thing. It was easy to translate. And I think that kids are not seeing that it's easy to translate and that's down to ignorance, as well as more complicated society. . . . It's really disheartening to see that black communities being racist to other black communities. It's just heartbreaking, absolutely heartbreaking. So that would be an issue that I would like to have looked into. . . . *How on earth do we bring our communities back?* (emphasis mine)[2]

Cross cutting black consciousness as expressed by Kelmsley seeks points of connection across the different iterations of racism experienced by different minority communities in Britain. Mutually reified abject differences—the "hijab"/"curly hair" analogy—are rearticulated as new metaphors and grounding for a post–War on Terror political blackness.

Since 2001, a continually expanding counterterrorism industry has arisen in England. Its activities overwhelmingly focus on racial profiling and conducting surveillance of Muslim communities. Most of these state-based initiatives and programs violate the classic norms of individual rights and the basic presumptions of abstract proceduralism in liberal justice. For example, an initiative called the Channel program in the United Kingdom was launched in 2010. Its stated purpose was "to provide support to people at risk of being drawn into violent extremism" (Home Office 2010). In 2016 this program referred some four thousand people, including children under nine years of age, who had not committed any terror offenses at all. They were, however, preemptively identified by state agents in child services or social services to be at risk for political "radicalization" and, based on that identification, subjected to a state- or community-based intervention (Kundnani 2012; House of Commons Home Affairs Committee 2014; Halliday 2016).

There have been numerous critiques of these prevention of terrorism programs that point to an illiberal, and Orwellian, dystopic democracy: the abrogation of free speech rights, the policing of political and intellectual thought, pseudoscientific notions that the state puts forward play an intimate role in shaping allowable political views and, particularly, the attempt to police British Muslims' political thought. As an NMP and Netpol activist, Kevin Blowe (2015), argued, the state's counterterrorism premise and strategy "is based on a lie: there is no inevitability about an 'escalator of radicalization' and youthful rebellion is never a guarantee of genuinely radical politics in later life." In 2015, some five hundred university lecturers and professors protested the government's proposal to impose a legal duty to prevent students from becoming radicalized and to require the vetting of visiting speakers' texts in advance of their presentation (Travis 2015).

In Newham proper, I, along with other NMP members and supporters, observed the penetration of the state's counterterrorism and counterradicalization agendas to be quickly permeating everyday life. I found the following statement in a local daycare and elementary school's newsletter. The school principal wrote it and it attests to the normalization of counterterrorism protocols as matters of local municipal governance: "I'm sure you have heard in the news about the Government's Prevent strategy, aimed at identifying and preventing radicalization of adults and young people. All staff and governors have now received Prevent training, which was aimed at keeping . . . pupils safe from these dangers."[3] These protocols normalize political surveillance as a continuation of the state's custodial duty for children. The following example from the British Home Office's own report further illustrates the slippages between state custodial duties and counterterrorism overreach that has become the basis of a new form of social contract:

> A member of the public told a Police Officer from their local Safer Neighbourhood Team of their concerns about a 15-year-old male who had recently converted to Islam. The information was initially vague and uncorroborated but the member of the public believed that the boy was prepared to give his life for his religion. Further research failed to reveal information indicating extremist tendencies, but did reveal violent behaviour and street gang affiliation. A panel meeting was held and the subject was referred to a provider specializing in working with young converts. Provision of support was conducted through a series of one to one meetings and group activities. Through this interaction the provider explored the boy's interpretation of Islam and following a period of working with the boy they became satisfied that he did not actually hold extreme and violent views. He was, however, vulnerable in other ways. The boy went into the care of foster parents and his school attendance and behaviour subsequently improved. The support provider remains in contact with him. (Home Office 2010:16)

In this Home Office account, no one questioned the power to seize and preemptively target a child within a counterterror program, on the basis of hearsay and flimsy evidence. The state's admission of errors in its original assessment, however, is redeemed by its own celebration of having picked up on other child protection concerns during the course of its counterterror operation. There is no accountability about the spurious basis of the Channel program's intrusive powers and slippery practices. Instead, the report self-validates the state's accumulation of power by normalizing the slippage between counterterrorism's transgression of children's rights and its child protective statutory duties.

As a result of a state-induced climate of suspicion and widespread derogation of basic civil liberties in counterterror operations, programs, and practices, British Muslims have been frequent targets of populist racial violence, largely perpetrated by white Britons (Littler and Feldman 2015:1). This reality has been so pervasive and indisputable that by 2015 the public was debating whether Britain was "lacking a sense of common humanity" in the light of numerous reports of bystanders who ignored the rising tide of virulent Islamophobic incidents on the streets and in public transport (Harris 2015). Measuring Anti-Muslim Attacks, or Tell MAMA, a reporting online portal and national phone-in service, started tracking the dramatic rise of interlinked online and offline Islamophobic abuse and threats in 2015.[4] Anti-Muslim attacks also appeared to be closely related to external "trigger" events, such as the Charlie Hebdo attacks in Paris and the Tunisian bombings in 2015 (Awan and Zempi 2015:6; Littler and Feldman 2015). The killing of the British Army soldier Lee Rigby in southeast London sparked a massive wave of collective retaliatory attacks on Muslim-looking people and symbolic Muslim spaces such as mosques. The Metropolitan Police in London recorded five hundred anti-Muslim hate crimes within just a few days following the event (Awan and Zempi 2015:10).

Former Prime Minister David Cameron was compelled to respond to official reports of surging Islamophobic hate crimes and stated, "I want to build a national coalition to challenge and speak out against extremists and the poison they peddle. I want British Muslims to know we will back them to stand against those who spread hate and to counter the narrative which says Muslims do not feel British" (Cameron 2015). The official state response to these events conformed to the formula outlined by the community cohesion policy, where anti-Muslim hate crimes were criminalized through new substantial laws and policies, while Muslims were generally presumed to be in need of more assimilation. In addition to the Racial and Religious Hatred Act of 2006, a new religion-based protocol for recording hate crimes was announced to separately monitor specific anti-Muslim crime statistics, akin to the way that anti-Jewish hate crimes were already recorded and monitored (Wintour 2015).

The state framework of conceptualizing anti-Muslim racism as aberrational and invidious hate crimes exempts from scrutiny the complicity of national security and war-making discourses in structuring anti-Muslim animus in the first place. An analysis of the Tell MAMA data by Mark Littler and Matthew Feldman (2015) describes the creeping social changes since the War on Terror, wrought by the cumulative, sometimes subtly embedded, anti-Muslim discourses within both the British state and society:

Initially the preserve of populist political movements at the fringes of acceptability (for example, the EDL [English Defence League],

Pegida, or Liberty GB), the low level rhetoric of anti-Muslim prejudice has increasingly spilled over into mainstream social and political debates, gaining greater traction and political capital as it becomes a more ingrained part of British political discourse. Particularly in the run-up to the 2015 elections . . . politicians of all stripes have been keen to adopt the language of "soft" nationalism and the promotion of "indigenous cultural identity," ranging from ministerial calls for the Muslim community to root out extremism to MEPs [members of the European Parliament] slurring a Muslim colleague by referring to them with the name of a known extremist. In the UK, this ratcheting up of political rhetoric has been accompanied by some evidence suggesting a rise in violent anti-Muslim activity. The socially marginal and politically disenfranchised have increasingly seized upon the Muslim community as a scapegoat for their broader social and political grievances, sometimes with violent consequences. (3)

Public policy responses, even pro-active reforms in which the liberal state performs its egalitarian protection of personhood against Islamophobic hate crimes, ignore how the British state society has itself been reoriented toward anti-Muslim racialization. Structurally, for example, Muslims have been rendered as an "entire category of citizens who for some reason cannot be integrated into the political system" (Agamben 2005:2). This racializing development is systemic, rather than a discrete hate crime against an individual Muslim.

Even the best empirical evidence of the disproportionate impact of the antiterrorism discourse on Muslim minority families and communities cannot dislodge or seriously call into question the now naturalized legitimacy of the national security state in western liberal democracies. In emergent anti-Muslim structures of racism, Muslim subjectivity and bodies are rendered suspicious, without corroborating grounds or "epistemological justification" (Buck-Morss 2006). Suspicion leads to social and racial differentiation. The very same state that aims to secure society against "Islamic terrorism" and also to protect British Muslims from anti-Muslim hate crimes (crimes engendered by its own structural tendencies) illustrates the now-normalized paradox of an illiberal liberal state.

For some British Muslims Islamophobia is perceived to be qualitatively different from the racism they experienced as black immigrants or second-generation children growing up in the 1970s, 1980s, or 1990s. Arzu Merali

(2013) of the Islamic Human Rights Commission, for example, notes, "Don't get me wrong, I grew up in a white working class area as one of a handful of *black kids as we were all known in those days* [emphasis mine] and there was racism aplenty, including threats from the far-right National Front. But we grew up and, so it seemed did most of society. Some of us even had the temerity to think that things had gotten better for a while before Islamophobia became so completely mainstream." In this view, the experience of anti-black racism as constructed during the post–World War II settlement of non-white colonial and former colonial subjects gave way to a reanimated western civilizational antipathy against the religion of Islam and Muslims. Islamophobia is presumed to be genealogically different from previous forms of anti-black racialization and racism.

It is important, however, to consider changes in the forms of racialization and racism as well as their historical continuities. Post-empire anti-black racial violence in Britain, which constructed South Asian, African, and African Caribbean communities as targets, did not simply dissolve with the passage of time or racial progress. Twenty-first-century anti-Muslim racism was built upon the preceding twentieth-century template of anti-black racism in Britain, where the post-empire trope of a defensive ethno-racial white British identity, rather than the civilizing mission of empire building, or the "white man's burden," energized discourses regarding anti-immigration, border control, and imperiled "Britishness." As Arif Dirlik (2008:1370) has argued, older forms of racism do not disappear: they become "a dynamic moment of the [new] reconfigured racism."

The British model of political blackness, with its tradition of pan-religious and pan-ethnic advocacy of antiracism, has been both valorized and critiqued in academic literature on race and resistance, as well as embraced and questioned by many inhabitants of Newham who relied on NMP. Political blackness, as a form of solidarity politics, offers many instrumental benefits, including the benefits of resource mobilization, localized communities of resistance, and what Robbie Shilliam (2015:3) has called a diasporically informed "global infrastructure of anti-colonial connectivity." As a theoretical weapon political blackness is a form of racial analysis that tries to understand and present the links among multiple forms of racism that are nonetheless interlocked in the politics of the state and in the dynamics of everyday political whiteness.

But political blackness in Britain often appears as a strange formation in relation to the more widely circulated and naturalized representations of race relations in the United States. Hence, the history of political blackness in Britain has often been dismissed as a compromised form of inauthentic and "imperfectly imagined" black identity (Eldridge 1997:37). Such critics would apply black identity solely and exclusively to African diasporic groups (Eldridge 1997; Andrews 2016). But other scholars have pointed out that Afro-Asian co-identifications and "polycultural" (Prashad 2001) formations have, in fact, occurred widely; they have manifested in Black Power social movements in South Africa, for example, as well as in the Caribbean and the Americas (Carmichael 1969; Kelley 2003; Slate 2012; Desai 2014; Shilliam 2015). In particular, Manning Marable (2016, chap. 16) argued that the example of cross-community black formation in Britain helps to mobilize broad non-white resistance to racism/white supremacy that goes beyond strategies "rooted implicitly in a competitive model of group empowerment," whereby different ethnic and racial minority groups "interpret their interests narrowly in divergent ways, looking out primarily for themselves rather than addressing the structural inequalities within the social fabric of the society as a whole."

As mentioned in the case of Newham, the tradition of political blackness has supporters and detractors within Britain. Julia Sudbury (1998), who carried out a pathbreaking, in-depth ethnographic study of politically black women's organizations in Britain, argued that the history of the construction of political blackness in Britain allows for a fruitful political reexamination of naturalized racial classifications:

> By insisting on using "black" to refer to two groups which have been defined as distinct "races" and today masquerade as ethnic groups with distinct and immutable boundaries, we create a dissonance which throws up contradictions in otherwise unquestioned social scientific categorization. The multiracial usage of blackness therefore serves as a sharp reminder of the social construction of taken-for-granted gendered racialized identities and forces us to question how and why the boundaries to such categories are created and maintained. (Sudbury 2001:46)

Sudbury also argued that the formations of political blackness in Britain are not settled affairs. Rather, the work of "reconstructing multiracial blackness" through overcoming divisions and fragmentation is a reiterative and permanent process that occurs in specific historical conditions. In fact, the racial conditions of the oppressed usually present both "common ground *and* mutual disaffection" (Yamamoto and Su 2002:386).

In contrast, Paul Gilroy (Yancy and Gilroy 2015) has argued for the development of antiracism that altogether goes beyond a "Manichean perspective" that is anchored in an absolutist black-white form of raciological thinking. Gilroy's concern would presumably exclude the re-racialization and binary oppositional politics with which political blackness engages in. The movement-building concerns of political blackness sit awkwardly with the social scientific search to achieve the "final deconstruction of race" as a spurious social category (Alexander and Knowles 2005:11). The academic and theoretical quest to denaturalize the categories of race would almost seem to contradict the continued, felt, need for varied forms of race-based social movements. As Gilroy (Yancy and Gilroy 2015) notes, the boundary-setting ethos of absolutist racial nationalism, even in forms propagated by oppressed communities, can lead to problematic contradictions in antiracist practice.

> Solidarity is an altogether trickier thing. It has to be made rather than assumed on racial grounds. . . . Let me raise a couple of difficult examples to illustrate the organizational and conceptual problems that we face in antiracist organizing. A couple of years ago, after the killing of Trayvon Martin, his mother came to Britain for a heavily publicized meeting with Baroness Lawrence, the mother of Stephen Lawrence. Her son was murdered by racists in a horrible, tragic case that has dominated the field of our racial politics for many years. The grieving mother whose loss has been compounded by the failure of the criminal justice system to bring redress is a very potent symbol. But when Anuj Bidve's parents came to Britain from India after his murder by racists in Manchester, I don't recall them meeting with anybody except the police and the mainstream politicians who were hungry for a photo op. The crisis of political imagination has real, disabling consequences.

Political blackness, however, has been the form of race-based antiracist organizing that has consistently incorporated the joint realities of multiple ethnic, racial, and religious minority communities suffering racism in Britain. Nonetheless, political formations like NMP have also been critiqued by British South Asian academics such as Tariq Modood (1994, 2005) as forcing a harmful lumping together that subsumes and erases South Asian cultural references and interests under the African Caribbean visibility in Britain. The consolidation of a British Muslim identity in public discourse has made even more tenuous the viability of solidarity politics among Britain's ethnic and racial minority communities, even within the pan-religious and pan-ethnic category of "British Asian," for which Modood had earlier argued for. Among non-Muslim South Asian communities in Britain, diasporic Hindutva fundamentalist movements and the demonization of Muslims by the War on Terror have also encouraged dis-identifications and social and political distancing from co-ethnic South Asian Muslims (Thomas 2011).

Political blackness has also long been critiqued by some Marxist scholars as a form of false consciousness and a species of detrimental "identity politics" that detracts from universalist, class-based social struggles (Shukra 1998; Cole 2009). As new immigrant groups have quickly diversified Britain's demographics, another critique of the activist traditions of political blackness is that it does not speak to newer communities such as Latin Americans (Fuentes 1997; Maylor 2009), or more culturally invisible ethnic minority groups such as the Chinese and others of East Asian descent, who were not even included within the census category of "Asian" until 2011, let alone the political category of black (Ang-Lygate 1997; Wilson, Andrews, and Chok 2016). As an a priori category of self-identification the political category of black is said to be unable to "capture the experiences of all those incorporated within the category" (Maylor 2009:384).

In 2016 and 2017 two controversies arose that again cast a spotlight on the question of the continued relevance of political blackness in British antiracist politics. The first involved the decision of the Kent University student union to include and feature the South Asian artist Zayn Malik and London mayor Sadiq Khan as celebrity symbols during Black History Month, which has increasingly become assumed as a celebration of African and African Caribbean heritage (Wilson, Andrews, and Chok 2016). The second controversy involved the casting of a popular South Asian actress, Freida Pinto, to play a 1970s British Black Panther radical activist in the television miniseries *Guerrilla*. Pinto's character was based on the historical personages of South Asian women like Mala Sen who were active leaders in the Brixton-based Black Panther group (Laura 2012; Obi 2017). However, the actual history of this group, which had constituted itself as a multiracial and multiethnic black formation in Britain was not well known or referenced in the debate that ensued. In fact, the actually lived history of political blackness as it operated along a range of grassroots social movements and intellectual, artistic, and women's groups, at different times and across different issues in post–World War II Britain, has been woefully understudied and underrepresented in popular culture.

Social media opprobrium quickly viralized following erroneous newspaper reportage that claimed that Pinto had been harassed to the point of tears by aggressive U.K. Black Lives Matter women activists at the premiere of *Guerrilla* (Qasim 2017). The furor led to a critique of political blackness as a silencing discourse against African and African Caribbean women, who were stereotyped in these newspaper accounts as "angry black women" as they raised critical questions about the erasure of women activists in the show's rare but fictionalized treatment of Black Power history in Britain (Qasim 2017). The journalists who raised the questions were not challenging the historical accuracy of casting a South Asian woman lead; they were, in fact, critiquing the paucity of representation and, when represented, the misrepresentation of the roles that were supposed to portray the numerous African and African Caribbean women who, as Elizabeth Obi (2017), an activist from the period argued, were the "backbone of the black movement." No actresses appeared as significant historical personages including Olive Morris, Althea Jones-Lecointe, Stella Dadzie, Beverley Bryan, or Barbara Beese.

As political blackness continues to be debated in Britain, it has also become more common to hear U.S.-derived racial terminology such as "people of color" and "black and brown" alongside depoliticized British state policy terms such as "BME," or "Black and Minority Ethnic," and "BAME," or "Black, Asian and Minority Ethnic." However, even these bureaucratic terms have not found a consensus among Britain's racial and ethnic minority communities and the question of racial categorization and political identification continues to be deeply unsettled (Okolosie, Harker, Green, and Dabiri 2015). The rejection of any shared inter-minority and antiracist political identity, including the U.S.-derived concept of "people of color," has also been sounded in the United Kingdom. One media commentator, for example, has argued that "'people of color' erases huge cultural differences, manufacturing an alleged sense of 'solidarity,' which I see little evidence of when it comes to concrete and practical gains for people of African descent" (Dabiri 2015).[5]

The topic of political blackness has also been intensely debated from 2015 onward within the ranks of the National Union of Students in Britain

(NUS), with some voices calling for the dismantling of the union's long-standing policy because it made "'ethnically' black students, feel their identities as well as their oppression(s) co-opted and monopolized" (Iheke 2017).[6] Although motions to dismantle political blackness within the student organization were defeated in the 2016 and 2017 NUS Black Students' Campaign annual conferences, the demands for an ethnological reconstruction of the term "black" to exclusively describe people of African descent, but not people of North African and Arab descent or South Asians and other non-white minorities in Britain, appears to be a tendency among some student activists in campus politics.

As suggested in the previous discussion, throughout its history, political blackness in its various social fields of operation has often been controversial and contested in the ways it disrupts naturalized racial reifications, multicultural representational politics, and the organization of different forms of race-based social struggles. Perhaps political blackness is best conceptualized from the perspective that Hazel Carby (1987:15) put forward in describing black British feminism, that it is "a problem and not a solution, as a sign that should be interrogated, a locus of contradiction." The problematizing of political blackness and racial terminology in Britain is itself a dynamic antiracist social movement tension that generates inquiry into contradictions and hierarchies that emerge among oppressed communities themselves. Through these critical practices, the ground of solidarity and movement building is potentially also strengthened.

In the context of the history of projects that support victims of racial violence, and state racism-monitoring organizations such as NMP, however, political blackness has been critical to mobilizing solidarities in multi-ethnic and multireligious contexts. To assess the relevance and viability of political blackness in the field of confronting white racial violence and racialized state violence, particularly in light of the changes wrought by the War on Terror, I turn to the perspectives and life-history reflections of an NMP activist whose involvement in the organization from the 1980s to the 2010s witnessed multiple moments of the composition and recomposition of political blackness.

Cilius Victor is an African Caribbean activist in his fifties, who grew up in Newham. He works as a computer programmer in central London and has been active in antiracist struggles across the country since his teens. He was a senior member of the NMP Management Committee, co-chair of the United Friends and Families Campaign, which deals with deaths in custody, and a board member of the Institute of Race Relations. Cilius's seniority, leadership, and considerable influence in the antiracist movement are based on his accumulated, extensive network of connections in the area of antiracism and his long-standing involvement.

Cilius narrated his turn toward antiracist activism as the slow evolution of a political blackness approach. In the process of becoming more involved in the spaces that facilitated black community activism, he described himself as gaining a more sophisticated understanding of what he termed the "subtle" manifestations of racism in his life. His earliest childhood memories of racism took shape around racial discrimination in schooling. This was a recollection that I often heard from other second-generation African Caribbean, African, and South Asian people in Newham who had grown up in the 1970s and 1980s.

Cilius related that his mixed primary school, Godwin Junior School in Newham, had a large black population in the 1970s, specifically of African Caribbean children. He remembered how the school would frequently polarize during recess into "black v. white" soccer games. He also recalled how his involvement as one of three black musicians in the school's otherwise all-white brass band provided disconcerting moments in band practice and when they traveled for competition around England. The presence of black people in rural areas and townships outside of London was considered an oddity. Cilius remembers that he and his friends received strange looks and questions. Whites would often wonder if they were celebrities, and white bandmates would subject them to name-calling. "Colgate!" was one familiar slur that Cilius recalled. (This particular insult was related to the stereotypical blackface images that were ubiquitously used in British Empire–era advertisements to promote toothpaste brands like Darkie, manufactured by the Colgate Company. The ads conveyed the message that the use of colonial hygiene products would aid in the empire mission of civilizing and literally cleaning dark-skinned Africans and Asians [see Ramamurthy 2003].) "You just let that wash over you, you never did anything, you never said anything," he explained.

As Cilius grew up, however, he became more aware of how race was constraining his life opportunities. On the whole, he argued that his growing up years were relatively safe in comparison to what he perceived to be more intense racial conflicts common for what he called his "African-American peers" in the United States.

Yet Cilius described going through the struggle against racial profiling occasioned by laws, such as "Sus" in the 1970s. The "Sus" laws allowed the police to stop and search people on the mere suspicion of criminal intent. The law became a key state-based policy to combat petty crime, such as mugging, and fueled a racialized panic around black "muggers" and criminality. Since then, African Caribbean males have been disproportionately cast as criminal elements who require police surveillance. Cilius reasoned that this police activity was also a way that black people were harassed to stay out of the tourist zones and symbolic capital zones of central London, and restricted to their "proper" place within the inner city.

"It was common knowledge among youngsters, fifteen, fourteen, you don't go to the West End because racially, as soon as you cross that boundary, east to west, you get arrested, you get nicked," he said. "That's what happened to black youngsters, and we were all conscious of that. I never went west as a young teenager because that was common currency."

Cilius today continues to work in the high-tech industry and maintains a highly active interest in Middle Eastern archaeology. He made the most of his talents, worked hard, and achieved conventional indicators of success. But his school years were also marked by the institutional dumbing-down of black students. He recalls academic segregation practices that selectively pushed black students into the bottom-rung non-science streams. Most of his black classmates, whom he described as "corralled" into nonacademic classes by the time they were eleven or twelve years old, did not have many opportunities to enter the sciences or have classes that put them on university tracks. "Typing was the most useful skill I left school with . . . which was useful in my later career with computer science since I could touch-type," he said.

At the age of sixteen or seventeen, however, Cilius encountered the novel *Black Boy* by Richard Wright as an extra assignment in his English class. This encounter was to have a significant impact on his consciousness. "You've got to remember that at the time anything written down black we gravitated towards because we weren't on television, we weren't around, we weren't visible externally in the white world," he added.

The encounter with a key literary text of black consciousness from across the Atlantic encouraged Cilius to get involved with African solidarity politics as soon as he left secondary school and entered the sixth form at East Ham College. East Ham College at the time was host to a number of Commonwealth scholarship students from the country then called "Rhodesia," now Zimbabwe. The contact with anticolonial African students and the ongoing struggle against the white supremacist regime of Ian Smith contributed to his growing awareness about the complexities of antiracist struggles and questions of black identity.

Cilius remembers that, at the time, even the African students were divided between two tendencies: one that categorically opposed the Smith regime, and one that argued for constructive collaboration and gradualist reforms. These complex politics and debates within African diasporic resistance introduced Cilius to nuanced understandings of multiple forms of politics that beckoned to young people of conscience at the time. Taking up a political position, therefore, meant more than assuming a predetermined, essentialist black identity. It also involved the need to negotiate a field of political identities within multiple ideological currents of diasporic African politics.

While his college years were characterized by an intense interest in the world beyond the inner city, Cilius recalls being scarcely aware of the local struggles in his own community. "I was still in Newham, and not yet engaged with the events taking place around me. Now this would have been the time of the Virk brothers and I had seen the riots on television."

On April 23, 1977, on St. George's Day, the far right National Front marched through the streets of London and on the same day five white youth racially abused and assaulted three South Asian brothers from the Virk family in front of their own homes in Newham. The brothers fought back and called the police, but when the police arrived, they did not arrest the white youths, but instead arrested the South Asian victims. The courts eventually found the brothers guilty of causing grievous bodily harm. Sukvinder Virk, aged seventeen, was sentenced to three months in a detention center while his older brothers were sentenced to a staggering three and seven years, respectively.

It was a time when many campaigns around the slogan "Self-Defence Is No Offence!" were erupting in response to the growing racist violence in Newham. New populations of stateless South Asians from Kenya and Uganda and other East African countries began to arrive in great numbers and added to the Indian, Pakistani, and African Caribbean communities already in Newham. The political hysteria against these newer arrivals spurred more mobilizations by the National Front, and racist harassment and attacks were commonplace (Thompson 1988).[7]

Similar uprisings took place in the inner cities of London and would climax with the Brixton rebellions in South London and elsewhere in the early 1980s. Cilius interpreted these events as interlinked, which quickened the development of his multiracial and political black consciousness. The contradiction between his identification with international Pan-African politics and his lack of awareness of race politics in his own neighborhood propelled him to search for analytical and practical ways to conjoin the numerous racial justice struggles he was encountering and with which he had begun to engage. As he studied international politics, he became more conscious of his missing connection to the struggles in Britain.

Upon finishing his sixth form, Cilius left London at the age of twenty and went to Wolverhampton Polytechnic near Birmingham. One of the main reasons for this decision was that he could be in a higher education setting with a large black population nearby—"the largest Rastafarian community in Europe," as he put it.

His initial involvement with other socially active students was in what he called a "culturalist organization" on campus, the Afro-Caribbean Society. He characterized his participation within this group as frustrating. The organization was largely oriented toward staging cultural variety nights and film shows, and it seemed to lack any connection to the racial violence and policing problems faced by black communities beyond the campus, in the inner cities of Birmingham itself. And after being engaged in transnational and diasporic anticolonial and anti-white supremacy struggles, Cilius found the society's lack of connection with international political issues, such as national liberation struggles in Africa, disappointing and bewildering too.

At this point, Cilius came into contact with a new social movement that was gathering momentum among the student body. A new black student organization, the National Black Student Alliance, had emerged on campus. The main group was at the University of Essex and it was in the process of forming itself as an autonomous entity within the national student movement. Drawn into the organization, Cilius attended a conference and encountered activists talking about a campaign called the "Newham 8."

Cilius recalled, "My ears just prick—I'm tuned in now because they're talking about my yard." It was also at this time that he met a Commonwealth student from Malaysia by the name of Jasbir Singh, who was canvassing nationally for the Newham 8 campaign. This resulted in Cilius's first major involvement with NMP. While affiliating with NMP, Cilius also returned to Wolverhampton for the remainder of his undergraduate years to organize a chapter of the National Black Student Alliance, which he recalls initially consisted of two South Asian women and a Jewish man.

In Cilius's time, however, black autonomy within the student movement typically meant departures from traditional coalition strategies with white students, and more in keeping with ways that recall the thesis put forward by Stokely Carmichael and Charles V. Hamilton (1967) in their classic text *Black Power*. Black student groups were arguing for restrictive membership, and wanted to create black-only political spaces in order to facilitate their own self-definitions and self-determined issues, agendas, and responses. This was in contrast to having to achieve these in negotiation with white liberal or white Marxist students who presumed progressive leadership, asserted the primacy of class-based identities and struggle, and subsumed questions of antiracism. However, both the white-dominated student movement, as well as a number of other ethnic minority groups who saw the strategy as separatist, opposed this position.

Cultural groups such as the Afro-Caribbean Society at Cilius's university objected because they had maintained a policy of open membership and cultivated the practice of encouraging broader white interest in their ethnic cultures. Such groups operated and still operate around a liberal theory that racism results from individual prejudice and ignorance, devoid of a political, structural, state, or racial group power dimension. Hence, their theory of antiracism argues that the promotion of deeper intercultural knowledge leads to better understanding among the races and thereby dissipates racism.

A group that termed itself "Pan-Africanist" also opposed the formation of the National Black Student Alliance, but on different grounds. Cilius recalled, "The Pan-Africanists had objected to the presence of a woman in a conference that the [alliance] organized who was of mixed Indian and African Caribbean background."

He explained, "They were questioning the African-ness of certain people who were at the meeting. . . . People are saying she is not black—this is for black people. So my thinking was, this is absurd, what are they talking about? I was first of all just perplexed by the argument. I wasn't angry, because I could not understand what they meant that she was not black. I am looking at her and I am saying what are we talking about? We ended up in a vicious argument about black and blackness. And these guys were basically mad. They were talking about genes, dilutions of blackness, and if this one bred with this one, and I'm saying this is crazy, this is nuts, who are these people?"

It was during the confusions arising out of this debate that Cilius went to seek the advice of Gus John, one of the leading activists in the African Caribbean community at the time, and a speaker at the conference. "So Gus John comes up and I take him to one side, explaining to him the battle that I had been having with these Pan-Africanists. Basically he agrees with me and says that it is really destructive. I am working my way now through the politics of being a member of the black community and asking, *where are you going with this?*"

Cilius's critiques of liberal culturalist groups and biological racial nationalists led him to opt for a third alternative: political blackness. The desire to bridge the gap between his transnational antiracist activism and the politics within his own local Newham context—his "yard," as he put it—pushed him to opt toward students who were organizing by a theory of political blackness.

"And had I not possibly gone to Essex, and been exposed to the arguments about being black as a political color as opposed to black as a genetic thing or African—remember I was a staunch Pan-Africanist—I had spent two years before with Africans in college talking about African liberation —it would have been very easy for me to travel down that line," Cilius reflected. "But when I heard the story of what happened to these Asian youths in Newham that these two Asian guys in Essex were talking about, I didn't really say this is not about me, this is not about black people," he recalled. "I said that this is something we have to deal with. It instinctively grabbed me that this was a one-ness that we have to deal with."

The student and anticolonial politics of the early 1980s also formatively influenced Cilius's sense of blackness, but not in a simple, mono-causal way. It is hard to agree with Stuart Hall's argument that the period of hegemonic unity across ethnic and cultural difference in the United Kingdom was a sign of the "the innocent notion of an essential black subject" (Hall 1996b: 443). There was no innocent black essentialism among African Caribbean, South Asian, and other marginalized non-white British communities in Newham, but, rather, a conscious history of solidarity making and joint struggles that arose from a political sensibility that appreciated their locally lived experience of white racial violence, state violence, and everyday political whiteness. The detailed histories of these local formations are occluded in contemporary British public consciousness. Hence, a generalized antiessentialist critique of political blackness has to be reexamined, given the contested and complex history of how such a black political consciousness emerged in different sites in Britain in the first place—through challenge, debate, and choice in the life trajectories of individual activists such as Cilius who grappled with a broad array of antiracist social movement contingencies and possibilities. These activists' embrace of political blackness was not an ingenuous, naïve default position or an "innocent notion."

Upon graduation from Wolverhampton, Cilius moved from Birmingham to Newcastle to take up an internship, also known as an industrial placement, and started to work for the local council there. The move to a different location in Britain away from the university campus in Birmingham brought him into contact with new kinds of antiracist issues that were specific to his own employment.

Cilius, now a qualified computer programmer, began this work when computer programming was a nascent field. His job brought him into contact with the workings of bureaucracies and the quite literal development of what today is called institutional racism. At the time, the Department of Health and Social Security was developing the first ethnic monitoring information systems for the local council in Newcastle, and Cilius was one of the programmers assigned to the task, largely, he reasons, due to his race.

In his computer programming work for the department, he witnessed the contradictions and limitations in the early forms of state antiracism. In those days, the state was instituting ethnic monitoring as a way to track diversity and to address questions of racial discrimination in employment. As a programmer, Cilius was instructed to create software that would track recruitment of ethnic minority staff.

Through his research, he identified a major problem in tracking recruitment—that of staff retention. Many black workers did not stay on the job, and the council was being perceived as an unwelcoming environment. His superiors shot down his attempts to convey these results and to propose software functions that would track retention rates in order to provide a more accurate picture of diversity issues. He was given stern orders not to create the software function that could provide a metric for ethnic minority staff retention rates. This way, the problem of black staff attrition could be concealed, and it was possible to publicly claim success in diversity recruitment. "It was a way to make the numbers of black people only go up, because it would appear that nobody ever left!" Cilius explained.

While working on this project at his day job, Cilius also helped establish a community-based police abuse and antiracist monitoring group in Newcastle. The project focused on working-class black communities living in Newcastle's infamous council estates. Racial inequities in social housing were glaringly apparent in the 1980s, as white families were routinely assigned superior housing, while immigrant and black families were given the leftovers—usually older, substandard, and decrepit accommodations.

In determining the social welfare provision of housing, some local councils even adopted policies that privileged relatives of current or former residents. Called the "sons and daughters" policy in public housing, these policies favored white British residents whose children were seeking housing. This seemingly race-neutral policy functioned as a de facto discriminatory tool against newly arrived immigrants and many second-generation black and Asian families, who could not claim kinship ties to long-standing social housing recipients.

During the period Cilius lived in Newcastle, he was involved in supporting a recently arrived group of Bangladeshi immigrants who were struggling to obtain public housing. Political blackness, which defines inclusion through one's lived experiences and concrete struggles against racial and state violence, was logically expanded to include this new group of Bangladeshi immigrants. The flexible and expansive ambit of black political identity also enabled Cilius to extend his organizing work to engage a community of mixed-race families whose children were being bullied in schools.

After a year in Newcastle, Cilius returned to London and became directly involved with NMP. He first formally joined the organization as a volunteer and then moved to its Management Committee, where he remained for the next ten years. Unlike some other NMP stalwarts, he did not become employed as a caseworker; he preferred to continue his career in computer programming in central London. However, he resettled in Newham and established his own residence in the Forest Gate neighborhood. As his activist involvement grew, he helped to found another antiracist body, the United Friends and Families Campaign, which continues to this day to work on campaigns for justice for the families of people killed in institutional custody—a disproportionate number of whom are of African or African Caribbean descent.

Both African Caribbean and South Asian youth in Newham in the 1970s and 1980s were targeted by white racial violence and state violence. African

Caribbean communities were more likely to be racially profiled by the police for criminal behavior than South Asian communities, while South Asians were more likely to be targeted for racial harassment and attacks. Both groups, however, were frequent targets of racial attacks and confronted local police who were likely to blame them, the actual victims. This often resulted in their arrests for public disorder offenses, or "affrays," when they had, in fact, simply defended themselves from attacks. Thus, these situations revealed the patterns of institutional racism that foiled protection, due process, or equal treatment.

The justice campaign for the Newham 7 (different from the earlier Newham 8 campaign) and the Justice for the Pryces campaign were the two major antiracist campaigns under way in Newham by the time that Cilius returned in 1985. On July 4, 1984, a group of white racists driving around in Newham carried out a spate of six random attacks against South Asians within a span of sixty minutes. The attackers used hammers and assaulted any South Asian person they encountered, including teenagers. A disabled youth was forcibly dragged into their car and brutalized. Panic-stricken and outraged South Asian residents later confronted the gang at the Duke of Edinburgh pub on Green Street. In the resulting violence, seven South Asian youth were arrested and spent weeks on remand, while the white attackers were given bail and eventually found guilty of the light offense of "common assault" and fined one hundred pounds. The police had taken a whole year to locate the white perpetrators and strenuously denied any racial motivation in the attacks. Following a lengthy trial, seven South Asian youth were convicted of public disorder. At the same time, however, the courts also recognized their actions not as "gang warfare" as the prosecution claimed, but as an exercise of the legal right to carry out a "pre-emptive strike in self defense" and in using reasonable force to prevent a crime (NMP 1985:24–38). The Newham 7 campaign was one of the most important campaigns of the 1980s in winning the right of the black community to defend itself in the face of brutal racial violence.

Also in 1984, on November 29, Eustace Pryce, a sixteen-year-old African Caribbean, was stabbed in his head outside Greengate pub on Barking Road as he and his brother, Gerald, went to aid some friends who had been racially attacked by a gang of youths. Eustace died from his wounds while Gerald, who had initially confronted the gang, was charged with public disorder. The white killer was eventually convicted only of manslaughter and not murder, and the police again tried to cast the events through the deracialized lens of "gang warfare" and a brawl (NMP 1985:39–44). Through joint public meetings, pickets, and demonstrations, the campaigns for the Newham 7 and Justice for the Pryces were symbolically and logistically fused. NMP worked hard to make outreach to South Asian and African Caribbean social, cultural, leisure, and religious organizations in order to mount mass mobilizations and protests. In the process, new and more intimate social relationships were formed between the two ethno-racial communities within Newham. On April 27, 1985, more than three thousand people gathered to march in support of the Justice for the Pryces campaign and the Newham 7—Self-Defence Is No Offence campaign.

Under these conditions, political blackness for Cilius was not reducible to an ethnological or boundary setting exercise. His life trajectory in antiracist activist work reveals a historically grounded engagement with multiple ethnic, racial, and religious minority communities because these were the actual communities he encountered who were suffering from racial violence and institutional racism in his "backyard."

His comfort with the shifting configurations of political blackness is perhaps best understood through the specific ways he translated global discourses of black power and black identity into the unfolding grassroots and justice-seeking campaigns against racial violence and state violence in the context of Newham.

As Cilius argued, "Communities experience racism differently in the sense that the practical, physical manifestation of what it deprives you of affects different groups in different ways. So, practical example—when I was growing up, the racism meted out lent itself to the stereotype that Asians were hard workers, shopkeepers, that their kids didn't really get into trouble and all the stuff about 'Sus' and policing was most associated with Afro-Caribbeans."

Cilius was referring to the police power to stop people on sight, which was utilized to racially profile African Caribbean people in the 1970s. It was subsequently repealed after the Brixton urban rebellions in 1981. "You transport the word 'Sus' to thirty years in the future, to now, where you have the antiterrorism legislation that is effectively 'Sus,' suspicion on sight because of what you look like focused now predominantly on Asians and Muslims," Cilius reasoned.

"The current hysteria around Muslims is one of the difficult scenarios we've been in," he added. "You tell someone that you need to support that person over there. They will say but he tried to blow up this building or this plane, are you mad? But then you have to say on what evidence?" Cilius argued. "People see the onslaught of the state. If you put your head up to say I will support this people—some supporters may say, 'I'm not ready for that kind of heat,' and keep quiet," he added.

Crucial to Cilius's understanding of the current divisions between Muslims and other racial and ethnic minorities suffering racism is the way that solidarity is thwarted through the repressive powers of the state and its authoritarian discourses. It is not simply a problem of ahistorical and naturalized representations of Muslim/non-Muslim incommensurability. "This problem runs right to the roots of NMP. Beyond Sus—the entire Muslim identity. The rhetoric behind Muslim is rhetoric behind the black community," Cilius reasoned.

His argument genealogically linked the collective profiling and surveillance of Muslims as potential terrorists to the collective profiling and surveillance of African Caribbean people as potential criminals. From the standpoint of social movement building, it is analytically important to recognize the homologous and related development of different racisms within British state policies and practices.

"These things go back and forth and it could easily switch back," Cilius continued. "So our communities, the different communities that make up the black community, experience the same onslaught in slightly different ways. The question is—is the difference enough to say that it is a completely different experience, that we have no points of connection and therefore have no interest to be connected? And I would say, no, that is not true. I would argue against that. I would turn it the other way around, what is it that is so different that says we don't have a point of interest? You still get arrested for no reason on the same basis of who you are and what you like and what we think you might do. Which is no different from what Sus used to do with Afro-Caribbean people," he concluded.

Cilius's analysis of racism, following a political blackness approach, finds points of connection between different forms and manifestations of racism. It is important to recognize the particularity of different racial experiences. At the same time, the mobilization of political blackness compels us to theorize how differential racisms in Britain are also historically and dynamically allied and affiliated. Hence, political blackness contributes a key insight into the color, culture, and religious identity dilemmas of antiracist organizing: it shows how the fear constructed by state repression is a critical factor in producing mutual isolation between suspect communities that are differently targeted, yet are all profiled.

Cilius also reflected on another changing context for racism, and that is the relative political invisibility of the racism that continues to affect African Caribbeans. He attributed this invisibility to emergent, mythic narratives of racial progress for African Caribbeans in Britain.

You could argue that if you take the number of lynchings that took place in America in 1938 and compare that to the number of lynchings that took place in 2001, that in hard numbers, the number is drastically different. But could you argue that things have got better for the black male when you compare the shootings downs by police or killings through the death penalty?

I have to say yes when the police in Britain say that they respond better to racial attacks now. Yes, because twenty years ago you did not even recognize the term while today you have things like the Racial Incidents squad, then in the broad framework of things—yes.

But thinking that this is progress also helps to subdue black people. So everyone is jumping up and down saying, oh look, you have black newscasters, black this and black that, black people advertising washing powder now! We're being told that things have got better, that we've been absorbed. You have to recognize when they've been concrete and unshakable steps forward, but you can't wrap it all up.

You have to pull it apart. What are we actually talking about? But when I look at our communities from a global scale—we have connections to other parts of the world and not just here in Newham—in the Caribbean, then you say no, you can't say that. If you're trying to persuade me that England, at the root core, is getting on top of this issue and genuinely trying to deal with itself or about Britishness, no way. My brother has a child, now this is the third generation born here, and the government still has fundamental problems in recognizing that black people are still here when they talk about having to integrate black people.

Cilius's critique of the state's citizenship, criminalization, and counterterrorism discourses (for example, about Muslim propensities for radicalization, or African Caribbean propensities for criminal behavior) is

understood as different elements within a complex equation of disempow-
erment. In many of my discussions and debates with Cilius, I would return
to the question of why it was necessary to continue the traditions, principles, and methodology of political blackness as a mode of antiracist activism
in Britain, despite its constraints. "Would it not be better to come up with
other idioms of antiracist struggle?"

"Let's go back to one of the guiding principles or concepts that I've
lived by—this concept of black," Cilius replied. "It is a very difficult line to
keep because this word 'black' is so damn strong. So I have to be careful
exactly in what context I say that because some of the people we try to help,
if I describe them as black would probably not understand what I really
mean by that."

An example Cilius referred to was a training session that I had participated in for new Emergency Service (ES) helpline volunteers. The twenty-
four-hour ES helpline was a hallmark attribute of NMP's presence in the
local community, as it provided full-time access for people who needed
immediate responses to police abuse and racial harassment. This service
would later close down.

The session had been organized by Titilayo Aloba, a fellow NMP caseworker, and drew people mainly from the African and specifically the Nigerian community with which she had ties. Other attendees included a
smaller number of South Asian volunteers. "At the NMP training session I
did use the term 'black' and then after I said that, I instantly said something
about all ethnic minorities in general, simply because in that environment
you're trying to unify people and actually it may not be a unifying core,"
Cilius said. "These things can destroy a campaign even before it gets off the
ground, even who turns up at your door wanting to help you. So you have
to acquiesce to the way the community currently operates because they feel
comfortable with somebody from their own particular background," he
continued.

"But the question is this," Cilius declared. "If political blackness is so
damn difficult, why do you keep it? This is the argument: just let it go.
A reasonable argument. But I'm an old dinosaur simply because I don't
fundamentally agree with dividing people up in their ethnic bits and pieces.
That does not mean that I don't recognize that people come from different
backgrounds, but in the struggle we are engaged in, the end product of
where this goes is people being divided into their own little constituent
groups to get what's coming to them," he said.

"The struggle then shifts to getting our slice for our people instead of talking of how you're going to transform society rather than getting a bigger portion for ourselves," he argued. "I'm a minority but I also still think that fundamentally we have to come back to this issue if we're going to advance as a group of people," he said. "Why Afro-Caribbean people are sometimes resistant to the notion of a wider black consciousness is that the past is so much about telling them that they don't exist as a group of people, that you're chattel, you're not even human, that you're the missing link between humanity and the apes, so for them they don't want anybody else encroaching on what they have spent quite a lot of blood struggling to grab for themselves," Cilius explained.

"But the practical reality for NMP in its work is that we don't have time for these arguments with the very people we're trying to help. Why? In the heat of the moment this is not what they want to hear, some intellectual argument. In the heat of the moment they want the police off their backs or they want to know who killed their son or daughter."

Conclusion

Endings and Beginnings

The British state plays a critical role in the social processes of racialization and the maintenance of racial hierarchies. State policies and practices, such as institutional racism, anticrime policing violence, ineffectual enforcement of antidiscrimination statutes, and legalized racial profiling in counter-terrorism, intersect with the construction of white British nativism and supremacy in everyday and institutional terms. In addition, the British state constructs adverse material conditions for any sustainable resistance against these racialized hierarchical patterns and tendencies.

Historically, the state's orientation toward politically black social movements has been antagonistic. A prime example of this is the state's stance toward independent community-based police and racism-monitoring groups such as the Newham Monitoring Project (NMP). NMP's militant pressure politics and racial justice advocacy on behalf of individual victims of racism, and its practice of mobilizing conjoined solidarity and direct action among African, African Caribbean, South Asian, Muslim, and other minority communities in Newham, have earned the ire of state institutions like the Metropolitan Police and Newham's municipal government. As an example, in 2014, a police whistle-blower who was working for a covert police program revealed that superiors had ordered him to infiltrate and collect intelligence on "black justice campaigns," including the Justice for Jean Charles de Menezes campaign organized by NMP (Blowe 2013; Evans and Dodd 2014).

Political surveillance and efforts to undermine black political groups are not new. Robin Bunce and Paul Field (2017) successfully declassified official archives that revealed the existence, between 1967 and the 1970s, of the "Black Power Desk" in Scotland Yard. Set up by a Labour Home Secretary, Roy Jenkins, the covert police operation worked to undermine black social movement organizations and leaders. Black Power activism in the 1970s was able to win the "first judicial acknowledgement of racial prejudice inside the Metropolitan Police" and assert the rights of black communities to legally engage in self-defense, without fear of criminalization, when confronted with white racial harassment and attacks (Cawthorne 2017). And yet the state has continued to utilize repression and political surveillance against such democratic struggles. A 2013 Freedom of Information request filed by an NMP activist, Kevin Blowe, in relation to the disclosure of the existence of the state's surveillance files on the group, was met with an official response of "neither confirm or deny," on the grounds of protecting national security.[1]

The liberal state's ambivalence and hostility toward black social movements, however, have also been reflected in the less covert but far more damaging pattern of gradually disappearing the public funding streams that support civilian-based police monitoring and projects that support victims of racial harassment. The contradiction of a declining public policy interest in combating racial violence and institutional racism, even when both are increasing in Britain, can be explained by the way that the contemporary British "performance of stateness" (Thiranagama 2011) has shifted toward centering white British nativism and national security in the War on Terror. These intertwined discursive frames help to drive the British state's retreat from antiracist justice and racial equality. Consequently, for NMP, the ease of being able to obtain and sustain the material resources needed for its operations, whether through direct public funding or through public foundations and charity-based funding, was tenuous at best and, in the 2010s, became sporadic and unreliable.

Black antiracist groups such as NMP initially broke into the British public sphere with the help of funding provided during the left wing–controlled Greater London Council (GLC) that governed between 1981 and 1986, at which time the Conservative government under Margaret Thatcher abolished it. This era, often referred to as the high point of "municipal socialism" and "municipal feminism" (Fisher 2012; Virdee 2014), led to the funding of numerous grassroots-led social equality projects. GLC-based antiracism support also emerged during the aftermath of the eruption of a number of significant urban rebellions in inner cities in London in 1981 and 1985 (termed the Brixton "riots" by the press). It was in this period that the GLC first provided funding to newly formed black community self-defense groups such as NMP (Rowe 2004:125).

The opposition-controlled local state governments then regarded investment in the political capacity building of racial and ethnic minority communities as a good thing, or the lesser of two evils, particularly in contrast to the specter of widespread social disorder and unrest. The black groups that emerged in this period were often city- and borough-based community self-defense groups, which sprang up all across London and in other major urban centers. NMP in the east and The Monitoring Group in the west were the longest-surviving organizations of this type in London.

The advent of neoliberal retrenchment and privatization of public services in the 1990s, however, made funding for racial harassment projects and police accountability groups scarce. These community-based organizations, which were unafraid to publicly criticize or stage pickets and protests against local councils and police forces, were a source of embarrassment to state authorities who preferred what they considered more respectable forms of community consultations. Tensions between NMP and Newham Council were constant throughout NMP's history, but the council continued to directly fund the operations of the group until 1997, when the election of New Labour saw the abrupt cancellation of NMP's funding (Hamid 1997). As the *Evening Standard* reported,

> The Blairite council has attacked the group for wasting public money and taking on political campaigns which go way beyond its remit of working for local people. NMP used £1,300 of public money to fly the body of a man who died in police custody home to Gambia. It spent £466 on a staff party, paid for a member of staff out of petty cash and paid for taxis and coaches to go to demonstrations as far away as Birmingham. . . . The final straw for Newham councilors was NMP adverts in local papers warning residents not to vote for the BNP [British National Party—a far-right political party] in a by-election. (Waugh 1997:17)

Newham Council wanted an antiracist organization that would not engage in direct action tactics and intervene in electoral politics. The council also preferred an organization that would set limits on its definition of care for the black community to those individuals with a strict citizenship status, even as it profited from the resettlement of asylum seekers like Ibrahim Sey, the Gambian man killed by the police. Following the cancellation of NMP's funding, the council eventually subcontracted its racial harassment support services to a private company called ALERT. This company's founders were former police officers and the enterprise folded after a short-lived period. Newham Council did not then find a replacement.

NMP activists interpreted the 1997 separation from local council funding as a mixed blessing. While funding uncertainties made the scale of its work shrink (the number of paid personnel, for example, was reduced and its well-known storefront office location was forced to move in order to lower rental costs), NMP activists agreed that the separation granted them greater critical independence to monitor state agencies. NMP's method of engaging both formal institutional channels and extra-institutional modes of protest politics was often cited as the main reason that Newham's city council deemed it too militant to be a suitable partner for community-oriented policing, or for inclusion in neoliberal public-private social service partnerships for municipal governance. For NMP, the dual strategy of engaging both institutional and extra-institutional political processes kept open a range of resistance options and an independence of action from bureaucratic or other constraints of respectability politics.

After the elimination of direct local government funding, NMP turned to grant awards from philanthropic foundations, principally the National Lottery and its Reaching Communities funding program. The Reaching Communities program had a funding stream that aimed to support third-sector (voluntary) organizations that provided services for socially disadvantaged groups. This new public policy framework included antiracist and antidiscrimination services no longer directly provided for by the state or private sector vendors. The program, however, was "ten times over-subscribed" (House of Commons Public Administration Select Committee 2008:285). Nevertheless, due to the work of NMP's director, Estelle du Boulay, the organization was successful in securing several grants until the advent of austerity politics. The Conservative–Liberal Democrat coalition that formed the national government between 2010 and 2015 made draconian spending cuts to social equality projects, and the trend continued with the 2015 election of the Conservative Party majority government. Antidiscrimination projects have suffered dramatic cutbacks, as have other social services, legal aid services, and the work that the voluntary sector undertakes to fill gaps in social services that the state is "unable or unwilling" to provide (House of Commons Public Administration Select Committee 2008:4).

The retrenchment of social services affected NMP's work in numerous ways. For example, the declining investment in public housing led to situations where people targeted for ongoing racial harassment and attacks in their homes could not secure alternative housing allocations from the local council, the entity statutorily tasked with providing safe accommodations.

In 2015, NMP caseworkers told me of desperate victims of racial harassment who had resorted to sleeping in NMP's offices because they had nowhere else to go.

The absorption of the Commission for Racial Equality into the generalized Equalities and Human Rights Commission (EHRC) also diminished the British state's focus on official antiracism. State-based antiracism in Britain was made into law through the 1965, 1968, and 1976 Race Relations acts. These laws made crimes of racist harassment and attacks. The 2000 Race Relations (Amendment) Act extended the de jure provision of nondiscriminatory service and positive duties toward promoting racial equality to apply to the police and other state agencies. Many NMP activists, however, were not fond of the whitewashing politics of the EHRC and its head, Trevor Phillips. In 2009, Phillips used his position to declare that London's Metropolitan Police was free from institutional racism. As he put it, "The Lawrence inquiry touched a deeper nerve when it accused the police of 'institutional racism'—a badge of shame that has hung over the service ever since. So today, ten years on, is the accusation still valid? I don't think so." He further declared Britain as "by far the best place in Europe to live if you are not white" (Phillips 2009). Such authoritative pronouncements were woven through a triumphalist (and nascent Euro-skeptic) nationalist narrative of British exceptionalism, and this narrative of racial progress necessarily muted the voices and standpoints of the victims of racial violence and racialized state violence.

When the force of austerity politics started to hit in 2012, the new EHRC budget and workforce were halved and the government was concomitantly "stripped of its duty to promote a society with equal opportunity" (Ramesh 2012). In light of allegations of financial impropriety, Phillips was fired. Antiracist activists and policy researchers whom I talked to expressed their alarm at how these policy changes resulted in what they perceived as the active "de-skilling" of antiracist activism and a loss of advocacy knowledge for racial, religious, and ethnic minority communities. Robert Berkeley, a former director of the Runnymede Trust, a leading research institute focusing on race issues, explained in a personal interview the ideological justifications behind austerity policy cuts on organizations like the Trust and other antiracist groups: "The new discourse is purportedly color-blind. If you do race analysis you are segregationist and racist yourselves."[2] He added that the public spending cuts effectively shut down public discussion of racism and racial equality as national priorities.

The state's ideology of retrenching antidiscrimination projects influenced the funding priorities of charities and foundations as well. In the 2010s, NMP struggled hard to secure its customary National Lottery funding for racial harassment and police abuse casework. Additionally, other charity foundations turned down most of NMP's grant applications. These public spending cuts and nonprofit-sector abandonment of antiracism ironically came at the very same time when race and religiously based hate crimes were rising sharply in London and in Britain as a whole. Even before the explosion of Brexit-related racial violence (Burnett 2016), racially and religiously aggravated harassment crimes, which are largely nonphysical incidents, had been on the rise. In a study of forty-one of forty-three police forces in Britain, the number of reported hate crimes in the nation were more than 47,000 for the three-year period between 2012 and 2015 (Stupples 2015). In London, the Metropolitan Police recorded a 60 percent spike in hate crimes over the same three-year period. A majority of the police forces in England and Wales in that same period saw a rise in the number of racial and religious hate crimes in their districts as well.

In 2013, a report by the Independent Police Complaints Commission concluded that even fifteen years after the Macpherson Royal Commission of Inquiry into its racist practices, the Metropolitan Police still failed to deal with the problem of racist behavior of police officers, and there was "an unwillingness or inability to deal with these [race] complaints robustly and effectively. Too often, complaints are dismissed without proper investigation or resolution, complainants are not properly engaged with, and lessons are not learnt" (2013a, 2013b). Momentum has slowed on state-based antiracism, which had been a brief municipal and national state concern in the 1980s. Official antiracist policies were jettisoned in favor of less contentious and more celebratory multicultural policies during the 1990s. By the 2000s, state-based antiracism was a residual policy concern, as the question of how to protect racial and ethnic minorities against racism was substituted with panics about the socio-cultural integration of minorities themselves ("community cohesion") and the expansion of counterterrorism programs. Antiracism, as a state-based policy paradigm, is rarely even a mention in the state's post-Brexit discourse.

The difference in the political economy of antiracism as compared to counterterrorism is staggering. In dramatic contrast to declining funding for antiracism and racial equality, funding for domestic counterterrorism policing alone has risen exponentially to 670 million pounds for 2016–17

(House of Commons Home Affairs Committee 2016:3). In 2015, the Conservative government announced a total increase of "counter-terrorism spending up to £15.1bn from £11.7bn over the course of the next parliament [5 years]" (Barber 2015). By design, this spending increase will expand national security-based state activity "across government departments, including the Home Office, intelligence services and defence" (Barber 2015). Since 2003, the British state has also implemented the Prevent strategy to "stop people becoming terrorists and supporting terrorism" and has created antiradicalization programs such as the controversial Channel and Prevent Professional Concern programs that impose a statutory duty on schools, universities, and health care providers, including doctors and psychologists, to monitor people whom the state considers to be at risk for future adoption of terroristic ideologies (Open Society Justice Initiative 2016). The Prevent strategy is not geared toward reasonable suspicions of imminent acts of terrorism, but toward surveillance to predict possible "radicalization."[3] Between 2011 and 2015 some 150 million pounds have been spent on the prevention of radicalization schemes, and each local municipality has received allocations to carry out these new legal duties (Home Office 2015a). Newham Council itself received more than one million pounds between 2009 and 2012, which it spent on counterterrorism programs with questionable human rights standards. This counterterrorism state funding arrived during a period when over 106 million pounds had been cut from the municipality's budget between 2010 and 2015 (Newham Council 2015b). The 2016–17 budget allocation alone required a cut of fifty million pounds.

Ironically, however, these counterterrorism programs are represented as substituting for social welfare services such as health, youth, sport, recreation, and library services. The state's repressive and surveillance-based counterterrorism discourse is couched in soft social service language. For example, counterradicalization programs are purported to "support individuals who are vulnerable to recruitment, or have already been recruited by extremists" (Open Society Justice Initiative 2016:23). Additionally, these programs are said to "improve resilience to extremism" and facilitate forums for "young people to engage in discussions on radicalization and extremism" (Office for Public Management 2010).

This intensive shift toward counterterrorism policies and programs in liberal governance combined with a retreat from antidiscrimination social objectives finally proved too much for a casework-driven and campaigning antiracist group like NMP. In August 2015 the group dismantled its thirty-five-year-old presence in Newham. Its office at the Harold Road Community Center was closed. Workers boxed up its small and wonderful community education library. They also shredded papers, campaign posters, and records. The organization's archives, however, were provided to the May-Day Rooms educational charity (2017), an "active repository, resource and safe haven for social movements, experimental and marginal cultures and their histories." Caseworkers wrapped up their outstanding cases and current cases abruptly ended. Some of these cases involved critical issues such as the rise in "gang"-related policing and the ongoing, disproportionate targeting of black communities under the police's renewed stop-and-search powers. The possibility of rebounding or resurrecting the organization, as had occurred following the local council abolishment of its modest but peak annual budget of 158,000 pounds in 1995, is remote.

In the wake of the final demise of a key antiracist organization like NMP, it is fair to ask whether its failure derived from the contradictions of the organization's reliance on state and philanthropic funding. The rise of austerity economics may have been the final straw, but the state grant-based and charity-sector model of funding racial justice projects also encourages organizations to drift toward a dangerous dependency. As Adjoa Florência Jones de Almeida has argued,

> We as activists are no longer accountable to our constituents or members because we don't depend on them for our existence. Instead, we've become primarily accountable to public and private foundations as we try to prove to them that we are still relevant and efficient and thus worthy of continued funding. . . . In theory, foundation funding provides us with the ability to do the work—it is supposed to facilitate what we do. But funding also shapes and dictates our work by forcing us to conceptualize our communities as victims. (Jones de Almeida 2007:186–87)

The NMP model of antiracist activism attempted to address the contradictions of the victim paradigm by going beyond service-oriented individual casework and embracing solidarity-based direct action strategies. In the process of moving from casework to campaigns, as the organization had done in Gillian's police abuse case or with Abdul Kahar and Abul Koyair in the Forest Gate Antiterror Raid, the NMP model was based on the theory that its purpose was to facilitate processes through which marginalized people could transform themselves from victims into social change agents who would utilize their lived experiences to construct antiracist resistance and social movements.

The model required at least a modicum of funding to pay skilled case-workers and effective grant writers (who were often paid irregularly). Without the possibility of funding, it is very unlikely that robust case-by-case advocacy through the liberal juridical system over issues such as everyday forms of racial harassment, racial violence, and police abuse can continue. Singular eruptions of protest over these issues are important as they help to disrupt the normalization of racism. But these uprisings and other acts of rebellion are no substitute for the daily work necessary to pursue practical remedies for individuals suffering from racial violence or state violence. And it also does not replace the years of campaigning and pressure politics that often are required to make changes to state policies and practices. For thirty-five years NMP was able to navigate and survive the funding and nonprofit conundrum that is common to many social movement organizations. But it was ultimately unable to break free of the dependence on state-based and philanthropic streams of financing. The question of how to alternately fund and sustain independent social movement organizations is still unclear. Following NMP's cessation, individual activists involved in the group were able to transition to other nonprofits such as the global anti-poverty organization War on Want, the national Network for Police Monitoring (Netpol), feminist groups such as Rights for Women, as well as civil liberties and human rights–oriented legal practices.

The resistance spaces created by political blackness in Britain enable justice-seeking connections that are constructed across differently racial-ized and ethnicized oppressions. As the stories in this ethnography illustrate, racism and white supremacy affect multiple communities in both differential and overlapping ways. Solidarity-based analysis and theories have the potential to socially emerge and become real when communities and activists find opportunities to practically engage in each other's struggles against racism. As a project of political blackness, the NMP space for me, and for many others, facilitated opportunities to practice concrete interracial, interethnic, intergender, and interreligious solidarity that went beyond the mutual disaffections, divisions, and unequal social relationships that otherwise characterize segmented and hierarchical western social orders.

My work as an activist anthropological researcher was to directly participate in the lived experience of political blackness in Britain and to record
the collaborative struggle against white racial violence and state violence
that this political tradition engendered. Political blackness is an inter-
minority and race-based social struggle that through its very practice challenged and transformed everyday reified and racialized social relationships
into temporary egalitarian and cooperative forms. C. R. Hensman (1992:
163), the late Sri Lankan Tamil transnational activist and onetime member
of the Institute of Race Relations in Britain, explained that "humans must
be related to be known. If there is human-related care . . . or if there is
human-like thought and creativity, it has to be learnt only in a relationship,
through mutually self-revelatory action."

For these mutually self-revelatory processes to take place, the building
of organizational spaces and social movement projects is critical. NMP's
care-based casework, campaigns, and solidary-building protest politics now
represent a critical archive of political blackness in Britain. The meaning of
this history does not lie in resolving once and for all the question of British
racial and ethnic terminology. Rather, it is situated in what João Costa
Vargas terms "the revolutionary component of Blackness" where activists
continue the restless search for and experimentation with "theories and
practices that project a nonhierarchical life world, one that does not depend
on tropes of difference associated with vertical scales of power and humanity" (Vargas 2010:138).

Will this legacy of political blackness in Britain become renewed or will
it be made to disappear, as one detractor has argued, into the "dustbin of
history"?[4] The question is not something that can be decided a priori. Walter Rodney (1990:86), a key twentieth-century anticolonial theorist of
African-Asian solidarity, made clear that "the sheer weight of analysis will
not itself make that position become valid. As you make your revolution,
the theory on which a practice was based has to be taken seriously." The
future of political blackness will rest on whether new generations critically
rediscover the archives of political blackness and then renew or discourage
this particular tradition of resistance.

As an activist and anthropology researcher who participated in political
blackness, I cannot agree with the "stand aside" or "stand above" objectivist
and positivistic premises of value-free social science. The dispassionate
standpoint of avoiding the "trap of a speaking position which ultimately
can be reduced to a form of advocacy" is untenable in antiracist research

(Back and Solomos 2001:386). Accountability to the multiple communities who suffer from the continuous cycles of white racial violence and the persistence of institutional racism necessitates ethnographic research and writing that align with the work of reenergizing solidarity and resistance.

The deployment of vigilant antiracist analysis of the white-aligned British state is also an important legacy. For example, in 2013, NMP's diligent monitoring of the state exposed how Newham Council had redacted the concept of racism from its official reports and state policy discourse. NMP activists examined a draft copy of Newham's Council document *Equalities and the Local Development Framework in Newham: December 2010* and found many instances where the council had made a "series of deletions and comments appear to reveal a pattern of targeting references to racism within the report and attempting to replace them with ambiguous terminology to downplay their significance" (NMP 2013). The council's report claimed to have carried out public consultations to ascertain the main social equality issues for Newham's youth. However, in NMP's examination of the report, it discovered that its authors substituted the public's references to racism with the British state's preferred color-blind or postracial policy speak.

For example, in the draft text that initially read, "Significantly, racism is within their top 3 issues facing Newham, just behind crime and the availability of jobs," the editor deleted the word "racism" and refashioned the sentence to read, "Crime, the availability of jobs and issues relating to promoting community cohesion are the top 3 issues facing Newham" (NMP 2013). The order in which the issues were listed also reemphasized the crime and law-and-order discourse at the expense of racism, which was now made to disappear into the framework of community cohesion. In its press release on this issue, NMP vigilantly criticized Newham Council's surreptitious act of racism denial.

> The edit mark-up in the Equalities Framework report shows an unmistakable pattern of downplaying or deleting references to racism. This is an appalling situation, which leads us to only one conclusion: that Newham Council has deliberately and cynically tried to push race off the agenda. The council has a duty to accurately report levels of inequality in the borough, instead it appears to have attempted to mislead the public by whitewashing the issue of racism.

If this is the case, it calls into question the legitimacy of Newham Council's agenda of recent years following the publication of this document, promoting policies of integration and cohesion as if they had public backing. These policies have been widely criticized locally for avoiding to address and deprioritize pressing issues of racism. They have resulted in a number of moves including the withdrawal of foreign language papers and cuts to translation and interpreting services. The outcome of this leaves black communities, suffering racism without recognition or support and left to spiral downwards, facing greater discrimination and greater levels of marginalization and deprivation. All communities should rightly be up in arms about this if it is proven there has been a calculated approach to undermine the representation of their needs by the public servants elected to represent them. (NMP 2013)

NMP's voice was not directed at simply representing a culturally homogeneous black community but, through analysis and activism, it created a ground for agreement against the processes of everyday political whiteness in liberal governance. Britain's racial, religious, and ethnic minority communities might not all self-identify as black. Or, they might even be against the ideology of political blackness. But their issues and interests were always imagined as included in the resistance and advocacy agendas of a group like NMP.

At this historical juncture, it is useful to ask what within the NMP experience opens new possibilities for reinvigorating antiracist resistance in Britain? The theory and praxis of political blackness as a form of dissident racial subjectivity confound dominant media and academic modes by which we understand the political imaginations and priorities of racial, religious, and ethnic minorities. Gerd Baumann (1996:1) has argued that the dominant British public sphere frequently seeks to "tribalize" racial minority social actors through "ethnic reductionism" where "whatever any Asian informant was reported to have said or done [is] interpreted with stunning regularity as a consequence of their 'Asianness,' their ethnic identity, or 'culture of their community.'" These hegemonic representations marginalize political blackness formations and voices from the dominant public sphere. Political blackness, however, also reappears in different guises and in alternative cultural realms.

The NMP-linked activist Benjamin Zephaniah illustrates one example of the diffusion of political blackness beyond the realm of community-based local activism. Zephaniah is a poet, musician, children's writer, and antiracist activist of Barbadian and Jamaican descent. He is one of the most popular and publicly visible performance poets in Britain and was declared as one of the *Times'* (2008) fifty greatest postwar writers. Zephaniah, who describes his style as "street politics" (Zephaniah, Hajdukowicz, and Sotinel 2011), has been deeply involved in multiple black British social movements—from the pivotal Handsworth Arts Movement in Birmingham, to community-based organizing around police abuse, to self-defense campaigns against racial violence in London. He was a long-time patron of NMP and he also has family ties to the Justice for Michael Powell campaign. Powell, Zephaniah's cousin, suffered from bouts of depression and was killed in 2003 by the West Midlands police who responded to Powell's mother's call for assistance. All the white police officers involved in the killing by asphyxiation were acquitted of criminal wrongdoing in 2006 (Zephaniah 2006).

In 2007, Zephaniah made an online-released music video entitled *Rong Radio*, based on his published poem and song of the same name, which was first released on the 2005 album *Naked* (by Little Indian Records). The establishing shot of the music video *Rong Radio* sets the mise-en-scène through the image of a "racially ambiguous" (Harpalani 2013) but clearly marked non-white man waiting at a train platform. The man is disheveled and unshaven and, while dark-skinned in the British context, is most likely to be racially interpellated as a South Asian or Muslim-looking subject. The figure in the video appears lonely and emotionally distraught as he waits to board the train.

The narrative arc of *Rong Radio,* as revealed in Zephaniah's poem, which he recites throughout the video, depicts a man returning from prison, traveling through London's subways and arriving at the home of his lover. In the video, Zephaniah creates a parallel between himself and the South Asian/Muslim-looking character. As Zephaniah speaks about his own struggles with internalized racism, critiquing the emotional and psychic damage of social phobias against African Caribbean males, the video often cuts to the Muslim-looking man who carries a mysterious package under his arm, an image that frequently conjures up anxieties concerning the imminent threat of terrorism.

The Muslim-looking man is framed against a background where a normative middle-class white male, dressed in a professional suit and carrying a briefcase, is going to work. The Muslim-looking man's early morning appearance is contrasted to the work identity inhabited by the ideal of the employed, middle-class, or professional white male, securely ensconced in the world of material respectability. As Zephaniah narrates the lines "I waz beginning to believe dat all black men were bad men," the corresponding images of the Muslim-looking subject create a double articulation of blackness, where the social figure of the non-normative male subject/enemy/deviant is coded as both African Caribbean and South Asian/Muslim.

The conjoined representation of abject blackness that is ascribed to Zephaniah as a criminalized African Caribbean subject, and the representation of the South Asian/Muslim-looking subject, provides an overlapping "politics of articulation" (Hall 1996a:118). As the video progresses, an analysis of comparative racialization and a critique of the War on Terror is invoked as part of Zephaniah's self-critique:

I waz beginning to believe dat all Moslems were terrorist
An Christian terrorists didn't exist,
I really did believe dat terrorism couldn't be done by governments,
Not our governments, not white governments,
I just could not see what waz rong wid me
I gave hungry people hamburgers you see,
I waz beginning to believe dat our children were better dan
Their children,
Their children were dying from terrorism
But I couldn't hear their children call
An a child from Palestine simply couldn't count at all,
What despair? No children
I waz not aware
      I've been listening to de rong radio station.

The music video then splices sequences of the Muslim-looking man's homeward journey with flashbacks of torture scenes, citing images associated with the Abu Ghraib and Guantanamo prisoner abuses. The implication here is that, while imprisoned, the Muslim-looking man himself has been subjected to such tortures. Rather than situating these violations within the dominant white, western frameworks of the unruly terrorist or Muslim-looking person, the video seeks to rehumanize the figure of the Muslim subject. This is accomplished through the construction of a solidarity-based analysis of racism and engendering co-identification through a shared blackness.

Rong Radio continues a long tradition of counter-stories that can be told within the context of racial and state violence in Britain. In this vein, and through the received tradition, the future of political blackness as a cultural-political process and as an uncompromising vision of entangled and mutual liberation can find new beginnings. Political blackness therefore requires a non-positivistic conception of struggle; it is not bound by what is already established as an immovable limit on identity or terminology. The unfolding processes of being the object of the process of racialization and racism and becoming the subject of racism's negation are not separable. Racialized political subjectivities do not naturally occur in a single or predetermined form. The emergence of new forms of racial and political subjectivity, centered on confronting the roots of white racial violence and racialized state violence in Britain, will depend on the type of antistructural projects, mobilizational strategies, and social movement solidarities and identities that are actively initiated in the social field.

By participating within NMP's political blackness I developed a many-sided consciousness of the experience of racial and state violence in Britain. The necessity of participating in making social change in immediate and practical terms with people similar to and different from me produced a daily awareness of racism as a totalizing social relationship that was greater than the sum of its parts.

Such a holistic antiracist standpoint, however, cannot seek to dissolve into slogans or grand theories and stage an escape from the concrete problems of effective day-to-day struggle. Antiracists in Britain must answer serious practical questions: How do we stop the ongoing scourge of racial attacks? How do we stop the sexual assaults of the police against black women? How do we interrupt the intersectional oppressions of racial domination and gender domination, as they emerge interlocked within subordinated racial, religious, and ethnic minority communities? How do we stop the harassment of women wearing the hijab on the streets? How do we disrupt the state's expansive juridical regimes of surveillance, torture, and violence that are proliferating within the War on Terror? How do we stop the dismemberment of diasporic refugee and asylum-seeking families? We are compelled to create practical everyday answers to these many-sided questions of antiracism rather than to leave them as intergenerational grief to be passed down.

The ethnographic account presented in this study is composed of a limited set of stories about the pain and screams that emanate from the racism that occurs when the antiterror police, trigger-happy and ready to dole out death-dealing violence, smash their way into an innocent Muslim family's home as they sleep; when one black woman's son is rendered mute by hearing his mother insulted as a "Paki-whore," "wog's meat," "black cunt"; when another black woman looks out of her kitchen window and wonders if yet another police officer is going to be coming to assault and sexually molest her; or when a Muslim woman sets out in the morning dressed in a hijab and worries about being greeted by harassment, insults, assaults, and confinements.

Stories, as opposed to ossified political positions and reified certainties, only require that we listen and thus begin the rediscovery of our inter-subjective contingency. The "imagination to listen," as Mariana Mora (2003) points out, is an important component of progressive political prac-tice and it can alter our received notions of what it means to struggle, where we think the struggle is located, and where we assume there are no points of struggle. Listening, as an activist practice, further opens up a path to realizing a phenomenological form of interconnected dignity and human-ity. Accordingly, the impact of listening strengthens our capacity for multi-sided negotiations and negations of domination and oppression. That is, rather than seeking a dismissive ground above the subjective horrors of suffering, we must be moved so as to ground our theorizing from the stand-point of the multiple screams we tune into with our listening.

As an activist anthropologist in east London, I learned that developing the capacity for listening to people's screams and becoming accountable to their sufferings and hopes for justice evolved my own subjective parame-ters. The question of what to do was never an abstraction or an anachro-nism that could be reflected upon in tranquility or through received foreclosures of identity. Instead, the task of making connections between the different screams and thereby developing an adequate and expansive consciousness became the ground of constructing my own autonomy in a daily world full of people, some very similar and some very different from myself. What theorization, therefore, will enable antiracists to build their own capacity and power for both their short- and long-term struggles against violent and interlocking forms of racial domination? To privilege, in the end, the political question of antiracism, rather than abstract theory building for its own sake, is to become grounded again in the practices of practical and engaged solidarity.

Antiracism in Britain will need to continue to grapple with the task of creating political protagonists out of researchers, activists, and communities who confront racialized violence and state violence, as well as the normalized processes of everyday political whiteness that work to block access to justice. Ongoing white racial violence and the continuation of the state's discriminatory discourses in anticrime and counterterrorism operations will require it.

Twenty-one years after Ibrahim Sey was killed by the Newham police through suffocation and spraying of CS gas at close range, another young black man and a father, Edir Frederico (Edson) Da Costa, was similarly killed in an instance of excessive force and the use of CS gas during a police stop-and-search. On June 25, 2017, demonstrators again took to the streets of Newham with placards that read "How Many More???" (Rawlinson 2017).

In the same month, thirty-three years after white racists drove around in a car and attacked South Asians in Newham with hammers, a white British man knocked on Jameel Mukthar and Resham Khan's car window and threw acid on their faces and bodies. The two cousins had been celebrating Resham's twenty-first birthday when they were attacked. Jameel was put into an induced coma as he was treated for his excruciating injuries, while his cousin underwent skin grafts. The attack occurred in the context of four other acid attacks that had taken place in the area on the same day and amidst a growing perception in east London that Muslim-looking people were becoming targeted for revenge attacks in the War on Terror (Hartley-Parkinson 2017; Lusher 2017).[5]

Disclosure of the alleged suspect's social media posts revealed white racist imaginings: "A sleeping lion can only be provoked so much before it wakes up and attacks . . . and so will us British" (Dearden 2017). But the Newham police initially denied that the attack was racially motivated and did not take statements from Resham for several days (Dearden 2017). The story did not hit the national news for an entire week. As Jameel stated, "If this was an Asian guy like myself, going up to an English couple in a car and acid attacking them, I know for a fact and the whole country knows that it would be classed as a terror attack. . . . There'd be a national manhunt. . . . I've been left here, and my cousin's been left here to just shrivel up and wait" (Channel 4 News 2017; Dearden 2017).

There are no absolute phenotypical requirements, passports, or work identities necessary for participating in the long and enduring struggle for racial freedom and justice. The challenges of new activist projects and campaigns that seek to mobilize along the lines of racial justice or political blackness are considerable but they can be informed by history. An examination of contradictions such as activists' drift into day-to-day clientelism with victims of racism rather than constantly building and sustaining grassroots involvement and collaborations; the continued subordination of women's intersectional experiences of racism as political priorities; over-reliance on high-profile, usually male, charismatic activist leaders; and the contradictions of anti-African phobias and Islamophobia within and among minority communities are all salient issues. There are, of course, many other contradictory tendencies that will emerge in the process of resistance building and they need to be named and bravely confronted. A degradation of the tradition would be the use of political blackness as dogma or a silencing mechanism against those who dissent. Political blackness, by its very unsettled character, cultivates a political imagination that is based on engaging the problematics of unity and solidarity, not simply celebrations of diversity.

Political blackness offers a particular horizon for mutually self-revelatory and self-transforming antiracist action and practice. To illustrate this I will recount the story of the Justice for the Pryces campaign that NMP carried out and the political tenets that this campaign produced for its time. After Kenny Pryce's brother Eustace was murdered by white racists in 1984, two founding NMP activists, Hardev Singh Dhesi and Herbie Boudier, a South Asian Sikh immigrant from India and an African Caribbean immigrant from Jamaica, respectively, came to see Kenny, who would later become an antiracist activist himself and go on to become a chair of NMP. Kenny provided a testimonial to the character of his relationship with the late Mr. Dhesi:

> Mr. Dhesi helped us to use our voice, helped us to use it to demand justice and make changes, from a time when we had been overwhelmed with grief and helplessness. He had a gentle, calm and dignified way of encouraging the confidence and strength to do it. He was a role model showing young people how to use their own

experience, not to be frightened and find the courage to speak out boldly. As I got to know him he showed me that racism was far broader than I had thought, the massive effect institutional racism has across so many areas of life, from policing to education. He was an excellent ambassador from his community, before that, I had little contact with Asian people. He was like a teacher and a fatherly friend encouraging so many people to develop their own skills and fight for justice. He worked tirelessly to do that, he wasn't interested in creating a high profile for himself. That is his legacy. (NMP 2000:25)

The legacy of political blackness is encapsulated in this humble ethic of showing up and working to forge solidarities that do not as yet exist. It is demonstrated in the commitment to sustain intimacy with each other and each other's struggles against the pain and grief of racism and its interlocked structures of domination. The power that such solidarities have to transform our social relationships provides an undefeatable point and purpose of political blackness in Britain today. In this resistance against forgetting and in the coming struggles, a new future for political blackness begins.

NOTES

Preface

1. I draw on a tradition of postcolonial and feminist ethnographic research critiques to examine racial violence and racialized state violence in Britain, a liberal juridical polity that predicates itself upon principles of egalitarian citizenship and objective rule of law. Modern historians, such as Lorraine Daston and Peter Galison (1992, 2007), however, argue that the notion of "objectivity" is itself historically constructed. Objectivity came to signify an eminent moral discourse specifically with the rise of positivistic scientism in the late nineteenth and twentieth centuries, but its forms are many and its registers are rather fluid, signifying "everything from empirical reliability to procedural correctness to emotional detachment" (Daston and Galison 1992:81). Black feminist research in Britain (Sudbury 1998) and feminist research in general have historically critiqued the construction of scientist objectivity by pointing toward the socially "situated" (Haraway 1988) character of all social research. Challenges to masculinist and authoritative regimes of objectivity in the social sciences therefore are not neutral regarding the broader conditions of social conflict, but rather are mediated through multiple lines of power struggles for representation and discursive control. Furthermore as Linda Tuhiwai Smith (2012) argues, the colonial model of research objectivity emerges precisely through a moral discourse that valorizes imperial bureaucracy's social and emotional distance.

2. The concept of stories as "lived experiences" (Eastmond 2007) helps to frame our understanding of the victims of racial violence and state violence as knowledge-producing subjects themselves. When victims of racial and state violence tell their own stories, or counter-stories (Bell 1987), an alternative account and epistemology emerges in the aporia between the dynamics of white domination and overidealized theories of color-blind and individual rights–based liberal justice (Mills 2005).

3. Critical attention to the processes of building antiracist resistance is an urgent corrective foci for ethnic studies and the anthropology of race, especially as white nationalist violence and racialized state violence in border control, policing, and counterterrorism are resurgent in both the United Kingdom and the United States (Burnett 2016; Potok 2017).

Introduction

1. A workless household is one that is economically inactive; that is, it is one in which no adult is working or seeking work (for any of a number of reasons).

2. This definition was found in an internal Newham Monitoring Project (n.d.a) document, entitled "NMP's Nine Absolutes: Or How to Save Ourselves from Ourselves."

3. There are discrepancies between the 2001 Census figures and the Greater London Authority (GLA) ethnic-group projections of 2005. While the 2005 GLA figures placed the white British population at 33.2 percent, the 2001 Census stated it was 39.4 percent (for a discussion of the discrepancies, see London Borough of Newham 2007:26). I utilize the GLA data for the Asian, African, and Caribbean population figures that follow.

Chapter 1

1. "DSS" stands for "Department of Social Security," which is an obsolete term. However, it is still often used in everyday speech to refer to offices where people go to claim government assistance.

2. As Paul Gilroy (2005) argues, British public culture often retreats to an ahistorical nostalgia, or what he terms "postcolonial melancholia," that evacuates the past and present of its own entanglements with empire.

3. As Patrick Bratlinger (2007) points out, Rudyard Kipling's poem, written in 1898 and sent to President Theodore Roosevelt, meant to encourage the United States' conquest of the Philippines from Spain. The white man's burden was therefore seen as a shared and globalized Anglo-American enterprise to establish colonial relations to uplift the colonized, who were associated with cultural backwardness and racial inferiority.

4. The 1948 British Nationality Act was passed as the British Commonwealth was coming into being and created the single citizenship category of Citizen of the United Kingdom and Colonies. The act included both Britons and colonial subjects whose rights to enter the United Kingdom were enshrined (Hansen 1999). Successive anti-Commonwealth immigration legislation, however, eroded and ultimately eliminated these rights by 1981.

5. Thatcher (1978) recognized the appeal of the National Front's immigration-control logics and sought to absorb them into the Conservative Party. As she stated in 1978,

> In my view, that is one thing that is driving some people to the National Front. They do not agree with the objectives of the National Front, but they say that at least they are talking about some of the problems. Now, we are a big political party. If we do not want people to go to extremes, and I do not, we ourselves must talk about this problem and we must show that we are prepared to deal with it. We are a British nation with British characteristics. Every country can take some small minorities and in many ways they add to the richness and variety of this country. The moment the minority threatens to become a big one, people get frightened.

6. The narrative of white Britons becoming "swamped," or overwhelmed by the number of immigrants, has become a recurrent trope in British politics (Syal 2014).

7. The construction of "good" or "bad" non-white and non-western subjects is part of the disciplinary power/knowledge nexus of western discourses as it has been shaped in the post-9/11 era, where unruly nonwestern identities have come to occupy a central place in western global geopolitics. See Mamdani (2005).

8. Such idealizations, however, help to suture over persistent racialized social inequalities and racialized power differentials in liberal democratic western societies. As Charles Mills (1997, 2008) has argued, however, a more historicized theorization of western liberal democratic polities reveals the operation of a "racial contract" as the basis for governance and state formation.

9. Mehta's (1999:46–49) full argument is as follows:

In its theoretical vision, liberalism, from the seventeenth century to the present has prided itself on its universality and politically inclusionary character. And yet, when viewed as an historical phenomenon, the period of liberal history is marked by systematic and sustained political exclusion of various groups and "types" of people. . . . [T]he exclusionary basis of liberalism does, I believe, derive from its theoretical core, and the litany of exclusionary historical instances is an elaboration of this core. It is so not because the ideals are theoretically ingenious or concretely impractical, but rather because behind the capacities ascribed to all human beings exists a thicker set of social credentials that constitute the real basis of political inclusion.

10. Glean was also known by her maiden name (Marion Patrick Jones) and as Marion O'Callaghan.

11. In 2003, I assisted in organizing focus group research on what victims of racial and police violence needed in terms of support, beyond the casework service that the NMP provided. The project's aim was to identify areas of holistic support needed by victims of police abuse, racist harassment, and attacks. This research-based information led to the creation of a short-lived project within the organization that utilized volunteers to provide companionship and moral support and to address some of the resulting daily life complications that arose when people fell victim to racist violence or police abuse.

My research consisted of semistructured interviews I conducted with dozens of local ethnically based social and leisure groups in order to assess the cross-community experiences of racist violence in Newham. NMP used these data to identify local communities' experiences of racial violence and the strategies they pursued to protest and combat these incidents. Follow-up outreach training and education workshops occurred after the research encounters. One of these training workshops, held for and with Muslim women wearing the hijab, supplied much of the material I discuss in Chapter 4.

My growing familiarization and analysis of NMP's work influenced my focus on the dynamics of racist violence and state violence as the two interlinked issues of racism historically affecting largely working-class, black communities in Newham. These two themes were identified as the most recurrent in the daily casework and campaigning activities of the group as I worked in short periods with its members in 2003, again in 2005, and for all of 2006. This final period marked the time when I began to develop a more direct participatory role as a resident of Newham and as an NMP caseworker and an activist. I carried out short-term follow-up research in 2013 and 2016 and continued to maintain regular conversations with NMP activists through emails, social media, and hosting visits to the United States.

During the course of fieldwork, I became partly or wholly responsible for some twelve cases of individual people or families who suffered from racist violence and state violence and, in particular, police abuse. I also participated in organizing local community mobilizations in response to the wrongful Forest Gate Anti-terror Raid, carried out by the British state in June 2006.

Chapter 2

1. It is clear that ever since Powell was able to represent the phenomenon of non-white and non-western immigration and settlement as a racial, cultural, and national crisis for

whites, British political culture has become very sensitive to popular and white working-class based counternarratives against antiracist reforms. In 2009, for example, following the release of a report by the Department for Communities and Local Government, ministers in the New Labour government and the media sought to frame white working-class marginalization as the result of an undue policy favoritism and bias toward immigrants in social housing and jobs (Doughty 2009; *Telegraph* 2009).

2. The populist narrative of blaming immigrants for the long-term impact of de-industrialization, neoliberal retrenchment of social welfare services, and capitalist immiseration of the white working classes also enters into sociological and public policy analyses. There is a tendency to explain away white working-class racism in British sociology and cultural studies as forms of resistance against ruling class elites who allegedly favor immigrants through antiracist and multicultural policies at the expense of working-class whites (Bonnett 1996; Hewitt 2005; Dench, Gavron, and Young 2006). See Gillborn (2009) for a critique of the "white racial victimhood" narrative.

3. A helpful explanation of the temporary legal remedy of a restraining injunction is as follows:

> In general terms, when exercising its discretion to issue an injunction, the court will need to be persuaded that there is a good reason why the respondent's rights should be restricted before the court knows whether the applicant will succeed at trial. . . . Once it is satisfied that there is a serious question to be considered in the underlying claim, the court will exercise its discretion according to what it regards as the "balance of convenience." The court will weigh the likely inconvenience or damage which would be suffered by the applicant if the injunction is not granted against the likely inconvenience or cost for the respondent if it is. (Out-Law.com 2013)

4. An overall picture of the extent of the problem of racial violence and hate crimes in Britain and the effectiveness of the state in protecting the personhood of ethnic minority citizens can be gleaned from combining Home Office data (financial year), Association of Chief Police Officers reports (calendar year), British Crime Survey data, and news stories. Race hate crimes are generally considered to be underreported, but by utilizing a "face-to-face victimization survey" research instrument, the annual British Crime Survey estimates that there is an estimated 136,000 race hate crime incidents a year (Smith et al. 2012). In contrast, some 37,000 complaints of racial and religiously motivated offenses were recorded in England and Wales for 2010 and 2011 (Morris 2008; Williams 2012). The number of police-recorded offenses, since the peak rise between 2005–6 and 2006–7, appears to have decreased in subsequent years. However, since the advent of the Macpherson report and its reform recommendations issued in 1999, the Crime Prosecution Service has intensified its race hate crimes prosecutions, and race hate crimes now constitute a majority (83 percent) of all hate crime prosecutions undertaken by the state, peaking at over twelve thousand cases in 2010–11 (Crime Prosecution Service 2012). The British Broadcasting Corporation (BBC) has also published its own investigative research that collated data from ninety local municipal authorities and which revealed a figure of nearly eighty-eight thousand cases of racist bullying and incidents that occurred in Britain's schools between 2007 and 2011 (Talwar 2012).

A 2010 Institute of Race Relations (IRR) report further challenged common theories that proclaim that white aversion to non-whites, color-based racism, or "raw, crude racism" is on the decline in Britain. As the report stated, "Since Stephen Lawrence's death in April 1993, eighty-nine people have lost their lives to racial violence—an average of five per year" (Athwal, Bourne, and Wood 2010:3). Contrary to the cultural narratives of racial progress in contemporary Britain, the figures in the first decade of the twenty-first century (2000–2009) show an increase to sixty-four cases from the forty cases recorded in the previous decade (1990–99).

Throughout Britain's post–World War II period, South Asian males of different nationalities have composed the largest group of people who have been racially attacked and killed. This entrenched cultural and structural pattern of violent racial harassment and virulent racial antipathy continues with a growing emphasis on Muslim South Asians. My examination of the data of racist murders monitored by the IRR from 2000 to 2009 shows that South Asians were the victims in 50 percent of all racist murders and 21 percent of those murdered were of African Caribbean or African descent. The remaining victims were of Chinese, Turkish, Polish, Iranian, Iraqi, Kosovan, Traveller, and mixed-race backgrounds. There was one instance of a known racist killing of a white British youth by a South Asian gang. Since 1993, 44 percent of those who have died as a result of racist killings are also Muslims. Official statistics include racist incidents involving minority-on-white crimes as well, but the record shows that whites make up two-thirds of the perpetrators of all nationally recorded race hate crimes. The IRR report further estimated that, in an examination of 660 cases of racist violence reported in the press, 93 percent of the cases involved white perpetrators, while South Asians and African Caribbeans were represented at 3.8 percent and 2.8 percent, respectively.

According to an unpublished geo-information system and environmental modeling study commissioned by Newham Council and carried out by A. J. Brimicombe (2006) between January 2004 and July 2006, the borough's police flagged 1,324 incidents as race hate incidents in the local area, involving 1,179 victims (see also Brimicombe et al. 2001). This study significantly established that the majority of race hate crimes in Newham occurred within a proximate private context (i.e., within one hundred meters of the victims' homes). It also revealed that ninety of the cases, or 8 percent, were repeat victims of racist incidents.

Less than a third of the reported racist incidents against racial and ethnic minorities throughout London achieved a "clear up" or resulted in a "sanctioned detection" where an offender is brought to charge (Martineau, Brown, and Faulkner 2007). In Newham, the sanctioned detection figure was closer to one-fifth of cases reported. Recent studies suggest that 10–20 percent of Newham residents have been victims of racial harassment or attacks and, according to the Newham Household Panel Survey, almost a quarter of its residents claim that racial violence is a common feature of daily life (Newham Household Panel Survey 2006).

Chapter 3

1. Studies have shown that African Caribbean women who face domestic violence have been "reluctant to take formal routes for fear of betraying black men and black people by using the 'white system'" due to fears of racist treatment by the police and the lack of serious protection for women who do file complaints (Thiara and Gill 2012:61).

2. Of the total prisoners in the United Kingdom, 26 percent were racial and ethnic minorities, and African- and African Caribbean–descended prisoners accounted for 10 percent of the total prison population while South Asian–descended prisoners accounted for 6 percent (Prison Reform Trust 2016). In the youth justice system, young people from minority communities accounted for 40 percent of those being held (Sloan and Allison 2015).

3. The total number of women prisoners in England and Wales in 2016 was 3,861 (Prison Reform Trust 2016).

4. For a brief time in the 1980s the left wing–controlled Greater London Council's Police Committee Support Unit published the *Women and Policing in London* newsletter. The first edition was in March 1985. Articles in the newsletter covered topics such as women and immigration law, rape victims and the police, an attack on a women's center, making London safe for women, women and public order, and lesbians and policing projects. A key concept from this period of struggle was the notion of the "cult of masculinity" that prevailed in the police force (*Women and Policing in London* 1985:1). This civilian oversight effort was part of a parallel "municipal feminist" movement that was prematurely halted when the Thatcher government managed to dissolve the Greater London Council in 1986 (Gelb 1989).

5. See Gargi Bhattacharyya's *Tales of Dark-Skinned Women* (1998) for an analysis of how success stories and exceptional achievements do not change negative racial stereotypes and cultural invisibility. See also Mirza (2014).

6. "Foreigner talk" is a comical and stereotyping practice of constructing and mocking a nonstandard English accent. See D'Cruz and Steele (2000).

7. The Defend the Deane Family campaign involved an Indo-Caribbean mini-cab driver from the island of St. Vincent, whose son was brutalized by the police at the Forest Gate police station. See NMP (1992).

8. The everyday territorial control of London's urban neighborhoods through the deployment of white racial harassment and racial violence has been well documented as modes of British "neighborhood nationalism" (Back 1996).

9. Even the complaints framework was enveloped within the European Union legal structure, and Commonwealth countries could not utilize that framework to contest the eligibility requirements for social security benefits (see O'Neill 2011).

10. All police complaints data cited are from the IPCC's 2006–7 annual report (see Gleeson and Grace 2007).

Chapter 4

1. An ongoing national debate about Britishness abets an anxious and hostile relationship to everyday signs of British Muslim religiosity, ranging from the very presence of mosques in Britain to the existence of parochial Muslim schools that are said to promote radicalization and cultural incommensurability (Kundnani 2014).

2. As Ashis Nandy (2010:2) notes, the colonizer-colonized relationship is formed through processes that "alter the original cultural priorities on both sides and bring to the center of the colonial culture subcultures previously recessive or subordinate in the two confronting cultures."

3. The hijab has a polyvalent history. As Faegheh Shirazi (2003) has argued, the practice of the hijab for Muslims has acquired a "flexible semantics" throughout its history, starting from its earliest known record in the Assyrian laws of the thirteenth century BCE, before the advent of Islam, where it was a status symbol and restrictively conferred on the women of wealthy families who did not have to work.

4. In France it is estimated that only some two thousand women actually wear the niqāb (British Broadcasting Corporation 2010). There are no official estimates as to how many of Britain's one million Muslim women wear the hijab, but some online discussions estimate

about half the population, but the percentage wearing the full veil, the niqāb, is small in Britain as well.

5. But the socioeconomic picture of Muslim women in the borough is not as freewheeling as the author implies. The fact of the matter is that some 76 percent of all Muslim women, inclusive of women who wear the hijab and do not wear the hijab, in the borough are economically inactive compared to 50 percent of the overall female population. Some 46 percent of Muslim women state that their primary occupation is home work and family care (see Harriss 2006).

6. *Green Street Hooligans*, also known as *Hooligans* in its U.S. release, was a 2005 independent film directed by Lexi Alexander. The film did not portray the ethnic and racial dimensions of the impact of football hooliganism in the community, nor did it represent the community as the multiethnic space that it is in contemporary reality.

7. "Yobs" is a colloquial term for rude young people and is part of the current moral panic around the rise of antisocial behavior.

Chapter 5

1. The understanding of "radical evil," as an aberration in the politics of the west has been critiqued on several grounds. Hannah Arendt (2006) argued that the rise of Nazism was not only the responsibility of totalitarian and charismatic leaders, but that it was fueled by the "banality" of bureaucratic dispositions and anti-intellectual conformity that shaped the subjectivity of modern state functionaries. Aimé Césaire ([1972] 2001:36), however, argued that twentieth-century European fascism was not a rupture with its preceding moral history but continuous with the genocides of its empire building.

> Yes, it would be worthwhile to study clinically, in detail, the steps taken by Hitler and Hitlerism and to reveal to the very distinguished, very humanistic, very Christian bourgeois of the twentieth century that without his being aware of it, he has a Hitler inside him, that Hitler *inhabits* him, that Hitler is his *demon*, that if he rails against him, he is being inconsistent and that, at bottom, what he cannot forgive Hitler for is not *crime* in itself, *the crime against man*, it is not *the humiliation of man as such*, it is the crime against the white man, the humiliation of the white man, and the fact that he applied to Europe colonialist procedures which until then had been reserved exclusively for the Arabs of Algeria, the coolies of India, and the blacks of Africa [emphasis in the original].

2. See Lowe (2015).

3. Abdul Kahar's account was published in Sky News (2006).

4. Norman Tesbitt was a Conservative Party politician who in 1990 declared, "A large proportion of Britain's Asian population fails to pass the cricket test. Which side do they cheer for? It's an interesting test. Are you still harking back to where you came from or where you are?" (Howe 2006). The "cricket test" referred to Tesbitt's allegation that British Asians had divided national loyalties due to the support they showed for India's and Pakistan's cricket teams.

5. Both the de Menezes family (Powell 2017) and the police monitoring group Netpol raised objections to Dick's appointment as Metropolitan Police Commissioner, on account of the operational failures during the July 7, 2005, antiterror operations. As Netpol argued,

The Metropolitan Police then lied about the circumstances of Jean's death and during subsequent investigations vital evidence went missing, including Cressida Dick's instructions to allow Jean into the station because he did not appear a threat. In 2007, the Met was eventually found guilty of breaking health and safety laws and endangering the lives of Londoners and a year later, an inquest jury decided that a series of police failures contributed to Jean's death. No individual officers were ever charged or disciplined. These events have never hindered Cressida Dick's rapid rise within the ranks. Although ultimately accountable for the string of errors that led to Jean's death, she was promoted soon afterward, in September 2006, with glowing tributes in the press and support from senior advisors to the then London mayor Ken Livingstone (who himself later praised her as a "potential future Commissioner"). Only a year after the inquest jury had flatly rejected the police's claims that Jean was lawfully killed, Cressida Dick was given a medal for "distinguished service." (Netpol 2017)

6. The history of the hearts and minds campaign within counterterrorism has deep roots in Britain's decolonization experience and its relationships with colonized races and their struggles for self-determination. Examples include the counterinsurgency campaigns against both the Mau Mau in Kenya and the Malayan Communist Party (Webster 2001).

7. Personal communication, November 14, 2006.

Chapter 6

1. Stated by the NMP activist Cilius Victor during his speech at the Forest Gate Anti-terror Raid protest, June 18, 2006.

2. Personal communication, June 27, 2003.

3. See Saint Stephen's School and Children's Centre (2016).

4. As Littler and Feldman (2015:1) report,

Of the 402 online incidents recorded, the majority were coded as anti-Muslim abuse (385), with significant numbers of attacks also coded for the dissemination of anti-Muslim literature (372). Threats of offline action remained comparatively rare (only 78 cases in total). Where recorded, the victims of online incidents were generally reported to be male. Less than half (186 of 402, or 45%) of all recorded online incidents were coded as having been reported to the police. . . . Offline anti-Muslim attacks were overwhelmingly reported to have been perpetrated by white (68, versus 5 BME) males (59, versus 21 female perpetrators). The victims of offline anti-Muslim attacks were generally female (48 reports). A significant number (44) of victims reported being targeted while wearing distinctively Muslim dress. The offline attacks reported were overwhelmingly characterized by abuse (103 cases). Significant numbers were also coded for property damage (15), threats (29), and assault (21). Less than 10% (7) of cases reported the use of extreme violence.

5. For a similar critique in the U.S. context, see Sexton (2010).

6. The Center for Migration and Diaspora Studies (2015), at the School of Oriental and African Studies of the University of London (SOAS), organized a panel on the question of

political blackness in British student politics, presenting arguments for and against, and similar panels have been organized at other universities (see also Hamilton 2016).

7. There were numerous racial attacks and murders in east London during the period. In 1978, ten-year-old Kenneth Singh left his home in Plaistow to go to the local cornershop for his parents and never returned. He was found dead several days later. During the same month a nine-year-old South Asian boy had his face cut open from his left eye across to his left ear in an attack perpetrated by five white boys. In 1980, twenty-nine-year-old Akhtar Ali Baig was attacked by a skinhead gang and stabbed fatally in his heart by his killer who was heard to have boasted, "I have just gutted a Paki," while the local police initially categorized the crime as a mugging gone wrong. In 1982, a group of South Asian schoolchildren who escorted younger children home from school to protect them from recurrent racial attacks in Newham were themselves attacked by plainclothes police officers and racially abused and charged with public disorder (Bethnal Green and Stepney Trades Council 1978; Thompson 1988).

Conclusion

1. Freedom of Information Request reference no. 2014070001055. Request made by Kevin Blowe on July 10, 2014 (see WhatDoTheyKnow 2014).

2. Personal communication, July 10, 2013.

3. See Kundnani (2012) for a critique of the notion of radicalization.

4. See the debates that emerged with the airing of the television series *Guerrilla*, and its controversial treatment of the history of black power social movements in Britain (Obi, Okolosie, Andrews, and Amrani 2017).

5. Throughout east London, acid attacks in general have been on the rise with Newham alone accounting for 398 of total acid-related incidents between 2011 and 2016, the highest in the city (Lusher 2017). Despite fears that have been circulating on social media that a number of these attacks are racially motivated, there is not yet any dedicated state recognition and action concerning this crisis that is making east Londoners afraid to leave their homes (Lusher 2017).

REFERENCES

Abu-Lughod, Lila. 2006. "The Muslim Woman: The Power of Images and the Danger of Pity." *Eurozine.* http://www.eurozine.com/articles/2006–09–01-abulughod-en.html. Accessed April 28, 2011.

———. 2013. *Do Muslim Women Need Saving?* Cambridge, Mass.: Harvard University Press.

Adesina, Zack, and Oana Marocico. 2015. "Islamophobic Crime in London 'Up by 70%.'" *BBC News.* http://www.bbc.com/news/uk-england-london-34138127. Accessed May 22, 2017.

Afzal-Khan, Fawzia. 2004. "The Female Body as a Site of Attack: Will the 'Real' Muslim Woman's Body Please Reveal Itself?" In *Interventions: Activists and Academics Respond to Violence,* ed. Elizabeth A. Castelli and Janet R. Jakobsen, 187–95. New York: Palgrave Macmillan.

Agamben, Giorgio. 2005. *State of Exception.* Stanford, Calif.: Stanford University Press.

Ahmad, Muneer. 2004. "A Rage Shared by Law: Post-September 11 Racial Violence as Crimes of Passion." *California Law Review* 92 (5): 1261–1330.

Ahmed, Sara. 2015. "Feminist Consciousness." *Feministkilljoys.* http://feministkilljoys.com/. Accessed June 23, 2017.

Aitch, Iain, and Colette Bernhardt. 2015. "Vijay's Chawalla." *Guardian.* https://www.theguardian.com/lifeandstyle/2015/mar/21/this-weeks-best-food-and-drink. Accessed May 22, 2017.

Aldridge, Hannah, Theo Barry Bon, Adam Tinson, and Tom MacInnes. 2015. *London's Poverty Profile 2015.* London: Trust for London and New Policy Institute.

Alexander, Claire, and Caroline Knowles. 2005. "Introduction." In *Making Race Matter: Bodies, Space and Identity,* ed. Clare Alexander and Caroline Knowles, 1–16. Basingstoke: Palgrave Macmillan.

Alexander, Jacqui. 2006. *Pedagogies of Crossing: Meditations on Feminism, Sexual Politics, Memory and the Sacred.* Durham, N.C.: Duke University Press.

Ameli, Saied, and Arzu Merali. 2006. *Hijab, Meaning, Identity, Otherization and Politics.* Wembley, U.K.: Islamic Human Rights Commission.

Amin, Ash. 2003. "Unruly Strangers? The 2001 Urban Riots in Britain." *International Journal of Urban and Regional Research* 27 (2): 460–63.

Amnesty International. 1995. "UK—Death in Police Custody of Joy Gardner." https://www.amnesty.org/download/Documents/172000/eur450051995en.pdf. Accessed July 6, 2017.

Andrews, Kehinde. 2016. "Resisting Racism: The Black Supplementary School Movement." *Ethnic and Racial Studies* 39 (11): 56–73.

Ang-Lygate, Magdalene. 1997. "Charting the Spaces of (Un)location: On Theorizing Diaspora." In *Black British Feminism: A Reader*, ed. Heidi Safia Mirza, 168–86. New York: Routledge.

Anidjar, Gil. 2003. *The Jew, the Arab: A History of the Enemy*. Stanford, Calif.: Stanford University Press.

———. 2014. *Blood: A Critique of Christianity*. New York: Columbia University Press.

Arendt, Hannah. 2006. *Eichmann in Jerusalem: A Report on the Banality of Evil*. New York: Penguin.

Aretxaga, Begoña. 1995. "Dirty Protest: Symbolic Overdetermination and Gender in Northern-Ireland Ethnic Violence." *Ethos* 23 (2): 123–48.

———. 1997. *Shattering Silence: Women, Nationalism, and Political Subjectivity in Northern Ireland*. Princeton, N.J.: Princeton University Press.

———. 2003. "Maddening States." *Annual Review of Anthropology* 32: 393–410.

Armstrong, Bruce. 1989. *A People Without Prejudice? Experience of Racism in Scotland*. London: Runnymede Trust.

Arshad, Rowena. 2003. *States of Scotland*. Glasgow: ICS Books.

Asad, Talal. 2015. "Reflections on Violence, Law and Humanitarianism." *Critical Inquiry* 41 (2): 390–427.

Athwal, Harmit, Jenny Bourne, and Rebecca Wood. 2010. *Racial Violence: The Buried Issue*. London: Institute of Race Relations.

Awan, Imran, and Irene Zempi. 2015. "We Fear for Our Lives: Offline and Online Experiences of Anti-Muslim Hostility." https://www.tellmamauk.org/wp-content/uploads/resources/We Fear For Our Lives.pdf. Accessed November 26, 2017.

Back, Les. 1996. *New Ethnicities and Urban Culture*. London: University College London Press.

Back, Les, and John Solomos. 2001. "Doing Research, Writing Politics: The Dilemmas of Political Intervention in Research on Racism." In *Race and Ethnicity*, ed. Harry Goulbourne, 3: 378–99. London: Routledge.

Bagguley, Paul, and Yasmin Hussain. 2008. *Riotous Citizens: Ethnic Conflict in Multicultural Britain*. New York: Routledge.

Banton, Michael. 1967. *Race Relations*. London: Tavistock.

Barber, Lynsey. 2015. "Autumn Statement 2015: George Osborne Promises £3.4 Billion Extra Counter-terrorism Spending in Wake of Paris Attacks but No Police Cuts Commitment." *City A.M.* http://www.cityam.com/229260/autumn-statement-and-comprehensive-spending-review-2015-george-osborne-promises-30pc-increase-in-counter-terrorism-spending-in-wake-of-paris-attacks. Accessed November 26, 2017.

Basarudin, Azza. 2015. *Humanizing the Sacred: Sisters in Islam and the Struggle for Gender Justice in Malaysia*. Seattle: University of Washington Press.

Baumann, Gerd. 1996. *Contesting Culture: Discourses of Identity in Multi-Ethnic London*. Cambridge: Cambridge University Press.

Bell, Derrick. 1987. *And We Are Not Saved: The Elusive Quest for Racial Justice*. New York: Basic Books.

Benhabib, Seyla. 2002. *Claims of Culture: Equality and Diversity in the Global Era*. Princeton, N.J.: Princeton University Press.

Berkeley, Robert, Omar Khan, and Mohan Ambikaipaker. 2006. *What's New About New Immigrants in 21st Century Britain?* York, U.K.: Runnymede Trust.

Bernstock, Penny. 2014. *Olympic Housing: A Critical Review of London 2012's Legacy*. London: Ashgate.

Bethnal Green and Stepney Trades Council. 1978. *Blood on the Streets: A Report by Bethnal Green and Stepney Trades Council on Racial Attacks in East London*. London: Bethnal Green and Stepney Trades Council.

Bhattacharyya, Gargi. 1998. *Tales of Dark-Skinned Women: Race, Gender and Global Culture (Race and Representation)*. London: University College of London Press.

———. 2008. *Dangerous Brown Men: Exploiting Sex, Violence and Feminism in the "War on Terror."* New York: Zed.

Biko, Steve. (1978) 2002. *I Write What I Like: Selected Writings*. Chicago: University of Chicago Press.

Blitz, James. 2017. "Post-Brexit Delusions About Empire 2.0." *Financial Times*. https://www.ft.com/content/bc29987e-034e-11e7-ace0-1ce02ef0def9. Accessed November 26, 2017.

Blowe, Kevin. 2013. "We Must Have Far-Reaching Inquiry into Police Spying." *Red Pepper*. http://www.redpepper.org.uk/we-must-have-a-far-reaching-inquiry-into-police-spying/. Accessed November 26, 2017.

———. 2015. "Newham Labour Nominates the 'Prevent' Candidate for London Assembly Selection Battle." *Random Blowe*. http://www.blowe.org.uk/2015/07/newham-labour-nominates-prevent.html. Accessed November 26, 2017.

Bonilla-Silva, Eduardo. 2014. *Racism Without Racists: Colorblind Racism and the Persistence of Racial Inequality in America*. New York: Rowman and Littlefield.

Bonnett, Alastair. 1996. "Anti-racism and the Critique of 'White' Identities." *Journal of Ethnic and Migration Studies* 22 (1): 97–110.

Boo, Su-Lyn. 2015. "Marina Mahathir: Malaysia Undergoing 'Arab Colonialism.'" *Malay Mail Online*. http://www.themalaymailonline.com/malaysia/article/marina-mahathir-malays ia-undergoing-arab-colonialism. Accessed May 22, 2017.

Bowcott, Owen. 2006. "Muslims Who Want Sharia Law 'Should Leave.'" *Guardian*. http://www.guardian.co.uk/uk/2006/feb/27/religion.islam. Accessed April 28, 2011.

Bowling, Benjamin. 2001. *Violent Racism: Victimization, Policing and Social Context*. Oxford: Oxford University Press.

Bowling, Benjamin, and Coretta Phillips. 2001. *Racism, Crime and Criminal Justice*. London: Longman.

Bratlinger, Patrick. 2007. "Kipling's 'White Man's Burden and its Afterlives.'" *English Literature in Translation 1880–1920* 50 (2): 172–91.

Brimicombe, A. J. 2006. *Racial Harassment in Newham*. Paper presented at the REIN Race Hate Crime conference, Newham, London, November 30.

Brimicombe, A. J., Martin P. Ralphs, Alice Sampson, and Hoi Yuen Tsui. 2001. "An Analysis of the Role of Neighbourhood Ethnic Composition in the Geographical Distribution of Racially Motivated Incidents: Implications for Evaluating Treatment." *British Journal of Criminology* 41 (2): 293–308.

British Broadcasting Corporation. 2010. "Should France Ban the Full Veil?" *BBC News*. http://www.bbc.co.uk/blogs/haveyoursay/2010/07/should_france_ban_the_veil.html?page=2. Accessed May 2, 2011.

———. 2014. "Police Handling of Discrimination Complaints 'Poor.'" *BBC News*. http://www.bbc.com/news/uk-27707625. Accessed June 23, 2017.

Brogan, Benedict. 2005. "It's Time to Celebrate Empire, Says Brown." *Daily Mail.* http://
    www.dailymail.co.uk/news/article-334208/Its-time-celebrate-Empire-says-Brown.html.
    Accessed June 22, 2017.

Brown, Jacqueline Nassy. 2005. *Dropping Anchor, Setting Sail: Geographies of Race in Black
    Liverpool.* Princeton, N.J.: Princeton University Press.

Buck-Morss, Susan. 2006. *Thinking Past Terror: Islamism and Critical Theory on the Left.* New
    York: Verso.

Bunce, Robin, and Paul Field. 2017. *Renegade: The Life and Times of Darcus Howe.* London:
    Bloomsbury.

Burnett, Jon. 2016. "Racial Violence and the Brexit State." *Institute of Race Relations.* http://
    www.irr.org.uk/app/uploads/2016/11/Racial-violence-and-the-Brexit-state-final.pdf.
    Accessed May 27, 2017.

Cacho, Lisa Marie. 2012. *Social Death: Racialized Rightlessness and the Criminalization of the
    Unprotected.* New York: New York University Press.

Cameron, David. 2011. "PM's Speech at Munich Security Conference." https://www.gov.uk/
    government/speeches/pms-speech-at-munich-security-conference. Accessed June 23,
    2017.

———. 2015. "I Want to Build a National Coalition to Challenge and Speak Out Against
    Extremism." *Prime Minister's Office.* https://www.gov.uk/government/news/prime-minister
    -i-want-to-build-a-national-coalition-to-challenge-and-speak-out-against-extremism.
    Accessed December 12, 2015.

Campbell, Marie, and Frances Gregor. 2002. *Mapping Social Relations: A Primer in Doing
    Institutional Ethnography.* Aurora, Canada: Garamond Press.

Cantle, Ted. 2008. *Community Cohesion: A New Framework for Race and Diversity.* Basing-
    stoke, U.K.: Palgrave Macmillan.

Cantle, Ted, and the Independent Review Team. 2001. *Community Cohesion: A Report of the
    Independent Review Team.* London: Home Office. http://resources.cohesioninstitute
    .org.uk/Publications/Documents/Document/DownloadDocumentsFile.aspx?recordId
    =96&file=PDFversion. Accessed April 28, 2011.

Carby, Hazel V. 1987. *Reconstructing Womanhood: The Emergence of the Afro-American Novel-
    ist.* New York: Oxford University Press.

Carmichael, Stokely. 1969. "Black Power and the Third World." In *The New Revolutionaries,*
    ed. Tariq Ali, 91–103. New York: William Morrow.

Carmichael, Stokely, and Charles V. Hamilton. 1967. *Black Power: The Politics of Liberation in
    America.* New York: Vintage.

Carter, Bob, Clive Harris, and Shirley Joshi. 1987. "The 1951–55 Conservative Government
    and the Racialization of Black Immigration." *Immigrant and Minorities* 6 (3): 335–47.

Cawthorne, Ellie. 2017. " 'Guerrilla' and the Real History of British Black Power." *History
    Extra.* April 13. http://www.historyextra.com/article/feature/guerrilla-real-history-british
    -black-power. Accessed June 10, 2017.

Center for Migration and Diaspora Studies. 2015. "Departure Point: Political Blackness and
    Solidarity Between People of Colour in the UK." https://www.soas.ac.uk/migration
    diaspora/seminarsevents/seminarseries/18mar2015-departure-point-political-blackness
    -and-solidarity-between-people-of-colour-in-the-uk.html. Accessed June 20, 2017.

Césaire, Aimé. (1972) 2001. *Discourse on Colonialism: A Poetics of Anticolonialism.* New York:
    Monthly Review Press.

Chahal, Kusminder, 2003. *Racial Harassment Support Projects: Their Role, Impact and Potential*. York, U.K.: Joseph Rowntree Foundation.

Chakraborti, Neil, and Jon Garland. 2011. *Rural Racism*. New York: Routledge.

Channel 4 News. 2017. "'Acid Attack Was a Hate Crime': London Victim Speaks Out." https://www.youtube.com/watch?v = 9_X6WlSthsY&feature = youtu.be. Accessed July 4, 2017.

Chigwada-Bailey, Ruth. 1991. "The Policing of Black Women." In *Out of Order? Policing Black People*, ed. Ellis Cashmore and Eugene McLaughlin, 134–50. New York: Routledge.

———. 2003. *Black Women's Experiences of Criminal Justice: A Discourse on Disadvantage*. Winchester, U.K.: Waterside Press.

Clifford, James. 1997. *Routes: Travel and Translation in the Late Twentieth Century*. Cambridge, Mass.: Harvard University Press.

Cole, Mike. 2009. *Critical Race Theory and Education: A Marxist Response*. New York: Palgrave Macmillan.

Collins, Patricia Hill. 1998. *Fighting Words: Black Women in Search of Justice: Contradictions of Modernity*. Minneapolis: University of Minnesota Press.

Connolly, Paul, and Romana Khaoury. 2010. "Whiteness, Racism and Exclusion in Northern Ireland: A Critical Race Perspective." In *Northern Ireland After the Troubles: A Society in Transition*, ed. Colin Coulter and Michael Murray. Manchester, U.K.: Manchester University Press.

Conservative Party (UK). 2015. "Strong Leadership, a Clear Economic Plan, a Brighter, More Secure Future." https://www.conservatives.com/manifesto. Accessed December 10, 2015.

Cornell, Drucilla. 2004. *Defending Ideals: War, Democracy, and Political Struggles*. New York: Routledge.

Cox, Jane, and Katherine Sacks-Jones. 2017. *"Double Disadvantage": The Experiences of Black, Asian and Minority Ethnic Women in the Criminal Justice System*. London: Women in Prison and Agenda, the Alliance for Women and Girls at Risk. http://www.womeninprison.org.uk/perch/resources/double-disadvantage-1.pdf. Accessed June 7, 2017.

Crime Prosecution Service. 2012. *Annual Reports and Accounts 2011–12*. London: Crime Prosecution Service.

Dabiri, Emma. 2015. "I Do Not Identify with Others on the Basis That Neither of Us Is White." *Guardian*. https://www.theguardian.com/commentisfree/2015/may/22/black-asian-minority-ethnic-bame-bme-trevor-phillips-racial-minorities. Accessed June 28, 2017.

Daston, Lorraine, and Peter Galison. 1992. "The Image of Objectivity." *Representations* 40 (1): 81–128.

———. 2007. *Objectivity*. New York: Zone.

Davenport, Justin. 2006. "Met Chief: We Got It Wrong with Raid at Forest Gate." *Evening Standard*. June 29.

Dawson, Michael C. 1995. *Behind the Mule: Race and Class in African American Politics*. Princeton, N.J.: Princeton University Press.

D'Cruz, J. V., and William Steele. 2000. *Australia's Ambivalence Towards Asia: Politics, Neo/Post-colonialism, and Fact/Fiction*. Monash: Monash Asia Institute, Monash University Press.

Dear, Paula. 2004. "Women Vow to Protect Muslim Hijab." *BBC News*. http://news.bbc.co.uk/2/hi/uk_news/3805733.stm. Accessed May 2, 2011.

Dearden, Lizzie. 2017. "Muslim Man Who Was Attacked with Acid Wants to Know Why It's Not Labelled a Terror Attack." *Independent.* http://www.independent.co.uk/news/uk/crime/muslim-man-acid-attack-victim-why-not-terror-attack-east-london-jameel-muhktar-resham-khan-21st-a7816331.html. Accessed July 4, 2017.

Dench, Geoff, Kate Gavron, and Michael Dunlop Young. 2006. *The New East End: Kinship, Race and Conflict.* London: Profile Books.

Desai, Ashwin. 2014. "Indian South Africans and the Black Consciousness Movement Under Apartheid." *Diaspora Studies* 8 (1): 37–50.

Dirlik, Arif. 2008. "Race Talk, Race, and Contemporary Racism." *PMLA* 123 (5): 1363–79.

Donoghue, Jane. 2010. *Anti-social Behavior Orders: A Culture of Control?* London: Palgrave Macmillan.

Doughty, Steve. 2009. "Britain's 'Betrayed' White Working Classes Believe Immigrants Receive Better Treatment." *Daily Mail.* http://www.dailymail.co.uk/news/article-1104046/Britains-betrayed-white-working-classes-believe-immigrants-receive-better-treatment.html. Accessed June 11, 2017.

Duncan, Tom. 2006. "Learning to Live with Evil." *Newham Recorder.* August 16.

Eastmond, Marita. 2007. "Stories as Lived Experience: Narratives in Forced Migration Research." *Journal of Refugee Studies* 20 (2): 248–64.

Edwards, Jeff. 2006. "Hunt for Poison Bomb." *Daily Mirror,* June 3.

Eisenstein, Zillah. 2004. *Against Empire: Feminisms, Racism and the West.* New York: Zed.

Eldridge, Michael. 1997. "The Rise and Fall of Black Britain." *Transition* 74: 32–43.

Elgot, Jessica, and Matthew Taylor. 2015. "Calais Crisis: Cameron Condemned for 'Dehumanising' Description of Migrants." *Guardian.* http://www.theguardian.com/uk-news/2015/jul/30/david-cameron-migrant-swarm-language-condemned. Accessed December 12, 2015.

Evans, Rob, and Vikram Dodd. 2014. "Undercover Police Gathered Evidence on 18 Grieving Families." *Guardian.* https://www.theguardian.com/uk-news/2014/jul/24/undercover-police-spying-justice-campaigns-20-years. Accessed May 27, 2017.

Falk, Richard, Irene Gendzier, and Robert Jay Lifton, eds. 2006. *Crimes of War: Iraq.* New York: Nation Books.

Fanon, Frantz. 1965. *A Dying Colonialism.* New York: Grove.

Fisher, Tracy. 2012. *What's Left of Blackness: Feminisms, Transracial Solidarities and the Politics of Belonging in Britain.* New York: Palgrave Macmillan.

Fitzpatrick, Pamela. 2006. "Right to Reside—New Rules." http://www.cpag.org.uk/content/right-reside-%E2%80%93-new-rules. Accessed May 22, 2017.

Foley, Douglas E., and Angela Valenzuela. 2005. "Critical Ethnography: The Politics of Collaboration." In *The Sage Handbook of Qualitative Research*, ed. Norman K. Denzin and Yvonna S. Lincoln, 217–34. Thousand Oaks, Calif.: Sage.

Forman, James. 2017. *Locking Up Our Own: Crime and Punishment in Black America.* New York: Farrar, Strauss and Giroux.

Fuentes, Consuelo Rivera. 1997. "Two Stories, Three Lovers, and the Creation of Meaning in Black Lesbian Autobiography: A Diary." In *Black British Feminism: A Reader*, ed. Heidi Safia Mirza, 216–25. New York: Routledge.

Garcia, Feliks. 2016. "Ivy League Economist 'Suspected of Terrorism' While Doing Maths Aboard American Airlines Plane." *Independent.* http://www.independent.co.uk/news/

world/americas/american-airlines-ivy-league-economist-suspected-of-terrorism-while-doing-math-a7018686.html. Accessed May 23, 2017.

Gelb, Joyce. 1989. *Feminism and Politics: A Comparative Perspective*. Berkeley: University of California Press.

Gillan, Audrey. 2005. "Ghettoes in English Cities 'Almost Equal to Chicago.'" *Guardian*. http://www.theguardian.com/uk/2005/sep/23/race.world. Accessed December 12, 2015.

Gillborn, David. 2008. *Racism and Education: Coincidence or Conspiracy*. New York: Routledge.

———. 2009. "Education: The Numbers Game and the Construction of White Racial Victimhood." In *Who Cares About the White Working Class?* ed. Kjartan Páll Sveinsson, 15–21. London: Runnymede Trust.

Gilmore, Ruth. 2002. "Fatal Couplings of Power and Difference." *Professional Geographer* 54 (1): 15–24.

———. 2008. "Forgotten Places and Seeds of Grassroots Planning." In *Engaging Contradictions: Theory, Politics, and Methods of Activist Scholarship*, ed. Charles R. Hale, 31–61. Berkeley: University of California Press.

Gilroy, Paul. 2005. *Postcolonial Melancholia*. New York: Columbia University Press.

Glean, Marion. 1973. "Whatever Happened to CARD?" *Race Today* 5 (1): 13–15.

Gleeson, Emily, and Kerry Grace. 2007. *Police Complaints: Statistics for England and Wales*. London: Independent Police Complaints Commission.

Goodchild, Sophie, and Francis Elliot. 2006. "Tip-off by Police Informer Led to Forest Gate Raid." *Independent*. June 11.

Goulbourne, Harry. 1991. *Ethnicity and Nationalism in Post-Imperial Britain*. Cambridge: Cambridge University Press.

Grice, Will. 2015. "Canadian Sikh Man 'to Sue News Outlets' After He Is Wrongly Labelled a Terrorist After Paris Attacks." *Independent*. http://www.independent.co.uk/news/world/americas/sikh-mans-image-photoshopped-to-make-him-look-like-isis-paris-attacker-a6735266.html. Accessed June 28, 2017.

Guardian. 2007. "1,166 Anti-terror Arrests Net 40 Convictions." http://www.guardian.co.uk/uk/2007/mar/05/politics.terrorism. Accessed April 28, 2011.

Gupta, Rahila. 2003. *From Homebreakers to Jailbreakers: Southall Black Sisters*. London: Zed.

Gusterson, Hugh. 1997. "Studying Up Revisited." *PoLAR: Political and Legal Anthropology Review* 20 (1): 114–19.

Hale, Charles R. 2006. "Activist Research v. Cultural Critique: Indigenous Land Rights and the Contradictions of Politically Engaged Anthropology." *Cultural Dynamics* 21 (1): 96–120.

Hall, Catherine. 2011. "Macaulay: A Liberal Historian?" In *The Peculiarities of Liberal Modernity in Imperial Britain*, ed. Simon Gunn and James Vernon, 19–36. Berkeley: University of California Press.

Hall, Kathleen D. 2002. *Lives in Translation: Sikh Youths as British Citizens*. Philadelphia: University of Pennsylvania Press.

Hall, Ruth E. 1985. *Ask Any Woman: A London Inquiry into Rape and Sexual Assault: Report of the Women's Safety Survey Conducted by Women Against Rape*. Bristol, U.K.: Falling Wall Press.

Hall, Stuart. 1996a. "Minimal Selves." In *Black British Cultural Studies*, ed. Houston A. Baker Jr., Manthia Diawara, and Ruth H. Lindeborg, 114–19. Chicago: University of Chicago Press.

————. 1996b. "New Ethnicities." In *Stuart Hall: Critical Dialogues in Cultural Studies*, ed. David Morley and Kuan-Hsing Chen, 441–49. New York: Routledge.

Halliday, Josh. 2016. "Almost 4,000 People Referred to UK Deradicalisation Program Last Year." *Guardian.* https://www.theguardian.com/uk-news/2016/mar/20/almost-4000-people -were-referred-to-uk-deradicalisation-scheme-channel-last-year. Accessed June 23, 2017.

Hamid, Sameera. 1997. *Silencing an Independent Voice of the Community? An Analysis of the Decision by the London Borough of Newham Council to Withdraw Funding from the Newham Monitoring Project.* Master's thesis, London School of Economics.

Hamilton, Antony. 2016. "Politically Black Is Back." *Socialist Review.* http://socialistreview.org .uk/415/politically-black-back. Accessed June 20, 2017.

Hansen, Randall. 1999. "The Politics of Citizenship in 1940s Britain: The British Nationality Act." *Twentieth Century British History* 10 (1): 67–95.

Haraway, Donna. 1988. "Situated Knowledges: The Science Question in Feminism and the Privilege of Partial Perspective." *Feminist Studies* 14 (3): 575–99.

Harnecker, Marta. 2007. *Rebuilding the Left.* New York: Zed.

Harpalani, Vinay. 2013. "DesiCrit: Theorizing the Racial Ambiguity of South Asian Americans." *New York University Annual Survey of American Law* 69 (1): 1–112.

Harris, Sarah Ann. 2015. "Islamophobic Abuse Ignored by Bystanders, Prompting Claims We're Missing 'a Sense of Common Humanity.'" *Huffington Post.* http://www.huffington post.co.uk/2015/10/17/islamophobic-muslims-islamophobia-abuse-tell-mama_n_8293 904.html. Accessed December 12, 2015.

Harrison, Faye V., ed. 1997. *Decolonizing Anthropology: Moving Further Toward an Anthropology of Liberation.* Arlington, Va.: Association of Black Anthropologists/American Anthropological Association.

Harriss, Kaveri. 2006. *Muslims in the London Borough of Newham.* Oxford: University of Oxford—COMPAS.

Hartley-Parkinson, Richard. "Man Wanted After Acid Attack on Two People in East London." *Metro News.* http://metro.co.uk/2017/06/29/man-with-crying-tattoos-and-a-large-left -ear-wanted-over-two-acid-attacks-6742567/. Accessed July 4, 2017.

Hayman, Andy. 2006. "Report to MPA Full Authority on 29/06/2006—Operation Volga." Presented at a press conference at the Metropolitan Police Authority, London. June 29.

Hazareesingh, Sandip. 1986. "Racism and Cultural Identity: An Indian Perspective." *Dragon's Teeth* 24: 4–10.

Hensman, C. R. 1992. *New Beginnings: The Ordering and Designing of the Realm of Freedom. Vol. I—Captivity.* Mount Lavinia, Sri Lanka: Third World Perspectives.

Hesse, Barnor. 2014. "Escaping Liberty: Western Hegemony, Black Fugitivity." *Political Theory* 42 (3): 288–313.

Hesse, Barnor, Dhanwant K. Rai, Christine Bennett, and Paul McGilchrist. 1992. *Beneath the Surface: Racial Harassment.* Brookfield, Vt.: Avebury.

Hewitt, Roger. 2005. *White Backlash and the Politics of Multiculturalism.* Cambridge: Cambridge University Press.

al-Hibri, Azizah. 2000. "Deconstructing Patriarchal Jurisprudence in Islamic Law." In *Global Critical Race Feminism: An International Reader*, ed. Adrien Katherine Wing, 221–33. New York: New York University Press.

Hills, Sarah. 2006. "Blair: I Back 'Terror' Raid Police 101%." *Metro.* June 7.

Home Office. 2010. "Channel: Supporting Individuals Susceptible to Recruitment by Violent Extremists." http://tna.europarchive.org/20100419081706/http://security.homeoffice.gov .uk/news-publications/publication-search/prevent/channel-guidance?view = Binary. Accessed May 24, 2017.

———. 2015a. "Home Office Funding of the Prevent Programme from 2011 to 2015." https://www.gov.uk/government/publications/home-office-funding-of-the-prevent -programme-from-2011-to-2015. Accessed June 23, 2017.

———. 2015b. "2010 to 2015 Government Policy: Counter-terrorism." https://www.gov.uk/ government/publications/2010-to-2015-government-policy-counter-terrorism/2010-to -2015-government-policy-counter-terrorism. Accessed June 23, 2017.

Hopkins, Peter. 2004. "Everyday Racism in Scotland: A Case Study of East Pollockshields." *Scottish Affairs* 49 (1): 88–103.

House of Commons Joint Committee on Human Rights. 2007. "Counter-Terrorism Policy and Human Rights: 28 Days, Intercept and Post-Charge Questioning: Nineteenth Report of Session 2006–07." https://www.gov.uk/government/uploads/system/uploads/attachment _data/file/243174/7215.pdf. Accessed November 27, 2017.

House of Commons Home Affairs Committee. 2014. *Counter-terrorism: Seventeenth Report of the Session 2013–14.* http://www.publications.parliament.uk/pa/cm201314/cmselect/ cmhaff/231/231.pdf. Accessed December 12, 2015.

———. 2016. *Radicalisation: The Counter-Narrative and Identifying the Tipping Point: Eighth Report of Session 2016–17.* https://www.publications.parliament.uk/pa/cm201617/cmselect /cmhaff/135/135.pdf. Accessed June 29, 2017.

House of Commons Public Administration Select Committee. 2008. "Third Sector Commissioning: Written Evidence." https://www.parliament.uk/documents/commons-committees/ public-administration/tscwrittenevidence-final.pdf. Accessed November 26, 2017.

Howe, Darcus. 2006. "Tebbit's Loyalty Test Is Dead." *New Statesman.* http://www.newstates man.com/node/164689. Accessed July 2, 2017.

Human Rights Watch. 1991. "Needless Deaths in the Gulf War: Civilian Casualties During the Air Campaign and Violations of the Laws of War." https://www.hrw.org/reports/ 1991/gulfwar/INTRO.htm. Accessed May 12, 2017.

Iheke, Amarachi Ninette. 2017. "NUS Black Students' Conference 2017: Politically Anti-Black." *Gal-dem.* http://www.gal-dem.com/nus-black-students-conference-2017-politically -anti-black/. Accessed June 20, 2017.

Independent Police Complaints Commission (IPCC). 2006. *IPCC Independent Investigation into the Shooting of Muhammad Abdulkahar on Friday 2 June 2006.* London: Independent Police Complaints Commission.

———. 2013a. "IPCC Report Concludes the Metropolitan Police Service Is Failing to Deal Effectively with Race Complaints." https://www.wired-gov.net/wg/wg-news-1.nsf/0/ 484216FFE81C8E9B80257BAC00220E34? OpenDocument. Accessed November 26, 2017.

———. 2013b. "Report on Metropolitan Police Service Handling of Complaints Alleging Racial Discrimination." http://www.ipcc.gov.uk/sites/default/files/Documents/investigation _commissioner_reports/Report_on_Metropolitan_police_Service_key_statistical_info .PDF. Accessed December 10, 2015.

Jackson, Cassandra. 2011. *Violence, Visual Culture, and the Black Male Body.* New York: Routledge.

Jawad, Haifaa, and Tansin Benn. 2003. *Muslim Women in the United Kingdom and Beyond: Experiences and Images.* Boston: Brill.

Jeremy, Antony. 2007. "Practical Implications of the Enactment of the Racial and Religious Hatred Act." *Ecclesiastical Law Journal* 9 (2): 187–201.

Jivraj, Stephen. 2013. "Geographies of Diversity in Newham." *Center on Dynamics and Ethnicity (CoDE).* http://www.ethnicity.ac.uk/medialibrary/briefings/localdynamicsofdiversity/geographies-of-diversity-in-newham.pdf. Accessed November 11, 2015.

Johnson, Boris. 2016. "Speech to the Conservative Party Conference 2016." *Spectator.* http://blogs.spectator.co.uk/2016/10/full-text-boris-johnsons-conference-speech/. Accessed June 23, 2017.

Jones, Nigel. 2012. "Cameron, Churchill, Race . . . and a Historical Howler." *Daily Mail.* http://www.dailymail.co.uk/debate/article-2114950/Cameron-Churchill-Race--historical-howler.html. Accessed March 28, 2017.

Jones de Almeida, Adjoa Florência. 2007. "Radical Social Change: Searching for a New Foundation." In *The Revolution Will Not Be Funded: Beyond the Non-profit Industrial Complex,* ed. INCITE! Women of Color Against Violence, 185–96. Cambridge, Mass.: South End Press.

Joyce, Patrick. 2003. *The Rule of Freedom: Liberalism and the Modern City.* New York: Verso.

Joyce, Peter. 2002. *Politics of Protest: Extra-Parliamentary Politics in Britain Since 1970.* New York: Palgrave Macmillan.

Kahf, Mohja. 1999. *Western Representations of the Muslim Woman.* Austin: University of Texas Press.

Kelley, Robin D. G. 1996. *Race Rebels: Culture, Politics and the Black Working Class.* New York: Free Press.

———. 2003. *Freedom Dreams: The Black Radical Imagination.* Boston: Beacon.

Kellner, Douglas. 2016. *Media Spectacle and the Crisis of Democracy: Terrorism, War and Election Battles.* New York: Routledge.

Kipling, Rudyard. (1899) 1993. "The White Man's Burden." In *Rudyard Kipling: Selected Poems,* ed. Peter Keating, 82–83. New York: Penguin.

Kundnani, Arun. 2001. "From Oldham to Bradford: The Violence of the Violated." *Institute of Race Relations.* http://www.irr.org.uk/news/from-oldham-to-bradford-the-violence-of-the-violated/. Accessed December 10, 2015.

———. 2012. "Radicalization: The Journey of a Concept." *Race and Class* 54 (2): 3–25.

———. 2014. *The Muslims Are Coming!* New York: Verso.

Lamrabet, Asma. 2015. "An Egalitarian Reading of the Concepts of Khilafah, Wilayah, and Qiwamah." In *Men in Charge? Rethinking Authority in the Muslim Legal Tradition,* ed. Ziba Mir-Hosseini, Mulki Al-Sharmani, and Jana Rumminger. London: Oneworld.

Laura, Ana. 2012. "Brixton Black Panthers Movement." https://libcom.org/history/brixton-black-panthers-movement. Accessed May 10, 2017.

Lentin, Alana. 2008. *Racism: A Beginner's Guide.* London: Oneworld.

Leonardo, Zeus. 2004. "The Color of Supremacy: Beyond the Discourse of 'White Privilege.'" *Educational Philosophy and Theory* 36 (2): 137–52.

Linning, Stephanie. 2015. "Shocking Moment Hijab-Wearing Girl Is Attacked from Behind and Knocked to the Floor Unconscious as Police Reveal Huge Rise in Hate Crimes Against Muslims." *Daily Mail.* http://www.dailymail.co.uk/news/article-3225020/Shocking

-moment-hijab-wearing-woman-attacked-knocked-floor-unconscious-police-reveal -huge-rise-hate-crimes-against-Muslims.html. Accessed December 12, 2015.

Lipsitz, George. 2006. *The Possessive Investment in Whiteness: How White People Profit from Identity Politics.* Rev. and expanded ed. Philadelphia: Temple University Press.

Little, Kenneth Lindsay. 1968. "Some Aspects of Color, Class and Culture in Britain." In *Color and Race,* ed. John Hope Franklin, 234–48. Boston: Houghton Mifflin.

Littler, Mark, and Matthew Feldman. 2015. "Tell MAMA Reporting 2014/15: Annual Monitoring, Cumulative Extremism and Policy Implications." Teesside University's Centre for Fascist, Anti-fascist, and Post-fascist Studies. http://tellmamauk.org/wp-content/uploads/ pdf/Tell%20MAMA%20Reporting%202014-2015.pdf. Accessed December 12, 2015.

London Borough of Newham. 2007. "Focus on Newham: Local People and Local Conditions." http://s3.amazonaws.com/zanran_storage/www.newham.info/ContentPages/46961415 .pdf. Accessed June 27, 2017.

Lowe, Lisa. 2015. *The Intimacies of Four Continents.* Durham, N.C.: Duke University Press.

Lusher, Adam. 2017. "What Is the Truth Behind Claims Muslims Are Being Targeted by Right-Wing Acid Attackers in London." *Independent.* http://www.independent.co.uk/ news/uk/crime/east-london-acid-attacks-muslim-resham-khan-jameel-muhktar-south -asian-residents-race-hate-crimes-a7821701.html. Accessed July 4, 2017.

Macpherson, William. 1999. *The Stephen Lawrence Inquiry.* https://www.gov.uk/government/ uploads/system/uploads/attachment_data/file/277111/4262.pdf. Accessed June 23, 2017.

Maer, Lucinda. 2009. *The Racial and Religious Hatred Act 2006.* London: Library House of Commons.

Mahmood, Saba. 2005. *Politics of Piety: The Islamic Revival and the Feminist Subject.* Princeton, N.J.: Princeton University Press.

Maldonado-Torres, Nelson. 2008. *Against War: Views from the Underside of Modernity.* Durham, N.C.: Duke University Press.

Mamdani, Mahmood. 2005. *Good Muslim, Bad Muslim: America, the Cold War and the Roots of Terror.* New York: Doubleday.

Marable, Manning. 2016. *Beyond Black and White: From Civil Rights to Barack Obama.* New York: Verso. Kindle edition.

Marshall, Stephen. 2012. "The Political Life of Fungibility." *Theory and Event* 15 (3). https:// muse.jhu.edu/article/484457. Accessed June 23, 2017.

Martineau, Frances, Valerie Brown, and Sam Faulkner. 2007. *Race Hate Crime.* Paper presented at the Crime and Disorder Reduction Partnership, Newham, London. http:// mgov.newham.gov.uk/mgConvert2PDF.aspx?ID = 12279. Accessed December 10, 2015.

Mason, Rowena. 2015. "Number of Syrian Refugees Brought to UK Passes 1000." *Guardian.* https://www.theguardian.com/uk-news/2015/dec/16/number-syrian-refugees-uk-1000 -david-cameron. Accessed June 7, 2017.

MayDay Rooms. 2017. "Archives." http://maydayrooms.org/archives/. Accessed June 19, 2017.

Maylor, Uvanney. 2009. "What Is the Meaning of Black? Researching Black Respondents." *Ethnic and Racial Studies* 32 (2): 369–87.

Mbembe, Achille. 2003. "Necropolitics." *Public Culture* 15 (1): 11–40.

Mehta, Uday. 1999. *Liberalism and Empire: A Study in Nineteenth-Century British Liberal Thought.* Chicago: University of Chicago Press.

Merali, Arzu. 2013. "No-one Expects the Spanish Inquisition: Except Muslims and Jews." Islamic Human Rights Commission. http://www.ihrc.org.uk/blogs/arzu/10874-no-one -expects-the-spanish-inquisition-except-muslims-and-jews. Accessed December 12, 2015.

Mernissi, Fátima. 2003. "The Meaning of Spatial Boundaries." In *Feminist Postcolonial Theory: A Reader*, ed. Reina Lewis and Sara Mills, 489–501. New York: Routledge.

Metropolitan Police Service. 2006. *MPS Communities Together Strategic Engagement Team Community Engagement Timeline—Newham (Operation Volga)*. London: Metropolitan Police Service.

Miller, Peter, and Nikolas Rose. 2008. *Governing the Present: Administering Economic, Social and Personal Life*. Malden, Mass.: Polity.

Mills, Charles. 1997. *The Racial Contract*. Ithaca, N.Y.: Cornell University Press.

———. 2005. " 'Ideal Theory' as Ideology." *Hypatia* 20 (3): 165–84.

———. 2008. "Racial Liberalism." *PMLA* 123 (5): 1380–97.

Mills, Heather. 1999. "A Life Without Joy." *Guardian*. https://www.theguardian.com/cell deaths/article/0,2763,195387,00.html. Accessed May 22, 2017.

Mir-Hosseini, Ziba, and Mukti Al-Sharmani, eds. 2015. *Men in Charge? Rethinking Authority in Muslim Legal Tradition*. New York: Oneworld.

Mirza, Heidi Safia. 1992. *Young, Female, and Black*. New York. Routledge.

———, ed. 1997. *Black British Feminism: A Reader*. New York: Routledge.

———. 2009. *Race, Gender and Educational Desire: Why Black Women Succeed and Fail*. New York: Routledge.

———. 2014. " 'The Branch on Which I Sit': Heidi Safia Mirza in Conversation with Yasmin Gunaratnam." *Feminist Review* 108: 125–33.

Modood, Tariq. 1994. "Political Blackness and British Asians." *Sociology* 28 (4): 859–76.

———. 2005. *Multicultural Politics: Racism, Ethnicity and Muslims in Britain*. Minneapolis: University of Minnesota Press.

Mohanty, Chandra Talpady. 2003. *Feminism Without Borders: Decolonizing Theory, Practicing Solidarity*. Durham, N.C.: Duke University Press.

Mohanty, Satya. 1997. *Literary Theory and the Claims of History: Postmodernism, Objectivity and Multicultural Politics*. Ithaca, N.Y.: Cornell University Press.

Monitoring Group. 2011. "A Handbook for Victims of Racial Harassment." http://www.tmg-uk.org/?page_id=806. Accessed May 2, 2011.

Mora, Mariana. 2003. "The Imagination to Listen: Reflections on a Decade of Zapatista Struggle." *Social Justice* 30 (3): 17–31.

Morris, Nigel. 2008. "Huge Rise in Number of Racist Attacks." *Independent*. http://www .independent.co.uk/news/uk/home-news/huge-rise-in-number-of-racist-attacks-862944 .html. Accessed April 29, 2011.

Mutua, Kagendo, and Beth Blue Swadener. 2004. *Decolonizing Research in Cross-Cultural Contexts: Critical Personal Narratives*. Albany: State University of New York Press.

Nandy, Ashis. 2010. *The Intimate Enemy: Loss and Recovery of Self Under Colonialism*. Oxford: Oxford University Press.

Naples, Nancy A. 2003. *Feminism and Method: Ethnography, Discourse Analysis and Activist Research*. New York: Routledge.

National Counter Terrorism Security Office (UK). 2015. "Public Vigilance." https://www .gov.uk/government/publications/public-vigilance/public-vigilance. Accessed April 18, 2017.

National Union of Students. 2011. "National Union of Students (NUS) Black Students Campaign." http://www.nus.org.uk/en/Campaigns/BlackStudents/. Accessed May 1, 2011.

National Union of Students' Black Students' Campaign. 2011. "Why We Need a Black Students' Campaign." http://www.nus.org.uk/en/Campaigns/BlackStudents/Why-do-we-need-a-black-students-campaign/2006. Accessed May 1, 2011.

Nayak, Anoop. 2004. *Race, Place and Globalization: Youth Cultures in a Changing World*. New York: Berg.

Neal, Sarah. 2009. *Rural Identities: Ethnicity and Community in the English Countryside*. Burlington, Vt.: Ashgate.

Netpol. 2017. "Wave of Impunity Carries Cressida Dick into Commissioner's Job." https://netpol.org/2017/02/23/cressida-dick/. Accessed May 23, 2017.

Newham Council. 2010. "Newham, London: Local Economic Assessment." http://www.newham.info/Custom/LEA/Demographics.pdf. Accessed March 26, 2017.

———. 2015a. "English Indices of Deprivation 2015." http://www.newham.info/Indicesof deprivation2015. Accessed March 26, 2017.

———. 2015b. "Newham's Budget Challenge Q & A's." https://www.newham.gov.uk/Docu ments/Council%20and%20Democracy/BudgetChallengeFAQs.pdf. Accessed May 27, 2017.

Newham Household Panel Survey (NHPS). 2006. *Wave 4 Report*. London: London Borough of Newham.

Newham Monitoring Project (NMP). n.d.a. "NMP's Nine Absolutes: Or How to Save Ourselves from Ourselves." Personal NMP archives.

———. n.d.b. "What We Mean by Community Resistance." Personal NMP archives.

———. 1985. *Annual Report 1985*. London: Newham Monitoring Project.

———. 1992. *Annual Report 1991/2*. London: Newham Monitoring Project.

———. 1993. *Annual report 1992–93*. London: Newham Monitoring Project.

———. 2000. *Twentieth Anniversary Joint Annual Report 1999–2000*. London: Newham Monitoring Project.

———. 2006. *Aftermath of the Anti-terrorism Police Raids in Forest Gate on 2 June 2006*. London: Newham Monitoring Project. http://www.statewatch.org/news/2007/mar/uk -forest-gate-raids-nmp-report.pdf. Accessed April 29, 2011.

———. 2013. "Newham Council in Alleged Racism 'Whitewash' of Its Equalities Agenda." http://www.nmp.org.uk/2013/11/07/newham-council-in-alleged-racism-whitewash-of -its-equalities-agenda/. Accessed May 27, 2017.

New Policy Institute. 2015. "London's Poverty Profile: Newham." http://www.londonspoverty profile.org.uk/indicators/boroughs/newham/. Accessed March 27, 2017.

———. 2015b. "Poverty Has Not Left East London, but It Has Changed." http://www.npi .org.uk/blog/income-and-poverty/poverty-has-not-left-east-london-it-has-changed/. Accessed March 27, 2017.

Nicol, Mark. 2014. "Secret SAS 'Kill Room' Bunker Revealed." *Daily Mail*. http://www.daily mail.co.uk/sciencetech/article-2614045/Secret-SAS-kill-room-bunker-revealed-Elite-unit -build-futuristic-20million-training-complex-beneath-base.html. Accessed October 8, 2015.

Norshahril, Saat. 2016. "Exclusivist Attitudes in Malaysian Islam Have Multifarious Roots." *ISEAS Perspective* 39: 1–12.

Obi, Elizabeth. 2017. "I Was There, and I Find the Portrayal of Black Women Unforgiv-
    able." *Guardian.* https://www.theguardian.com/commentisfree/2017/apr/14/guerilla-fight
    -racial-equality. Accessed May 10, 2017.

Obi, Elizabeth, Lola Okolosie, Kehinde Andrews and Iman Amrani. 2017. "What Does *Guer-
    rilla* Teach Us About the Fight for Racial Equality Today?" *Guardian.* https://www.the
    guardian.com/commentisfree/2017/apr/14/guerilla-fight-racial-equality. Accessed May
    10, 2017.

Office for Public Management. 2010. "Research into Best Practice in Preventing Violent
    Extremism and Understanding the Causes of Violent Extremism: Final Report, London
    Borough of Newham." https://www.newham.gov.uk/Documents/Misc/Research-Extrem
    ism.pdf. Accessed June 10, 2017.

Okolosie, Lola, Joseph Harker, Leah Green, and Emma Dabiri. 2015. "Is It Time to Ditch the
    Term 'Black, Asian and Minority Ethnic' (BAME)?" *Guardian* https://www.theguardian
    .com/commentisfree/2015/may/22/black-asian-minority-ethnic-bame-bme-trevor
    -phillips-racial-minorities. Accessed May 10, 2017.

O'Neill, Ruari Cahir. 2011. "Residence as Condition for Social Security in the United King-
    dom: A Critique of the UK Right to Reside Test for Accessing Benefits and How It Is
    Applied in the Courts." *European Journal of Social Security* 13 (2): 226–47.

Open Face Films. 1986. *The Dividing Line* (booklet for the film). London: Open Face Films.

Open Society Justice Initiative. 2016. *Eroding Trust: The UK's Prevent Counter-extremism
    Strategy in Health and Education.* New York: Open Society Foundations.

Out-Law.com. 2013. "Interim Injunctions." https://www.out-law.com/topics/dispute-resolu
    tion-and-litigation/injuctions/interim-injunctions/. Accessed June 27, 2017.

Patterson, Sheila. 1963. *Dark Strangers: Sociological Study of the Absorption of a Recent West
    Indian Migrant Group in Brixton, South London.* London: Tavistock.

Pérez Huber, Lindsay. 2010. "Using Latina/o Critical Race Theory (LatCrit) and Racist Nativ-
    ism to Explore Intersectionality in the Educational Experiences of Undocumented Chi-
    cana College Students." *Educational Foundations* (Winter-Spring): 77–96.

Perlez, Jane. 2007. "Head-to-Toe Muslim Veil Tests Tolerance of Secular Britain." *New York
    Times.* http://www.nytimes.com/2007/06/21/world/europe/21iht-veil.4.6263112.html.
    Accessed May 2, 2011.

Phillips, Trevor. 2009. "Why Britain Is Now the Least Racist Country in Europe." *Daily Mail.*
    http://www.dailymail.co.uk/debate/article-1121442/TREVOR-PHILLIPS-Why-Britain
    -LEAST-racist-country-Europe.html. Accessed June 23, 2017.

Pool, Hannah. 2007. "The Police Are Meant to Be on My Side, But I Am More Than a Little
    Frightened of Them." *Guardian.* http://www.guardian.co.uk/uk/2007/mar/09/ukcrime
    .gender1. Accessed April 29, 2011.

Potok, Mark. 2017. "The Year in Hate and Extremism." *Intelligence Report.* https://www
    .splcenter.org/fighting-hate/intelligence-report/2017/year-hate-and-extremism. Accessed
    June 7, 2017.

Powell, Enoch. (1968) 2007. "Rivers of Blood." *Daily Telegraph.* http://www.telegraph.co.uk/
    comment/3643823/Enoch-Powells-Rivers-of-Blood-speech.html. Accessed May 23, 2017.

Powell, Tom. 2017. "Family of Jean Charles de Menezes Slam Cressida Dick's Appointment
    as Met Police Commissioner." *Evening Standard.* http://www.standard.co.uk/news/crime/
    family-of-jean-charles-de-menezes-slam-cressida-dicks-appointment-as-met-police
    -commissioner-a3473656.html. Accessed May 23, 2017.

Prashad, Vijay. 2001. *Everybody Was Kung-fu Fighting: Afro-Asian Connections and the Myth of Cultural Purity.* Boston: Beacon.

Presser, Lizzie. 2016. "What's Behind the Huge Fall in Deprivation in East London? And No, It's Not Gentrification." *Guardian.* https://www.theguardian.com/society/2016/jan/12/what-behind-deprivation-east-london-newham-unemployment. Accessed March 27, 2017.

Prison Reform Trust. 2016. "Prison: The Facts. Bromley Briefing Summer 2016." http://www.prisonreformtrust.org.uk/Portals/0/Documents/Bromley%20Briefings/summer%2020 16%20briefing.pdf. Accessed June 7, 2017.

———. 2017. "Why Focus on Reducing Women's Imprisonment?" http://www.prisonreform trust.org.uk/Portals/0/Documents/Women/whywomen.pdf. Accessed June 29, 2017.

Puar, Jasbir. 2007. *Terrorist Assemblages: Homonationalism in Queer Times.* Durham, N.C.: Duke University Press.

Pugliese, Joseph. 2006. "Asymmetries of Terror: Visual Regimes of Racial Profiling and the Shooting of Jean Charles de Menezes in the Context of the War in Iraq." *Borderlands e-journal* 5 (1). http://www.borderlands.net.au/vol5no1_2006/pugliese.htm. Accessed October 7, 2015.

Qasim, Wail. 2017. "Freida Pinto's Casting as Only Lead Female Character in *Guerrilla* Erases Women from the History of Black Power." *Independent.* http://www.independent.co.uk/voices/guerilla-freida-pinto-casting-criticism-asian-black-women-black-power-move ment-uk-a7677811.html. Accessed May 24, 2017.

Quijano, Anibal. 2000. "Coloniality of Power, Eurocentrism and Latin America." *Nepantla: Views from the South* 1 (3): 533–80.

Ramamurthy, Anandi. 2003. *Imperial Persuaders: Images of Africa and Asia in British Advertising.* Manchester, U.K.: Manchester University Press.

Ramesh, Randeep. 2012. "Equalities and Human Rights Commission Has Workforce Halved." *Guardian.* http://www.theguardian.com/society/2012/may/15/equality-human-rights -commission-cuts. Accessed December 10, 2015.

Rana, Junaid. 2011. *Terrifying Muslims: Race and Labor in the South Asian Diaspora.* Durham, N.C.: Duke University Press.

Rawlinson, Kevin. 2017. "Demonstrators Confront Police over Da Costa Death." *Guardian.* https://www.theguardian.com/uk-news/2017/jun/25/demonstrators-confront-police-in -east-london-over-da-costa-death. Accessed June 27, 2017.

Rawls, John. 2005. *Political Liberalism.* New York: Columbia University Press.

Razack, Sherene. 2008. *Casting Out: The Expulsion of Muslims from Western Law and Politics.* Toronto: University of Toronto Press.

Reese, Stephen D., and Seth C. Lewis. 2009. "Framing the War on Terror: The Internalization of Policy in the US Press." *Journalism* 10 (6): 777–97.

Revesz, Rachael. 2016. "Southwest Airlines Kicks Muslim Off a Plane for Saying 'Inshallah,' Meaning 'God Willing' in Arabic." *Independent.* http://www.independent.co.uk/news/world/americas/muslim-passenger-southwest-airlines-khairuldeen-makhzoom-arabic -phone-uncle-baghdad-cair-statement-a7347311.html. Accessed May 23, 2017.

Reynolds, Tracey. 2002. "Re-thinking a Black Feminist Standpoint." *Ethnic and Racial Studies* 25 (4): 591–606.

Richardson, Theresa. 2011. "John Locke and the Myth of Race in America: Demythologizing the Paradoxes of the Enlightenment as Visited in the Present." *Philosophical Studies in Education* 42: 101–12.

Ritchie, Andrea. 2006. "Law Enforcement Violence Against Women of Color." In *Color of Violence: The INCITE! Anthology*, ed. INCITE! Women of Color Against Violence, 138–56. Cambridge, Mass.: South End Press.

Roach, Kent. 2011. *The 9/11 Effect: Comparative Counter-terrorism*. New York: Cambridge University Press.

Rodney, Walter. 1990. *Walter Rodney Speaks: The Making of an African Intellectual*. Trenton, N.J.: Africa World Press.

Rothstein, Edward. 2002. "Kipling Knew What the U.S. May Now Learn." *New York Times*. http://www.nytimes.com/2002/01/26/books/kipling-knew-what-the-us-may-now-learn .html. Accessed June 20, 2017.

Rowe, Michael. 2004. *Policing, Race and Racism*. Cullompton, U.K.: Willan.

Saint Stephen's School and Children's Centre. 2016. *Headteacher's Newsletter*. April 12.

Samantrai, Ranu. 2002. *AlterNatives: Black Feminism in the Postimperial Nation*. Stanford, Calif.: Stanford University Press.

Sexton, Jared. 2010. "People-of-Color-Blindness: Notes on the Afterlife of Slavery." *Social Text* 28 (2): 31–56.

Shaikh, Thair. 2006. "Brothers Arrested in 'Terror Raids' Are Freed Without Charge." *Independent*. June 10.

Shilliam, Robbie. 2015. *The Black Pacific: Anti-Colonial Struggles and Oceanic Connections*. New York: Bloomsbury.

Shirazi, Faegheh. 2003. *The Veil Unveiled: The Hijab in Modern Culture*. Gainesville: University Press of Florida.

Shukra, Kalbir. 1998. *The Changing Pattern of Black Politics in Britain*. London: Pluto Press.

Siddiqui, Hannana. 2000. "Black Women's Activism: Coming of Age?" *Feminist Review* 64 (1): 83–96.

Sivanandan, A. 1990. *Communities of Resistance: Writings on Black Struggles for Socialism*. New York: Verso.

Sky News. 2006. "Man Shot in Terror Raid Speaks Out." *Sky News*. http://news.sky.com/story/ 434957/man-shot-in-terror-raid-speaks-out. Accessed October 2015.

Slate, Nico, ed. 2012. *Black Power Beyond Borders: The Global Dimensions of the Black Power Movement*. New York: Palgrave Macmillan.

Sloan, Alastair, and Eric Allison. 2015. "Sharp Rise in Proportion of Young Black and Minority Ethnic Prisoners." *Guardian*. https://www.theguardian.com/society/2015/jun/24/rise -proportion-black-ethnic-minority-young-prisoners-stop-and-search. Accessed May 22, 2017.

Smith, Evan, and Marinella Marmo. 2011. "Uncovering the 'Virginity Testing' Controversy in the National Archives: The Intersectionality of Discrimination in British Immigration History." *Gender and History* 23 (1): 147–65.

Smith, Linda Tuhiwai. 2012. *Decolonizing Methodology: Research and Indigenous Peoples*. London: Zed.

Spivak, Gayatri. 1999. *A Critique of Postcolonial Reason: Toward a History of the Vanishing Present*. Cambridge, Mass.: Harvard University Press.

Stokoe, Elizabeth, and Derek Edwards. 2007. "'Black This, Black That': Racial Insults and Reported Speech in Neighbor Complaints and Police Interrogations." *Discourse and Society* 18 (3): 337–72.

Stratford Guardian. 2006. "Met Police Sorry for Disruption to Residents." June 15.

Stupples, Ben. 2015. "Racial and Religious Hate Crimes Spike in Two Years." *RT News.* https://www.rt.com/uk/259065-hate-crime-increase-uk/. Accessed December 9, 2015.

Sudbury, Julia. 1998. *"Other Kinds of Dreams": Black Women's Organization and the Politics of Transformation.* New York: Routledge.

———. 2001. "(Re)constructing Multiracial Blackness: Women's Activism, Difference and Collective Identity in Britain." *Ethnic and Racial Studies* 24 (1): 29–49.

———. 2016. "Rethinking Anti-violence Strategy: Lessons from Black Women's Movement in Britain." In *Color of Violence: The INCITE! Anthology,* ed. INCITE! Women of Color Against Violence, 13–24. Durham, N.C.: Duke University Press.

Syal, Rajeev. 2014. "British Towns Being 'Swamped' by Immigrants, Says Michael Fallon." *Guardian.* https://www.theguardian.com/uk-news/2014/oct/26/british-towns-swamped-immigrants-michael-fallon-eu. Accessed May 18, 2017.

Talwar, Divya. 2012. "More Than 87,000 Racist Incidents Recorded in Schools." *BBC Asian Network/BBC News.* http://www.bbc.co.uk/news/education-18155255. Accessed June 23, 2017.

Taylor, Charles. 1994. *Multiculturalism: Examining the Politics of Recognition.* Princeton, N.J.: Princeton University Press.

Telegraph. 2009. "Britain's Betrayed Tribe: The White Working-Class." http://www.telegraph.co.uk/comment/telegraph-view/4077465/Britains-betrayed-tribe-the-white-working-class.html. Accessed June 11, 2017.

Thatcher, Margaret. 1978. "TV Interview with Granada *World in Action.*" http://www.margaretthatcher.org/document/103485. Accessed March 28, 2017.

Thiara, Ravi K., and Aisha K. Gill. 2012. *Domestic Violence, Child Contact and Post-separation Violence: Issues for South Asian and African-Caribbean Women and Children: A Report of Findings.* London: National Society for the Prevention of Cruelty to Children. https://www.nspcc.org.uk/globalassets/documents/research-reports/domestic-violence-child-contact-post-separation-violence-report.pdf. Accessed June 7, 2017.

Thiranagama, Sharika. 2011. *In My Mother's House: Civil War in Sri Lanka.* Philadelphia: University of Pennsylvania Press.

Thomas, David. 2001. "I Hate the Term 'Asian.'" *Daily Telegraph.* http://www.telegraph.co.uk/culture/4724609/I-hate-the-term-Asian.html. Accessed April 30, 2011.

Thompson, Keith. 1988. *Under Siege: Racial Violence in Britain.* London: Penguin.

Times. 2008. "Benjamin Zephaniah, Features." January 5.

Townsend, Mark, Anushka Asthana, Antony Barnett, and David Smith. 2006. "Angry Families Threaten Legal Action Against Police over Anti-terror Raid." *Guardian.* http://www.guardian.co.uk/uk/2006/jun/04/terrorism.world. Accessed April 28, 2011.

Travis, Alan. 2015. "University Professors Decry Theresa May's Campus Anti-terrorism Bill." *Guardian.* http://www.theguardian.com/uk-news/2015/feb/03/professors-letter-protest-counter-terrorism-campuses. Accessed June 23, 2017.

Twine, France Winddance. 2011. *A White Side of Black Britain: Interracial Intimacy and Racial Literacy.* Durham, N.C.: Duke University Press.

Vargas, João H. Costa. 2004. "Hyperconsciousness of Race and Its Negation: The Dialectics of White Supremacy in Brazil." *Identities* 11 (4): 443–70.

———. 2008. "Activist Scholarship: Limits and Possibilities in Times of Black Genocide." In *Engaging Contradictions: Theory, Politics, and Methods of Activist Scholarship,* ed. Charles R. Hale, 164–82. Berkeley: University of California Press.

————. 2010. *Never Meant to Survive: Genocide and Utopias in Black Diaspora Communities.* New York: Rowman and Littlefield.

Vargas-Silva, Carlos, and Yvonni Markaki. 2016. *Briefing: EU Migration to and from the UK.* Oxford: Migration Observatory, University of Oxford.

Vertovec, Stephen. 2007. "Super-diversity and Its Implications." *Ethnic and Racial Studies* 30 (6): 1024–54.

Virdee, Satnam. 2014. *Racism, Class and the Racialized Outsider.* New York: Palgrave Macmillan.

Volpp, Leti. 2002. "The Citizen and the Terrorist." *UCLA Law Review* 49: 1575–1600.

Wallace, Michele. 2015. *Black Macho and the Myth of the Superwoman.* New York: Verso.

Waugh, Paul. 1997. "How New Labour Newham Rocked Anti-racist Rebels." *Evening Standard.*

Webster, Colin. 2003. "Race, Space and Fear: Imagined Geographies of Racism, Crime, Violence and Disorder in Northern England." *Capital and Class* 27 (2): 95–122.

Webster, Wendy. 2001. " 'There'll Always Be an England': Representations of Colonial Wars and Immigration, 1948–1968." *Journal of British Studies* 40 (2): 557–84.

Wemyss, Georgie. 2009. *The Invisible Empire: White Discourse, Tolerance and Belonging.* Farnham, U.K.: Ashgate.

WhatDoTheyKnow. 2014. "Surveillance on Black Justice Campaigns." https://www.whatdo theyknow.com/request/surveillance_on_black_justice_ca. Accessed June 22, 2107.

Wild, Rosalind Eleanor. 2008. " 'Black Was the Color of Our Fight': Black Power in Britain, 1955–1976." PhD dissertation, University of Sheffield.

Williams, Nigel. 2012. "Hate Crime." http://www.civitas.org.uk/content/files/factsheet-hate crime.pdf. Accessed December 12, 2015.

Williams, Raymond. 1978. *Marxism and Literature.* New York: Oxford University Press.

Wilson, Amrit, Kehinde Andrews, and Vera Chok. 2016. "Is Political Blackness Still Relevant Today?" *Guardian.* https://www.theguardian.com/commentisfree/2016 /oct/27/political -blackness-black-history-month-zayn-malik-sadiq-khan. Accessed May 24, 2017.

Wilson, Elizabeth. 1991. *The Sphinx in the City.* Berkeley: University of California Press.

Wintour, Patrick. 2015. "Police Told to Treat Anti-Muslim Hate Crime in Same Way as Antisemitic Attacks." *Guardian.* https://www.theguardian.com/society/2015/oct/13/ police-must-record-anti-muslim-hate-crimes. Accessed June 23, 2017.

Women and Policing in London. 1985. "Why Women and Policing?" *Women and Policing in London* 1 (1).

Yamamoto, Eric, and Julie Su. 2002. "Critical Coalitions: Theory and Praxis." In *Crossroads, Directions and a New Critical Race Theory,* ed. Francisco Valdes, Jerome McCristal Culp, and Angela P. Harris, 379–92. Philadelphia: Temple University Press.

Yancy, George, and Paul Gilroy. 2015. "What 'Black Lives' Mean in Britain." *New York Times.* October 1. https://opinionator.blogs.nytimes.com/2015/10/01/paul-gilroy-what-black -means-in-britain/?_r=0. Accessed May 10, 2017.

Zaid Ibrahim. 2015. *Assalamualaikum: Observations on the Islamization of Malaysia.* Kuala Lumpur: ZI Publications.

Zainah Anwar. 2015. "Foreword." In *Men in Charge? Rethinking Authority in Muslim Legal Tradition,* ed. Ziba Mir-Hosseini, Mukti Al-Sharmani, and Jana Rumminger, vii–x. New York: Oneworld.

Zephaniah, B., T. Hajdukowicz, and J. Sotinel. 2011. "Benjamin Zephaniah: The People on the Street Are Very Angry People." http://www.thenewsignificance.com/2011/08/17/benjamin-zephaniah-the-people-on-the-street-are-angry-people/. Accessed December 10, 2015.

Zephaniah, Benjamin. 2001. "What Stephen Lawrence Has Taught Us." In *Too Black, Too Strong*, ed. Benjamin Zephaniah, 20–22. Highgreen, U.K.: Bloodaxe Books.

———. 2006. "You Can't Trust the Police with Your Children's Lives." *Guardian.* https://www.theguardian.com/commentisfree/2006/aug/05/comment.race. Accessed November 27, 2017.

Zine, Jasmin. 2006. "Between Orientalism and Fundamentalism: The Politics of Muslim Women's Feminist Engagement." *Muslim World Journal of Human Rights* 3 (1): 1–24.

INDEX

Abbott, Diane, 70
Abu Ghraib, 197
activism: antiracist, 40, 170, 175, 179, 182, 188, 191; black, 170; Black Power, 184; Newham Monitoring Project, xiii, 93, 191
activist(s): African Caribbea,n 169, 175; antiracist, xiii, 26–28, 32, 79, 92, 95, 98, 177, 179, 188, 196, 200–201; black feminist, 66–67; Black Lives Matter, 168; Black Panther, 167; community, 20, 159; Muslim, 140, 142; Newham Monitoring Project, xiii–xiv, 4, 28, 32, 64, 75, 87, 109, 121, 123, 125, 144, 148–50, 158–60, 169, 185, 187–88, 192, 194, 196, 201, 205 n.11, 210 n.1; organization(s), 75; and political blackness, 78, 142, 167, 176, 193; Sri Lankan 193; student, 169; women, 98, 168
Adil, 41, 43, 49
Afghanistan, 103–4; war in, 16
Africa, 8, 16, 18, 27; anticolonial movements in 15
African(s): colonies 16, 81; diaspora 165, 172; heritage 167; immigrant(s) 71; Muslim 159; politics 172; prisoners 66, 207 n.2; solidarity 171; student(s) 172, 175; women 67–68, 168. See also Pan-African
African-Asian solidarity, 193
African American, 170; social movement(s) 67
African Caribbean(s): activist(s), 169, 175; and Asian(s), 5, 39; colonies, 81; community, organizers, 26; heritage, 167; organization(s), 179; culture, 121; immigrant(s), 19, 158, 201; prisoners, 66, 207 n.2; and racism, 5, 39, 62; student(s), 114; surveillance of, 180; women, 66–68, 70, 75, 78, 88, 93, 168, 207 n.1; youth 5, 177. See also Caribbean; West Indian

African Caribbean-Asian solidarity, 77
Afro-Caribbean Society, 173–74
Afzal-Khan, Fawzia, 101
Ahmad, Muneer, 131
al-Amiriyah shelter, 123–24
al-Hibri, Azizah Y., 106
Albert, 13–14
ALERT, 186
Algeria, 111–12, 209 n.1; hijab in, 111
Algerian: society, 112; women, 112
Ali, Ishaque, 26
Alien Deportation Group, 69
Aloba, Titilayo, 182
Altab Ali Park, 26
Amina, ix–xii, 41–46, 49–58, 61–62, 64–65, 72, 117–22, 125, 147
Amos, Valerie, 70
Anglo-American civilization, 15
Anglo-Saxon capitalism, 21
Anklesaria, Kayimarz, 26
Anne, 13–15
anti-black hate speech 42
anti-immigration, 80; campaigns, 15; discourse, 16, 38; policies, 81
anti-Jewish, hate crime(s), 162
anti-Muslim politics, racialized, 105
Anti-Social Behavior departments, 62
Anti-Social Behavior Ordinances, 88
anti-terror raid: Forest Gate, 125, 128, 133–36, 140–41, 144–46, 150, 154–58, 191, 205 n.11, 210 n.1
anticolonial, 173; movements, 15, 28; politics, 175; resistance, 112, 117; student(s), 172
antiracism, 5, 25, 49, 52, 62, 139, 164, 166, 170, 174, 185, 189, 199–200; in Britain, 188, 195, 198, 200; and British state, 188; laws, 47; state, 57, 176, 188–89; in United Kingdom, 203 n.3

antiracist: activism, 40, 170, 175, 179, 182,
188, 191; activist(s), xiii, 26–28, 32, 79, 92,
95, 98, 177, 179, 188, 196, 200–201;
campaigns, 4–5, 7, 28, 32, 78, 172, 178,
196; casework, 32, 93, 121; demonstra-
tion(s), 122, 148; enforcement, 58;
group(s), 11, 35, 177, 185, 188, 191;
justice, 185; law(s), 43, 49, 56, 111; legislation, 59; monitoring, 177; movement(s),
66–67, 169–70, 175, 192; organization(s),
ix, 19, 78, 186, 191; policies, 189, 206 n.2;
politics, xiv, 3, 78, 123, 167–68, 175;
reform(s), 47, 59, 206 n.1; resistance, 4, 36,
78, 165, 184, 192, 194–95, 203 n.3;
services, 62–63, 65, 187; social move-
ment(s), 4, 66–67, 169, 176, 180, 192;
solidarity, 86, 166, 192, 198, 200; state, 45,
127; struggles, 78, 122, 169, 172, 182
antiradicalization campaigns, 139; and
British state, 190
antiterror: cases, 149; law, 131, 150; legislation, 129, 179; operation(s), 128, 132,
146; police, 32, 131–32, 149, 199; policing,
134, 140; raid(s), 98, 121, 125, 133, 141,
143, 145–46, 159
antiterrorism, 144; discourse, 163; policies,
32; powers, 132; violence, 146
Arab(s), 131, 169, 209 n.1; colonialism, 100
Arabization, in Malaysia, 101
Area 2 Territorial Support Group, 73
Aretxaga, Begoña, 117, 132
Asia, anticolonial movements in, 15. *See also*
South Asia
Asian(s): and African Caribbean(s), 5, 39;
British, xi, 42, 109, 167, 209 n.4; colonies,
16; Muslims, 119; women, 68, 88; youth,
175. *See also* East Asian(s); South Asian(s);
Southeast Asian(s)
Asian Friendship Centre, 143
Asianness, 195
Assembly for the Protection of Hijab, 101
assimilation, 18–19, 94, 162; cultural, 99
asylum seeker(s), 3, 5–6, 14–15, 20–21, 39,
186; Gambian, 122; Sri Lankan Tamil, 12,
14, 34; Syrian, 39
attacks, racist, 4–5, 28, 33, 36, 82, 156, 188
Australia, 23, 46
Azlan, x, xii, 8, 15, 24, 41

Baig, Akhtar Ali, 26, 211 n.7
Baker, Esme, 68

Bangla TV, 140
Bangladesh, 108
Bangladeshi(s), 7, 26, 128; immigrant(s),
177; Muslim, 138
Barbadian, 196
Baumann, Gerd, 195
Beckon, 114
Beese, Barbara, 168
Begum, Meanha, 99
Bend It Like Beckham, 8
Bengali, 109
Berkeley, Jackie, 68
Berkeley, Robert, 188
Bernstock, Penny, 1
Bhattacharyya, Gargi, 103
Bidve, Anuj, 166
Biko, Steve, 28
black: activism, 170; British, 8, 30, 66–67, 70,
169, 196; communities, 4, 20, 31, 48, 59,
68, 118, 143, 159, 173, 175, 178, 180,
185–86, 191, 195, 205 n.11; consciousness,
28, 159, 171, 173, 176, 183; essentialism,
175; feminism, 66, 169; feminist, 66–67,
70, 203 n.1; identity, 42, 165, 172, 177,
179, 195; immigrant(s), 40, 81, 163; and
justice, 46, 184; and law, 45; masculinity,
90; middle class, 30; others, 25; political
autonomy, 27; as political category, 167;
political group(s), 184, 186; politics, 123;
protagonism, 5; social movement(s), 19,
184–85, 196; student(s), 169, 171, 173–74;
subjects, 16, 175; women, 49, 51, 66–69,
70–72, 75, 78, 91, 93–95, 113, 165, 168,
198–99; working class, 30, 72, 177; youth,
68, 88, 171
Black, Asian and Minority Ethnic, 168
Black Boy (Wright), 171
Black History Month, 167
Black Lives Matter, 67; activist(s), 168
Black Panther, 167
Black Power, 179; activism, 184; in Britain,
28, 168, 184, 211 n.4; in Caribbean, 165;
social movement(s), 28, 165, 211 n.4; in
South Africa, 165; in United States, 28
Black Power (Carmichael and Hamilton), 174
Black Students' Campaign, 104, 169
Blair, Ian, 136
Blair, Tony, 91, 132–33
Blowe, Kevin, 144–45, 160, 185
Booth, Charles, 4

ACKNOWLEDGMENTS

Academics are not born but made through encouragement, opportunity, and support. I am grateful to have had many people who have advocated on my behalf and who have supported my journey. I would like to express a deep appreciation to the many institutions, people, and overlapping communities, stretching across several countries that have made this work possible.

This book project was funded in part by the Wenner-Gren Foundation's award of a fieldwork grant and a University Continuing Fellowship at the University of Texas at Austin (UT) that enabled time for writing. Publication of this book was also funded by a subvention grant awarded by the School of Liberal Arts at Tulane University. The John L. Warfield Center for African and African American Studies supported research through the award of multiple grants and fellowships both prior to and after fieldwork, and, most important, it provided the rare space where race and racism and the African diaspora could be rigorously thought about and debated intellectually. The Center for Asian American Studies at UT also enabled me to develop my own courses on black and Asian social movements and activist anthropological research. This was an invaluable opportunity and a clear reason why critical ethnic studies centers and programs are indispensable spaces for forms of knowledge production and teaching that otherwise would not take place.

In Britain, the opportunity to work with the Runnymede Trust in producing a major research report was a defining experience. I would like to thank Michelynn Laflèche, Robert Berkeley, Omar Khan, and Ros Spry for supporting my work there. Similarly, I am unable to forget the generosity of the late Stuart Hall, who facilitated introductions at the Centre for Urban and Community Research at Goldsmiths College. I want to especially thank its director at the time, Michael Keith, for the Centre's support and for engaging with my research project during his time as leader of the Tower

Hamlets Council. The early support provided by Heidi Mirza and the Center for Racial Equality Studies at Middlesex University is also deeply appreciated. At Tulane University, follow-up research for this project was supported through the award of a Lurcy Grant and travel grants from the University Senate Committee on Research.

I would like to thank the Department of Communication at Tulane University and in particular its former chair, Beretta Smith-Shomade, for her staunch institutional advocacy of my research and teaching interests. I would also like to thank the current chair, Mauro Porto, and my senior colleagues Ana López, Vicki Mayer, Michele White, Connie Balides, Frank Ukadike, Ferruh Yilmaz, Mary Blue, and Carole Daruna for their mentoring. Working with Eric Herhuth, Esra Özcan, Betsy Weiss, Kaiman Chang, Marie Davis, and Ava L'Herisse in the department has also been a pleasure. I am especially grateful to the passionate Tulane University undergraduate students in my Critical Race Theory and British Cultural Studies courses whom I have had the privilege to learn from and to teach. I have further enjoyed the opportunity of working with two outstanding graduate students, Dan Castilow and Octavio Barajas, who both will be amazing researchers and teachers in the universities lucky enough to hire them.

Throughout the long period of field research for this project, João H. Costa Vargas has been a constant source of critical feedback and encouragement. I have learned and continue to learn much from his determined radical politics that are anchored in the most utopian of humanistic spirits. I have also been incredibly fortunate to have the brilliant guidance of Sharmila Rudrappa, whose feminist intellectualism and compassionate teaching have been a model for me. I am further indebted to Douglas E. Foley for his mentoring in the arts of ethnography. Doug's books, his fieldwork stories, and his encouraging emails about writing have bolstered my determination to keep the ethnographic focus on storytelling. Edmund T. Gordon and Ben Carrington have also been supportive of this work in myriad ways.

The journey through academia would have been impossible without the friendships that have been made along the way. Mariana Mora has been a constant source of inspiration in helping to maintain the dream that another world is possible. Courtney Morris, for all intents and purposes, is family and for years has had my back and has chosen to see and value my political heart. From the time I met him, Jason Oliver Chang has been one of the most gracious people I have known in academia. From the lending of a coat for a job interview to gentle dispensations of counsel and advice, I have benefited tremendously from his knowledge and wisdom. My thanks also to Kushan Dasgupta for his work in transcribing my fieldnotes and for many years of conversation. I would also like to thank other fellow UT comrades: Alix Chapman, Amy Brown, Damien Sojoyner, Delia Avila, Gilberto Rosas, Gwendolyn Ferreti Manjarrez, Jennifer Goett, Korinta Maldonado Goti, Mathangi Krishnamurthy, Mónica Jimenez, Nick Copeland, Pablo Gonzalez, Peggy Brunache, Shaka McGlotten, Raja Swamy, Roger Reeves, Stephanie Lang, and Susy Chávez Herrera. A special shout-out also to Mauricio Rafael Magaña for advocating for this work. The organizing work of the Anthropology Graduate Student Association in 2009–11 in resisting the draconian budget cuts that threatened graduate student funding at UT was a critical site for the forging of solidarity and for continuing the unfinished struggle to decolonize and diversify the discipline of anthropology.

There were many supportive friends and family in Austin who provided a community without which the inception and long-term feasibility of this project would have been impossible. Thanks to Martha Diase and Ron Ayers for awarding the first grant to this project, which enabled me to have some British pounds in my pocket when I first set off in 2003. The friendship of Chris Milk Bonilla and Liliana Batista comprised a large part of the years spent in Austin, and the love of their children, Diana Isabel and Yashua Josué, humanized the travails of academia and put things in perspective. Thanks also to Richard Milk for his wise counsel and many intellectual conversations over coffee breaks and lunches. The friendships of Olga Milk and Mary Ann Harvey were also important pillars during the time that Austin was home.

This project would not have been possible without the inviting openness of the people I met and became friends with in the east London borough of Newham. I owe too much to the people whose stories I narrate in the book. Their willingness to share their experiences and feelings with me in the midst of great pain was never easy. I believe that it was selflessly undertaken in order for these stories to be known and to matter.

Zainab Kemsley, as director of the Newham Monitoring Project (NMP), first welcomed my application to carry out research with the organization. Kevin Blowe was a firm supporter of my project from the very beginning and generously shared his immense local knowledge of Newham and of antiracist history in Britain. I have similarly benefited from my conversations with Cilius Victor and Asad Rehman. I am indebted to Zareena Mustapha for training me to carry out antiracist casework and to Titilayo

Folosade Aloba for her camaraderie in the many cases we worked on together. Estelle du Boulay worked tirelessly to keep the organization going for many years and continued to welcome my visits with the warmest of feelings. The bond between caseworkers at NMP who did the daily grind was a truly special one.

Parmjit Singh and Yeşim Deveci were unimaginably hospitable when they opened their home to someone they barely knew, and their house on Monega Road became my first address in Newham. Ilona Aronovsky and Patrick Hickey are the sweetest of couples. Sunday roast and political discussions at their home and beautiful backyard garden in East Ham were a needed reprieve from the loneliness of fieldwork. I would also like to thank Alan Partridge of Wesley House Hostel in Stratford, where I was able to have a room, and Vivian Archer of the Newham Bookshop for running one of the most important community-based institutions in east London.

There were many other people in London who made my work possible. I offer special thanks to Mary James for allowing me to stay in her home when I first began this project. Alex Wisch was many times a friend in need and a familiar face from the past. The time of fieldwork also took an unusual turn with the rediscovery of a branch of my Sri Lankan Tamil/ Ceylonese diasporic family, who were displaced to London as refugees and asylum seekers because of the long-running civil war that ended brutally in 2009. Aunty Jeyanthy, especially, searched for and located me in London and brought me into the fold of her family's gatherings that also included my cousins Senan and Selvan and their families.

Throughout this improbable journey with many passages and sojourns, I had the benefit of the committed friendships of several people who have served as lifelong mentors. In particular I would like to thank Peter Schmidt and Aisha Khan for seeing something in me and for believing that I had a place in academia. My thanks also to the other encouragers I have met along the way: Broderick Webb, César Salgado, Glen Abbott, Harry Cleaver, Hirut Gebrekristos, Inderpal Grewal, Ismail Gareth Richards, Janarthanan Jayawickramarajah, John Mckiernan-Gonzalez, Lok Siu, Madeline Hsu, Mehnaaz Ali, Priyanshi Ritwick, Richard Flores, Shakiyla Smith, Shannon Speed, Subir Debnath, and Yosef Keleta. Judith Reyes also deserves my deepest thanks for the hours of patient and nonjudgmental listening.

Writing is most enjoyably undertaken in community. In Austin I had the pleasure of writing with Jodi Skipper, which has resulted in years of subsequent conversation. In New Orleans I would like to thank the writing group that I had with Ana Servigna and Jennifer Ashley, which jump-started the revisions that led to this book. Similarly, the writing group with Courtney Morris, Juli Grigsby, Alix Chapman, and Savannah Shange was instrumental in helping to revise Chapter 3. Thanks also to Nazia Hasan Kazi and Asma Lamrabet for feedback on Chapter 4. The book has bene-fited from the long-term dedicated editorial work of Eleanor Bernal, whose expertise and encouragement over the years in writing have been crucial to this and many other projects. She has been a sharp eye, a political ally, and a writing coach along with being a wonderful friend. I also want to thank Pamela Haag for her thorough reading and feedback on the organization of the book.

In Malaysia, I would like to thank all the friends and family who have given so much to me over the years. My aunts, uncles, and cousins who were there for us, and when I was away working on this book during the difficult period of my father's illness and eventual passing from cancer—words cannot repay the kindness they all showed. Thanks to Aunty Sangar-apillai, Cinta, Singam, Shyamala, Thaya, Dharshini, Nithi, Prashant, Vasi, Siva, Kumar-anna, Aunty Pillai, Uncle Dave, Uncle Pathy, Periamma, and Kumar. Thanks also to Uncle and Aunty Goh, Aunty Yashoda, Marion D'Cruz, Anne James, Bruno Pereira, Carmen Nge, Carolyn Lau, Ivy Josiah, Fahmi Fadzil, Gan Yen Sen, Jacqueline Ann Surin, Mark Teh, Masjaliza Hamzah, Navina Navaratnam, Ng Kwee Noi, Sivarasa Rasiah, Sujata Shas-hidaran, Yeoh Seng Guan, and Mr. Tong for the many years of back-home support and friendship. My thanks also to Gareth Ismail Richards and the amazing editorial team at Impress Creative & Editorial for their work and solidarity.

This book is made possible by many gifts of love. I would like to thank my in-laws, Jim and Ora Shay, for their kind and generous support over the years and for plenty of loving all around. I want to thank my mother, Kamala Devi Maniccam, for her devotion as we all tried to get over our grief after the passing of my father and for her loving care of our newborn children. Her labor made the writing of this book possible. I miss my father very much, but I draw daily on his legacy as a trade unionist and a fighter for justice.

And finally, but not in the very least, thank you, Briana, for everything you have done for me and with me. The beauty of your soul, the strength of your love, and your belief in my purpose have been resolute. This has been the ground beneath my feet, where I found my belonging. I definitely could not have completed this project without the presence of our children, Mallika Isabel and Ashwin Biko. All power to little people! Materially, spiritually, and physically, I could not have done this without all of you, and, without all of you, I would not have wanted to.

CPSIA information can be obtained
at www.ICGtesting.com
Printed in the USA
BVHW04*0311130618
518444BV00001B/1/P

9 780812 250305